There Once Was A Cook ...

First Printing   April 1985   10,000 copies

Additional copies may be obtained by addressing:

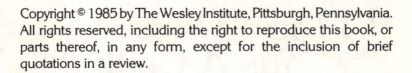

There Once Was A Cook ...

The Wesley Institute
Post Office Box 113445
Pittsburgh, Pennsylvania 15241

For your convenience, order blanks are included in the back of this book.

All proceeds from **There Once Was A Cook** ... will be used to benefit the children and youth serviced by the Wesley Institute.

ISBN 0-9614501-0-X

Printed in the United States of America
by
Moran Printing Company
Orlando, Florida

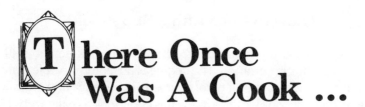

There Once Was A Cook ...

The Wesley Institute
Pittsburgh, Pennsylvania

INTRODUCTION
or
(How to Cook with a Storybook)

Cookbooks really are kinds of storybooks with characters, settings, moods, and actions in common. The degree of adventure and pleasure the reader has with each book relates, of course, to experience and motivation.

For every kind of cook we have made this cookbook as easy and relaxed an experience as possible, and we've used fairy tales, folk tales, and legends as stepping stones for enjoyment and learning just as we use them with our students.

If this cookbook
... inspires the reader to cook,
> then we are satisfied,
> or
... sends the cook to the library's children's literature shelves,
> then we are delighted,
> or
... is often found in the same room as the television set, or in bed with a child,
> then we are grateful,
> because
any one of these makes our effort worthwhile.

Cookbook Committee Personnel

AN INVITATION

The people of The Wesley Institute have always been interested in nourishment. With The Institute's variety of educational diets for children and young people, it is natural that we have developed a cookbook, for we realize and practice the need for a well-balanced approach to every student's educational and social development.

The Wesley Institute's menu of basic services includes:

THE HIGHLAND SCHOOL, education for students with special needs

HIGHLAND YOUTH SERVICES, therapy for Highland students

OAKDALE CENTER, refuge and retreat

PENN RESIDENCE, community-based care for boys

VILLAGE ACADEMY, academic fulfillment for high school students

... and we're still growing.

Satisfaction in giving the right nourishment comes from watching bloom and growth and fulfillment. We have satisfaction in observing the effects of The Wesley Institute's special diets, welcoming all to our table, and we sincerely wish the same for you as you enjoy this cookbook.

We would like to boast that the development of THERE ONCE WAS A COOK ... was a harmonious and confident work of our staff, Guild, and all. The truth is that the originators and supporters approached this task with the optimism and enthusiasm of a beaver's first bite into a giant sequoia. With flying sawdust we were brought together, each one working to carve this thing into an original. The effort gave us all another opportunity for challenge and romance and astonishment. We were already used to these, so like all good cooks - and beavers - we cleaned up and congratulated each other as we moved along.

With the gifts of talent and determination the committees expended on this cookbook, it might now exist as a pop-up, a scratch-and-sniff, or a punch-out-panorama variety. Not one of us would have been surprised.

We are all immensely proud of it.

Richard S. Schultz
Executive Director

Richard O. Whayland
President
Board of Directors

5

Featured Characters

DEVELOPMENT AND PRODUCTION COMMITTEE

Dorothy C. Baker   Teresa G. Meyer   Zuzanna K. O' Brien

ARTIST

Gary G. Baker

CREATIVE WRITER

Lora T. Spence

SPECIAL ADVISOR

Daniel F. Findley

TESTING

Patricia Smetanka, Chairman

Barbara Cooledge   Rosemary Kammerer
Norma Cottrill   Sheila S. Pasquantonio
Doris DePierre   Andreen Schneider
Lora T. Spence

PROOFREADERS

Joan Clark   Jennifer Drummy   Nancy Latshaw

MARKETING AND OPERATIONS COMMITTEE

June Ormiston, Chairman

Mary Benson   David Digby
Suellen Hicks   Nancy Johns   Shirley Norman
Frank Shonkwiler   David Smith

SPECIAL ASSISTANCE

Janet White, Chairman

Geraldine Bartelme   Ada Bates
Jean Getz   Penny Goldstein
Fern Jagger   Millicent McCathren
Linda Polito

TYPIST

Christine Hessler

Table Of Contents

ABOUT THIS COOKBOOK ...

Fairy tales, folk tales, and legends have always helped us lead our students, joyfully, step by step, into new understandings and experiences.

We invite our readers to follow a similar path through using this cookbook, for the fun, the pleasure, and the resulting togetherness each recipe may bring.

For all contributions, material and spiritual, we offer special thanks to:

Gary Baker	for	merriment and artistry
Lee O'Brien	for	perfect patience
Lora Spence	for	words and music
Eugene Spence	for	plowing and planting
The Brothers Grimm	for	their forgiveness

Now that this book belongs to you, we can only wish you every flavor of fun that we had cooking it up.

Dorothy C. Baker
Teresa G. Meyer
Zuzanna K. O'Brien

We lovingly dedicate these works to
All Young People of the Wesley Institute.

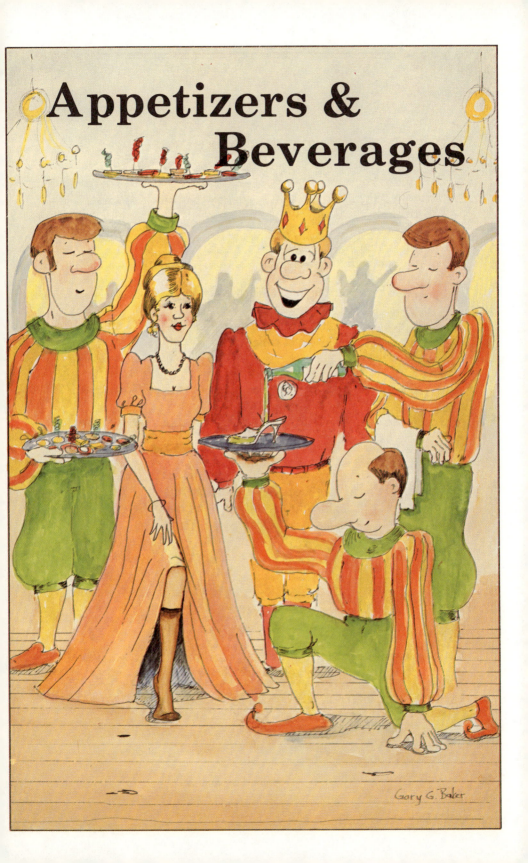

Appetizers & Beverages

Gary G. Baker

Chapter I

Cinderella's ... Appetizers and Beverages

What is that tinkling sound of glass -
That flash of rainbow light?
It could be Cinderella's toes,
or Tidbits of delight!

Cinderella couldn't have had that ball without her Fairy Godmother,
but
you can have one easily with any fitting combination of these niblets and
potions.

In your castle serve these anywhere
.. in the garden or by the fireplace
.. as a warm welcome or a first course.

Don't worry about arriving in a pumpkin coach; just make your entrance
with some of these dishes and —

NO ONE WILL NOTICE WHAT YOU'RE WEARING, EVEN WHEN THE
CLOCK STRIKES TWELVE!

CHEESE AND BACON HORS D'OEUVRES

16 slices white sandwich bread
1 pound Velveeta cheese
½ pound bacon, fried

1 medium onion
1 egg

Toast one side of bread in broiler. Cool. Grind cheese, bacon and onion in food grinder, or finely shred. Add egg and mix together. Spread cheese mixture on untoasted side of bread. Broil until bubbly. Immediately remove to freezer. When frozen, cut into quarters. Place in plastic bag. Will keep a long time in freezer. Heat before serving.

Janet White

CHEESE BUDS

½ pound Cracker Barrel mellow
   cheddar cheese
1 cup butter or margarine
2 cups sifted flour

¼ teaspoon red pepper
1 egg white, unbeaten
pecans, halved

Mix cheese and butter. Add sifted flour and red pepper. Roll out to ¼ inch thickness. Cut with the inside of a donut cutter. Brush tops with egg white. Place pecan half on each circle. Bake on ungreased cookie sheet at 425 degrees for 10 to 15 minutes.

Fern Jagger

CHEESE NIBBLES
(A good crunchy appetizer)

Thin sandwich bread
Butter, melted

Parmesan cheese
Sesame or poppy seeds, optional

Remove crusts from bread. Brush both sides of each slice with butter. Cut each slice into thirds. Sprinkle with Parmesan cheese, then seeds. Toast in 325 degree oven. Serve warm or cold, with soup, salad, or by itself.

Judy Douglass

COCKTAIL DEVIL TARTS

1 cup butter, softened
2 3-ounce package cream
  cheese, softened
2 cups flour
2 4½-ounce cans deviled ham

1 onion, finely chopped
½ cup grated Swiss cheese
2 eggs, beaten
2 tablespoons butter, melted
½ cup milk

Beat butter and cheese together until fluffy. Mix in flour. Roll into 24 1-inch balls. Press into miniature muffin tins to form a shell. Set aside. Divide deviled ham among shells. Divide onion and cheese among shells. Combine eggs, butter and milk. Pour over each tart as evenly as possible. Bake at 450 degrees for 10 minutes. Reduce heat to 350 degrees and bake for 15 more minutes.

Barbara Cooledge

GREEN CHILI APPETIZERS

4 4-ounce cans green chilies
1 pound cheddar cheese, grated

6 eggs

Butter oblong casserole. Line bottom with green chilies. Sprinkle top with cheddar cheese. Beat eggs until fluffy. Pour on top of cheese. Bake at 350 degrees for 45 minutes. Cool 10 to 15 minutes before cutting into squares. Serve on small square cocktail crackers, preferably Triscuits.

NOTE: These can be made ahead but do not add eggs until just
      before putting in oven.

Dotty France

HANKY PANKY

1 pound hot Italian sausage
1 pound ground beef
1 pound Velveeta cheese, grated
1 teaspoon oregano

1 teaspoon garlic salt
1 tablespoon Worcestershire
  sauce
2 loaves party rye bread

Brown meats separately and drain fat. Add cheese and remaining ingredients to meats. Mix well. Spread mixture on slices of party rye. Freeze on cookie sheets. After freezing, store in plastic bags. To use, heat in 300 degree oven for 15 to 20 minutes.

Ada Bates

PIZZA ORK
(Easy to prepare and so delicious)

1 2½-ounce jar chopped
   mushrooms, drained
½ cup chopped pepperoni
¼ cup chopped green pepper

¼ cup chopped black olives
1 cup shredded cheddar cheese
½ cup mayonnaise
nacho chips

Mix all ingredients. Spread on nacho chips. Put in microwave or broil until cheese melts.

Judy Oakley

SEAFOOD COQUILLE APPETIZER
(For an elegant evening)

Serves: 6

½ cup chopped onion
2 cloves garlic, crushed
½ cup butter
¼ cup flour
⅔ cup Sauterne wine
1 ⅓ cups milk

1 6½-ounce can crabmeat,
   drained
1 cup cleaned, cooked shrimp
8 tablespoons shredded Swiss
   cheese
2 tablespoons Parmesan cheese

Sauté onion and garlic in butter until tender. Remove from heat. Blend in flour. Cook over low heat, stirring until bubbly. Remove from heat, stir in wine and milk. Heat over low heat until the mixture boils, stirring constantly. Stir in crabmeat and shrimp. Divide into 6 individual baking dishes. Top each with cheeses. Broil for 4 minutes or until cheese is golden.

Susan Ferrell-Berman

Instead of hiring out, recruit the kids to help serve and make the hors d'oeuvres. After their job is complete, let them have their own party with a mini-tray of treats.

ZUCCHINI APPETIZERS

Yields: 4 dozen

3 cups thinly sliced zucchini
  (approximately 4 small)
1 cup Bisquick
½ cup chopped onion
½ cup grated Parmesan cheese
2 tablespoons snipped parsley
½ teaspoon salt

½ teaspoon seasoned salt
½ teaspoon marjoram or oregano
dash of pepper
1 clove garlic, finely chopped
½ cup oil
4 eggs, slightly beaten

Heat oven to 350 degrees. Grease 9 x 13 inch pan. Mix all ingredients. Spread in pan. Bake in 350 degree oven for 25 minutes or until golden brown. Cut into 2 x 1 inch pieces.

VARIATION: For a brunch or luncheon dish, spread into an 8 x 8 or 9 x 9 inch pan. Bake for about 35 minutes.

Anne Knoell

FRAN'S MUSHROOMS
(An easy marinated snack)

2 tablespoons vinegar
⅛ teaspoon salt
6 tablespoons oil or olive oil
1 small onion, sliced

1 pound mushrooms, cut as
  desired
1 package Good Seasons Italian
  Dressing mix

Mix all ingredients together. If possible, allow to marinate overnight.

Fran Schoemaker

MUSHROOM ROUNDS

1 cup finely chopped mushroom
  caps
1 ½ cups grated sharp cheese
¼ cup chopped green onion

½ cup mayonnaise
butter, softened
24 slices party rye bread

Combine mushrooms, cheese, onions and mayonnaise. Spread bread slices with a thin layer of softened butter. Spread mix on bread. Place on cookie sheet. Broil until cheese melts. Serve immediately.

NOTE: Can be made ahead of time and refrigerated until broiled.

Gail Holsinger

MUSHROOM SOUP HORS D'OEUVRES

1 loaf sliced white sandwich bread
1 10¾-ounce can cream of
  mushroom soup, undiluted
½ can evaporated milk
bacon strips

Trim crust from bread. Combine mushroom soup and milk in shallow pan. Press bread until flat. Dip bread in soup mixture and roll tightly. Wrap 3 small strips of bacon around roll to cover bread. Secure each with a toothpick. Cut bread roll between each piece of bacon. Place rolls on greased cookie sheet and refrigerate. Bake at 350 degrees for 20 minutes, or until brown.

NOTE: Can be frozen and used as needed.

Ruth Miller

SAUSAGE STUFFED MUSHROOMS
(Just terrific!)

2 pounds sausage, loose
¾ cup bread crumbs
garlic salt to taste
1 pound mushrooms
2 8-ounce cans tomato sauce
2 cups Sauterne wine
½ teaspoon oregano

Mix together sausage, bread crumbs, and garlic salt. Clean mushrooms and remove stems. If mushrooms are large, cut into 2 or 4 pieces. Roll meat mixture and place in mushroom cap. Ball should be approximately 1 inch in diameter. With mushroom side down, place in baking pan, one layer thick. Bake at 350 degrees for 30 minutes. Drain off excess grease. Mix tomato sauce, wine and oregano. Heat and add baked mushrooms. Mushrooms are best if left in sauce for at least 24 hours.

NOTE: These can be frozen.

Bonnie Emerick

STUFFED MUSHROOMS

16 to 18 large mushrooms
1 pound sausage, loose
1 pound cheddar cheese, grated
1 15½-ounce jar Ragu cooking
  sauce

Remove stems from mushrooms. Mix sausage and cheddar cheese. Form into 16 to 18 balls. Place balls in mushrooms. Bake on cookie sheet at 375 degrees for 15 minutes. Drain. Serve in hot Ragu cooking sauce.

Peggy Osborne

BAKED CRAB DIP
(You can never make too much)

1 8-ounce package cream
  cheese, softened
1 tablespoon milk
1 6½-ounce can crabmeat,
  drained

2 tablespoons chopped onion
½ teaspoon horseradish
¼ teaspoon salt
½ cup shredded cheddar cheese,
  and/or ⅓ cup toasted almonds

Blend all ingredients except cheddar cheese or almonds. Place in oven-proof dish. Top with cheese or almonds. Sprinkle with paprika, if desired. Bake at 350 degrees for 15 to 20 minutes. Serve with crackers.

NOTE: Has a white, fluffy appearance.

Pat Krivonak

BREAD DIP
(Gets reviews from "great" to "fantastic")

1 8-ounce jar Cheez Whiz
1 8-ounce package cream
  cheese, softened
¼ cup beer

¼ cup blue cheese salad
  dressing, or add to taste
1 round loaf unsliced rye bread

Mix together Cheez Whiz, cream cheese, beer and salad dressing on low speed until smooth. Cut a large hole from the top and center of the bread bread loaf. Pour cheese mixture into bread hole. Cut bread taken from loaf into cubes. Serve with bread cubes and cut vegetables.

NOTE: The bread loaf can be torn apart and eaten also.

Zuzanna K. O'Brien

CURRY DIP
(For curry lovers)

¾ cup mayonnaise
4½ teaspoons grated onion
4½ teaspoons ketchup

4½ teaspoons honey
4½ teaspoons lemon juice
1½ teaspoons curry powder

Mix all ingredients together. Refrigerate overnight. Serve with fresh vegetables.

NOTE: Keeps well in the refrigerator.

Pat Blair

DELICIOUS VEGETABLE DIP

1 24-ounce container small curd cottage cheese
2 generous tablespoons mayonnaise

1 package Hidden Valley Ranch or Original Ranch Style dressing mix
2 to 4 tablespoons milk

Put all ingredients in large mixing bowl. Beat with electric mixer on high until well-blended. Amount of milk added will determine desired consistency. Serve with raw vegetables.

Janet White

HOT BROCCOLI DIP
(Perfect for any party!)

1 10-ounce package chopped broccoli
1 small onion, sliced
½ cup almonds
2 tablespoons butter
1 2½-ounce can sliced mushrooms, drained

1 6-ounce roll garlic cheese spread
1 10¾-ounce can cream of mushroom soup, undiluted
½ teaspoon Tabasco sauce
1 teaspoon Worcestershire sauce
salt to taste
pepper to taste

Cook broccoli according to directions on package. Sauté onion and nuts in butter. Add mushrooms. Stir in drained broccoli. In a separate pan, melt cheese and soup together over medium heat, stirring constantly. Stir all ingredients into cheese-soup mixture. Heat. Serve warm with chips or crackers.

Dorothy Baker

HOT CLAM DIP

3 tablespoons butter
½ green pepper, chopped
1 medium onion, minced
1 7-ounce can of clams, drained
4 tablespoons ketchup

¼ cup processed cheese, cut in pieces
1 tablespoon Worcestershire sauce

Sauté pepper and onion in butter until tender. Add remaining ingredients. Cook over medium heat until cheese melts. Serve warm with crackers for dipping.

Barbara Cooledge

HOT PARTY DIP

1 8-ounce package cream
  cheese, softened
1 cup sour cream
2 tablespoons finely chopped
  onion

1 2½-ounce jar Armour dried
  beef, chopped
1 tablespoon finely chopped
  green pepper
6 to 7 black olives, chopped

Blend all ingredients. Bake at 325 degrees for 25 minutes. Serve with crackers.

Monica and Stu Hall

KING'S "HOT" TORTILLA CHIP DIP
(For the really daring)

2 tablespoons margarine
¼ cup chopped onion
1 8-ounce can stewed tomatoes,
  drained
½ 4-ounce can green chilies,
  chopped

½ teaspoon salt
dash of pepper
8 ounces cheddar cheese,
  shredded
20 pitted black olives, sliced
1 tablespoon hot taco sauce

Sauté onions in margarine in a 2-quart saucepan for 5 minutes. Add stewed tomatoes, green chilies, salt and pepper. Simmer for 10 minutes. Stir in cheese, olives and taco sauce. Cook until cheese is melted. Serve warm with plain tortilla chips.

NOTE: For the daring, try hot green chilies. For a milder dip, use mild taco sauce.

Nancy McCloskey

SHRIMP DIP

2 beef bouillon cubes
¼ cup water
1 8-ounce package cream cheese
½ cup sour cream

garlic salt to taste
1 4½-ounce can shrimp, drained
  and chopped

Boil bouillon cubes in water. Pour over cream cheese. Stir in sour cream. Mix well. Add garlic salt to taste. Mix in shrimp. Refrigerate at least 30 minutes before serving. Serve with plain crackers or chips.

Gail Holsinger

SPINACH DIP

1 10-ounce package frozen
   chopped spinach
1 package Knorr Vegetable Soup
   Mix

2 cups sour cream
2 tablespoons chopped scallions
   or onions
water chestnuts (optional)

Thaw spinach and drain thoroughly. Add other ingredients. Allow to sit for about 1 hour before serving. Good with pita bread, carrots and celery.

Joan Clark

TACO DIP
(It's hot but you'll never stop eating it)

2 8-ounce packages cream
   cheese, softened
1 8-ounce bottle hot El Paso
   Taco Sauce
1 green pepper, chopped
1 onion, chopped

1 tomato, chopped
shredded lettuce
10 ounces sharp cheddar cheese,
   grated
Tostidos or Doritos

Mix cream cheese and taco sauce. Form into a flat-topped ball. Set in the center of a large tray. Spread green pepper, onion, tomato and lettuce over top and sides of ball. Cover entire ball with grated cheese. Refrigerate. Arrange chips around tray.

NOTE: For a milder dip, use mild taco sauce.

Judy Oakley

FRUIT DIP
(A Cinderella pleaser)

1 8-ounce container Cool Whip
1 3-ounce box Americana Egg
   Custard instant pudding

1 teaspoon brandy extract
1 teaspoon rum extract
red food coloring, if desired

Mix all ingredients. Refrigerate. Serve with fresh fruit cut for dipping.

Monica and Stu Hall

GERRI'S FRUIT DIP

1 8-ounce package cream
  cheese, softened
10 ounces marshmallow cream
⅛ teaspoon ginger

2 teaspoons dried orange rind, or
  2 tablespoons fresh grated
  orange rind

Mix and blend ingredients well. Enjoy!

Gerri Bartelme

CHEESE BALL

8 ounces cheddar cheese, finely
  grated
1 3-ounce package cream
  cheese, softened
3 tablespoons sherry

½ teaspoon Worcestershire sauce
dash of onion salt
dash of garlic salt
dash of celery salt
½ cup chopped pecans or parsley

Mix all ingredients together at medium speed of an electric mixer. Shape into a ball. Roll in chopped nuts or parsley. Refrigerate.

Nancy Morgan

GARBANZO BEAN OR SPROUT SPREAD
(Will sprout many smiles)

4 cups cooked garbanzo beans
2 cloves garlic, pressed
¼ cup lemon juice
¼ cup oil
¼ cup tahini (roasted ground
  sesame)

cumin
paprika
salt
pepper
1 cup alfalfa sprouts

Press garbanzo beans through a food mill or blend in a food processor. In a large bowl, mix beans, garlic, lemon juice, oil and tahini. Add spices to taste. Gently fold in alfalfa sprouts. Mix thoroughly, being careful not to bruise bean sprouts. Spread heavily on whole wheat or bran bread.

VARIATION: Mean Green - Delete alfalfa sprouts. Add 1 cup packed, finely chopped parsley. Sprinkle with hot red bell pepper seed.

Don Polito

SHRIMP SPREAD
(Won't last until midnight)

½ cup chopped onion
½ cup chopped celery
½ cup mayonnaise
1 8-ounce package cream cheese, softened
½ can tomato soup, undiluted

1 envelope unflavored gelatin
2 tablespoons cold water
2 4½-ounce cans deveined pink shrimp or 1 9-ounce bag frozen shrimp

Put onion, celery, mayonnaise and cream cheese in medium mixing bowl. Mix with electric mixer. Heat tomato soup until warm, remove from heat. Mix gelatin with cold water and add to tomato soup. Add shrimp. Stir tomato soup mixture into cheese-mayonnaise mixture. Put into 1 quart mold. Chill well. Serve with crackers as a spread.

Janet White

PARMESAN CHEESE BREAD CUBES

1 loaf Pepperidge Farm very thin bread
2 eggs

milk
butter
Parmesan cheese

Cut crusts from bread, using 3 slices at a time. Beat eggs with a little milk. Dip 1 slice into egg mixture. Put between 2 dry slices. Cut into 1 to 1½ inch cubes. Dip each cube into melted butter. Roll each cube into Parmesan cheese. Put on cookie sheet and freeze. Remove to a plastic bag for storage in freezer. To serve, spray pan with Pam. Bake at 350 degrees for 8 to 10 minutes or until golden brown.

LaRue Weber

PARTY SNACK MIX

6 cups popped corn
1 6-ounce bag corn chips
2 cups small pretzels
1 cup soybeans
1 3-ounce can chow mein noodles

½ cup margarine or butter
2 tablespoons Worcestershire sauce
¼ teaspoon hot pepper sauce
1 clove garlic, minced

In large roasting pan, combine popped corn, corn chips, pretzels, soybeans and noodles. Melt margarine and stir in sauces and garlic. Pour over mixture. Mix well. Bake at 250 degrees for 1 hour, stirring several times.

Dottie Pierson

BAGNA CAUDA
(A fine fondue)

1 cup unsalted butter or
  margarine
¼ cup olive oil

6 large cloves garlic, minced or
  pressed
2 tablespoons chopped
  anchovies (optional)

Melt butter in saucepan. Add oil and garlic. Cook over low heat for 5 minutes. Do not let garlic brown. Add anchovies and cook for 5 more minutes. Transfer to fondue pot or electric wok. Double recipe may be required for wok.

NOTE: This recipe can be used for guests to cook their own small beet cubes, shrimp, mushrooms, sliced yellow squash, small zucchini slices, carrots, cauliflower, green pepper, pearl onions and celery. Each guest can use Syrian flatbread, Italian or sour dough bread to catch drippings from pot to plate or as an informal plate.

Gerri Bartelme

ANTIPASTO

1 cup oil
4 raw carrots, diced
4 green peppers, diced
2 large onions, diced
1 stalk celery, diced
1 pound mushrooms, diced
1 pound cauliflower, diced
1 7½-ounce can tuna fish,
  drained and flaked

1 pound crabmeat, drained
1 12-ounce bottle ketchup
2 12-ounce bottles chili sauce
½ cup green olives
½ cup ripe olives
3 cloves garlic, chopped
3 teaspoons salt
2 teaspoons Accent
juice of 2 lemons

Cook carrots, peppers, onions, celery, mushrooms and cauliflower in oil until tender. Stir in remaining ingredients. Simmer for 10 minutes. Serve hot or cold on plain crackers.

NOTE: Freezes well.

Dottie Pierson

CHAMPAGNE PUNCH
(Puts a sparkle in your holidays)

2 20-ounce cans crushed
   pineapple
4 bottles champagne, chilled
1 quart white rum
1 6-ounce can lemonade
   concentrate, frozen

1 46-ounce can pineapple juice,
   chilled
1 quart apple juice, chilled
1 pint lime or lemon sherbet
2 lemons, cut in slices

In punch bowl, combine pineapple, champagne, rum, lemonade concentrate, pineapple juice and apple juice. Stir until lemonade concentrate dissolves. Add sherbet. Garnish with lemon slices. Makes 40 servings.

Susan Ferrell-Berman

CITRUS PUNCH

1 6-ounce can lemonade
   concentrate, frozen
1 6-ounce can limeade
   concentrate, frozen
2 6-ounce cans orange juice
   concentrate, frozen

1 46-ounce can pineapple juice,
   chilled
6 cups cold water
½ teaspoon salt
2 7-ounce bottles club soda, chilled
1 fruit ring, frozen (if desired)

Combine juice, water and salt in punch bowl. Chill mixture. Before serving, stir in club soda. Add frozen fruit ring, if desired. Makes 32 servings

Fern Jagger

GUZZLE JUICE
(You can't get enough of it!)

1 46-ounce can pineapple juice,
   chilled

2 cups lemon blend, chilled
2 quarts ginger ale, chilled

Combine ingredients in punch bowl to make 25 servings.

1½ to 2 46-ounce cans pineapple
   juice, chilled

3 cups lemon blend, chilled
3 quarts ginger ale, chilled

Combine ingredients in punch bowl to make 36 servings.

Fern Jagger

SAUTERNE PUNCH

2½ cups sugar
2 cups lemon juice
1 medium pineapple, peeled and
   cut into ½ inch cubes
1 cup sugar
1 quart strawberries

1 block of ice
1 quart ice water
1 ⅘-quart bottle Sauterne, chilled
2 32-ounce bottles sparkling
   water, chilled
¼ cup brandy

In a large bowl, stir 2½ cups sugar into lemon juice until dissolved. In a separate container, sprinkle pineapple cubes with 1 cup sugar and let stand. Clean and slice strawberries and sweeten to taste. Refrigerate lemon mixture, pineapple and strawberries until ready to make punch. To serve punch, place ice in punch bowl. Surround ice with fruit pieces. Pour ice water, sauterne, sparkling water, brandy and lemon mixture over ice.

Millie McCathren

HOT SPICED CIDER
(From The Inn on Cove Hill in Rockport, Mass.)

Cider, without preservatives, if
   possible, as cider will have a
   sweeter taste

1 orange, sliced
2 sticks cinnamon
4 cloves

Combine ingredients. Heat on stove, on low heat, for approximately 1 hour. Keep heat low so cider does not boil.

Pat Krivonak

TEA BRANDY SLUSH

2 cups boiling water
3 tea bags
7 cups water
2 cups sugar
2 cups apricot or peach brandy

1 12-ounce can lemonade
   concentrate, frozen
1 6-ounce can orange juice
   concentrate, frozen
ginger ale or 7-Up

Place tea bags in boiling water and set aside. In a large pot, mix 7 cups water and sugar. Boil for 5 minutes. Cool. When cool, add brandy, lemonade concentrate and orange juice concentrate. Mix well. Add to tea mixture. Pour mixture into a large container and freeze. To serve, place 1 to 2 ice cream scoops of frozen mixture in a tall glass. Fill glass with ginger ale or 7-Up.

Elizabeth Pasquantonio

Breads

Gary Baker

CHAPTER II

Little Red Riding Hood's ... Breads

What brought that woodman to grandma's door?
"Red Riding Hood's cries," some have said.
But any cook knows that what made that man run,
was the **smell** from that **basket** of **bread**!

Watch your family and friends "wolf" down these goodies as fast as you can turn them out.

Cook's Note: Be sure to keep your windows closed while baking. We cannot be responsible for either wolves or woodsmen who pound at your door.

FRENCH BREAD

Yields: 2 loaves

2 cups warm water
1 package dry yeast
1 tablespoon sugar

2½ teaspoons salt
4 to 5 cups flour

Put warm water in large bowl. Add yeast to water and stir to dissolve yeast. Add sugar, salt and 3 cups of flour. Beat mixture 1 to 2 minutes, until smooth. Add enough flour to make a nice smooth dough (too much flour causes dough to be tough). Mix with spoon. Place dough on well-floured surface and knead until dough is smooth - about 8 minutes. Shape dough into ball and place in well-greased bowl. Cover dough with towel and set in warm place for 1 hour. Punch dough down. Divide dough in half and shape into smooth balls. Cover dough balls and let stand for 5 minutes. Use rolling pin and roll out dough ball to oblong shape. Starting at narrow end of dough, roll very tightly. Pinch the ends together to seal and pinch seam. Make sure ends and seam are well sealed; after sealing it helps to roll dough on flat surface a few times. Repeat steps with other dough ball. Place both loaves in well-greased French loaf pans. Make holes in top of loaves with fork - this releases air. Make 1 row of holes about 2 inches apart, the length of loaf. Cover loaves and let rise 1 hour. Bake at 400 degrees for 25 to 30 minutes.

Eleanor Towers

GRANDMA'S BROWN BREAD
(Conjures up sweet memories)

Yields: 5 loaves

3½ cups sugar
3½ cups unsifted flour
1 teaspoon salt
1 teaspoon ground cloves
1 teaspoon nutmeg
1 teaspoon cinnamon

2 teaspoons baking soda
4 eggs
1 cup oil
12 ounces apricot nectar
1 cup broken walnuts
1 cup raisins

Mix all ingredients together. Grease 5 1-pound coffee cans. Spoon batter into pans. Bake at 350 degrees for 1 hour. Cool for 10 minutes in pan before removing.

NOTE: Can substitute 1-pound loaf pans for coffee cans.

Fern Jagger

KANSAS BEER BREAD

Yields: 2 loaves

1 12-ounce can beer, warm
(preferably Coors)
3 cups self-rising flour

5 teaspoons sugar
4 teaspoons butter, melted

Combine beer, flour and sugar in large bowl. Mix well. Pour 2 teaspoons melted butter on dough. Do not stir butter in. Let stand for 15 minutes, then turn into 2 greased 5 x 9 inch loaf pans. Bake at 350 degrees for 1 hour or until brown. Remove bread from pan. Brush top with remaining butter.

Sue and Bill Law

MONK'S BREAD

(Cake-like, fragrant and perfect eaten fresh and warm. Needs no butter, but cries for jelly and jam!)

Yields: 2 loaves

½ cup water
1 cup milk
½ cup shortening or butter
4 cups sifted all-purpose flour,
divided
½ cup wheat germ

2 teaspoons nutmeg
½ cup sugar
2 teaspoons salt
2 packages dry yeast
3 eggs (at room temperature)

Preheat the oven to 350 degrees, 10 minutes before actual baking. Grease a 10-inch tube cake pan, bundt pan, or 2 loaf pans. Heat water, milk and shortening until warm - 120 degrees. The shortening does not need to melt entirely. Blend ⅓ cup of the flour with wheat germ, nutmeg, sugar, salt and dry yeast in large mixing bowl. Add the warmed liquid to the flour mixture. Beat with an electric mixer at medium speed for about 2 minutes, scraping sides of bowl occasionally. Add gradually ⅔ cup of the remaining flour and the eggs. Beat at high speed for 2 minutes. Add all the remaining flour and mix well. Batter will be thick, not stiff. Cover and let rise in a warm, draft-free place (about 85 degrees) until double in bulk - about 1 hour and 15 minutes. Beat the dough down. Turn into prepared pan(s). Cover and let rise in a warm, draft-free place until it has increased ⅓ to ½. Bake for 40 to 50 minutes at 350 degrees. Cool slightly, run a knife around the center and outer edges of the pan and turn onto a rack to cool.

Lora T. Spence

RYE BREAD

Yields: 2 loaves

3 ½ cups white flour
2 packages dry yeast
1 cup warm water
¾ cup milk
2 tablespoons shortening

2 ½ tablespoons sugar
3 teaspoons salt
1 egg
1 ½ cups rye flour
3 teaspoons caraway seed

Place 2 cups white flour in large mixing bowl. Add yeast. Stir to mix yeast evenly through flour. Mix water, milk, shortening, sugar and salt in saucepan. Heat until warm (130 degrees). Add warm mixture to flour and yeast. Add egg. Beat for 2 minutes. Stir in rye flour and caraway seed. Mix in enough white flour to make soft dough. Knead 8 minutes. Cover and let stand 20 minutes. Grease 2 5 x 9 inch loaf pans. Divide dough in half. Place in pans. Let rise in warm place for 50 minutes. Bake at 400 degrees for 25 to 30 minutes. Cool on rack.

VARIATION: Wheat Bread. In place of rye flour, use 1 cup whole wheat flour.

Eleanor Towers

WHOLE WHEAT BREAD
(Healthy and wholesome)

Yields: 3 to 4 loaves

4 cups milk
½ cup molasses
¼ cup margarine
½ cup sugar
4 teaspoons salt

¼ cup caraway seeds
½ cup whole wheat germ
2 packages dry yeast dissolved in
¼ cup warm water
10 cups whole wheat flour

Combine first 7 ingredients. Heat until steaming, stirring constantly. Cool. Stir in yeast mixture. Add flour, 1 cup at a time. Beat well after each addition. Place in large greased bowl. Let rise until double in size, about 1 ½ hours. Punch down. Let rise again 45 minutes. Turn out on board. Knead for 5 minutes. Divide into 3 or 4 loaves. Place in greased 5 x 9 inch loaf pans. Let rise until double in size. Bake at 350 degrees for 45 minutes.

NOTE: This recipe can be cut in half.

Janine and Mike Murphy

SCANDINAVIAN WHITE BREAD

Yields: 2 loaves

1 ½ packages dry yeast
¾ cup warm water (105 to 115 degrees)
2⅔ cups warm milk
¼ cup sugar

1 tablespoon salt
6 tablespoons shortening
9 to 10 cups flour
3 teaspoons grated cardamom
butter, softened

Dissolve yeast in warm water. Stir in warm milk, sugar, salt, shortening, 5 cups flour and cardamom. Beat until smooth. Mix in enough remaining flour to make the dough easy to handle. Turn dough onto a lightly floured board. Knead until smooth and elastic, about 10 minutes. Place in greased bowl, then turn greased side up. Cover. Let rise in a warm place until double, about 1 hour. Dough is ready if an impression lasts. Punch down dough. Divide in half. Roll each half into 9 x 18 inch rectangles. Roll up, beginning at the short side. With the side of hand, press each end to seal. Fold ends under loaf. Place seam side down in 5 x 9 inch greased loaf pan. Brush loaves lightly with butter. Let rise again until double in size, about 1 hour. Heat oven to 425 degrees. Place loaves on low rack so that the tops of the pans are in the center of the oven. Pans should not touch each other or the sides of the oven. Bake for 30 to 35 minutes or until the top is a deep golden brown. Loaves should sound hollow when tapped. Remove from pans. Brush loaves with soft butter. Cool on wire racks.

Dorothy Baker

DINNER BUNS

Yields: 2½ to 3 dozen

½ cup warm water
2 packages dry yeast
2 cups warm milk
7 tablespoons sugar

2 teaspoons salt
1 egg
½ cup oil
8 to 10 cups flour

Dissolve yeast in warm water. Add milk, sugar, salt, egg and oil. Add flour to make a soft dough. Knead until smooth. Let rise until double in size, about 1½ to 2 hours. Punch down. Let rise again. Shape into buns and place on greased cookie sheet. Let rise until double. Bake at 350 degrees for 20 minutes.

Doe Clark

BUNS, RAISIN BREAD, OR DINNER ROLLS

Basic Dough:

2 cups milk	2 packages dry yeast
½ cup sugar	½ cup warm water
2 teaspoons salt	2 eggs
4 tablespoons butter	6½ to 7 cups flour

Heat milk, sugar, salt and butter in saucepan (it should feel warm when a drop is put on wrist) and stir to dissolve sugar and salt. Mix yeast into warm water and stir to dissolve yeast. Add yeast mixture to milk mixture. Add eggs and stir. Put 4 cups flour into large pan. Add liquid mixture all at once and beat 2 minutes. Add remaining flour, 1 cup at a time and mix with spoon. (The amount of flour varies - only use enough to make a soft dough.) Place dough on well-floured surface and knead until dough is smooth - about 10 minutes. Place dough in greased pan and cover with towel. Let rise in warm place until double in size - about 1½ hours. Punch dough down then let set for 15 minutes. Dough is now ready to be baked into buns, raisin bread or rolls.

BUNS

Yields: 2 dozen

Shape by pinching off pieces of dough about the size of a tennis ball. Work dough with hands until nice and smooth - a little bit of oil on hands will help. Place dough on greased cookie sheet. Cover dough and let rise in warm place about 1 to 1½ hours. Bake at 425 degrees for 15 minutes.

RAISIN BREAD

Yields: 2 loaves

After first rising, add ½ cup raisins to dough. Shape dough into 2 loaves and place in greased loaf pans. Cover dough and let rise in warm place 1½ hours. Bake at 400 degrees for 25 to 30 minutes.

DINNER ROLLS

Yields: 2 to 2½ dozen

After first rising, pinch off pieces of dough about the size of ping pong balls and shape into balls. Place dough balls in greased muffin tins (2 pieces in each opening). Let dough rise 1½ hours. Bake at 400 degrees for 15 to 20 minutes.

Eleanor Towers

31

ICE BOX ROLLS

(Ice box in the city is commonly referred to as a refrig. or frig.)

Yields: 2 to 3 dozen

2 cups boiling water
½ cup sugar
2 tablespoons shortening
1 teaspoon salt

2 eggs, beaten
2 packages dry yeast
¼ cup warm water
6 to 7 cups sifted flour

Pour boiling water over sugar, shortening and salt. Let mixture cool until lukewarm. Add eggs to mixture. Dissolve yeast in warm water and add to mixture. Add flour and knead until elastic. Place dough in ice box overnight. Take pieces of dough and form into size of an egg. Put in muffin pan and let rise 3 hours. Bake at 400 degrees for 20 minutes.

Debbie and Frank McKenna

MOM'S ROLLS

Yields: 1 to 1½ dozen

1 cup boiling water
¼ cup sugar
1 teaspoon salt
1 tablespoon shortening
1 package dry yeast

⅛ cup warm water
1 tablespoon sugar
1 egg, beaten
4 cups flour
butter

Mix boiling water, ¼ cup sugar, salt and shortening. Cool until lukewarm. Dissolve yeast in warm water and sugar. Stir into sugar mixture. Add egg. Stir in 2 cups flour. Beat thoroughly. Stir in remaining flour. Mix, but do not knead. Form into a ball in the bowl. Brush top with butter. Allow to rise for 1 hour. Shape into rolls. Allow to rise again. Bake in a 350 to 375 degree oven for 10 to 15 minutes.

Dorothy Baker

Have your children form animals or other shapes from thawed frozen bread dough. Let them rise, bake, and eat them.

ANGEL BISCUITS
(Guaranteed to turn a wolf into an angel)

Yields: 1 to 1½ dozen

1 package dry yeast
¼ cup warm water
2½ cups flour
½ teaspoon baking soda
1 teaspoon baking powder

1 teaspoon salt
⅛ cup sugar
½ cup shortening
1 cup buttermilk

Dissolve yeast in warm water and set aside. Mix dry ingredients in order given. Cut in shortening. Stir in buttermilk and yeast mixture. Blend thoroughly. Refrigerate or roll into biscuits. Cut and place on greased pan and let rise slightly. Bake at 400 degrees for 15 minutes or until lightly browned.

Judy and Bill Alexy

BREAKFAST PUFFS

Yields: 1 dozen large or 2 dozen small

⅓ cup shortening
½ cup sugar
1 egg
1½ teaspoons baking powder
1½ cups sifted flour

½ teaspoon salt
¼ teaspoon nutmeg
½ cup milk
½ cup butter, melted

Cinnamon mixture:
⅓ cup sugar

1 tablespoon cinnamon

Grease 12 large or 24 small muffin tins. Cream together shortening, sugar and egg. Sift together baking powder, sifted flour, salt and nutmeg. Add flour mixture to shortening mixture, alternately with milk. Mix until smooth. Fill muffin tins ⅔ full. Bake at 350 degrees for 20 to 25 minutes, until light brown. Immediately remove from muffin tins. Roll in melted butter, then in cinnamon mixture.

Nancy Johns

33

APPLESAUCE LOAF

Yields: 1 loaf

½ cup butter or margarine
1 cup sugar
2 eggs
1¾ cups flour
1 teaspoon salt
1 teaspoon baking soda

½ teaspoon cinnamon
½ teaspoon nutmeg
1 cup sweetened applesauce
½ cup chopped walnuts
½ cup raisins

Cream butter or margarine to soften. Gradually add sugar, creaming till light. Add eggs. Beat until light and fluffy. Sift together dry ingredients. Add to creamed mixture, alternating with applesauce. Beat after each addition. Stir in nuts and raisins. Pour into lightly greased 9¼ x 5¼ x 3 inch loaf pan. Bake at 350 degrees for 55 to 60 minutes. Cool about 10 minutes, then remove from pan. When completely cool, wrap in clear plastic wrap or aluminum foil.

Peg Gillick

PECAN MUFFINS

Yields: 1 dozen

1 cup brown sugar
½ cup self rising flour
2 eggs, beaten

⅓ cup butter, melted
1 teaspoon vanilla
½ to 1 cup pecans

Mix all ingredients together. Pour into greased baking cups. Bake at 350 degrees for 25 minutes.

Joan Fullwood

 Using a spoon, drop pancake batter onto the griddle in shapes of animals or familiar objects. Turn with a spatula when puffed up and full of bubbles.

TWYLA'S REFRIGERATOR MUFFINS
(As simple as opening your refrigerator door)

Yields: ½ gallon batter

1 cup boiling water
1 cup Nabisco 100% bran
1¼ cups sugar
½ cup shortening
2 eggs
2 cups buttermilk

2½ cups flour
2½ teaspoons baking soda
¾ teaspoon salt
2 cups Kellogg's All Bran
½ pound seedless raisins
  (optional)

Pour boiling water over Nabisco Bran and set aside. Cream sugar and shortening. Add eggs, 1 at a time, to creamed sugar and shortening. Beat well. Add buttermilk and Nabisco Bran. Add sifted dry ingredients and Kellogg's Bran. Fold until just moist. Add raisins, if desired. Store in covered container 2 days (not really necessary). Batter will keep in refrigerator for 6 weeks · store in Tupperware-like container. Bake at 375 degrees for 20 to 25 minutes, or microwave at full power for 1¼ minutes per muffin.

Twyla Jagger

BANANA BREAD

Yields: 1 loaf

¾ cup butter or margarine,
  softened
1 cup sugar
2 eggs, lightly beaten

2 cups flour, sifted
½ teaspoon baking soda
1½ teaspoons baking powder
2 to 3 ripe bananas, mashed

Cream margarine and sugar. Add eggs, 1 at a time. Add dry ingredients, then bananas. Mix well. Grease 5 x 9 inch loaf pan. Turn batter into pan. Bake at 350 degrees for 1 hour.

Penny Goldstein

CINNAMON BREAD

Yields: 1 loaf

½ cup sugar
½ cup margarine, softened
1 egg
1 cup buttermilk
1 teaspoon baking soda

2 cups flour
⅓ cup sugar
1 tablespoon cinnamon
butter

Cream ½ cup sugar and margarine until smooth. Add egg and buttermilk. Mix well. Stir in baking soda and flour, forming dough. Mix ⅓ cup sugar and cinnamon. Divide dough into 3 parts. Place ⅓ of dough in greased 5 x 9 inch loaf pan. Sprinkle with ⅓ of the cinnamon-sugar mixture. Repeat procedure for the next 2 layers. Dot with butter. Bake at 350 degrees for 1 hour.

Zuzanna K. O'Brien

CRANBERRY NUT BREAD
(An excellent holiday snack)

Yields: 1 loaf

2 cups flour
½ teaspoon salt
1¼ teaspoons baking powder
½ teaspoon baking soda
1 cup sugar
1 cup cranberries

1 cup chopped nuts
rind of 1 orange, grated
2 tablespoons shortening
juice of 1 orange
¾ cup boiling water
1 egg, beaten

Combine flour, salt, baking powder, baking soda and sugar. Sift twice. Add cranberries and nuts. In a measuring cup, combine grated orange rind, shortening, orange juice and boiling water. Add to 1 beaten egg. Pour liquid ingredients into dry ingredients. Mix. Prepare a 5 x 9 inch loaf pan by greasing the sides and placing a piece of waxed paper on the bottom. Pour batter into loaf pan. Bake at 350 degrees for 1 hour.

Jeannette Johnson

DATE AND NUT BREAD

Yields: 2 loaves

1 ½ cups dates, washed, pitted,
cut in pieces
1 ½ cups boiling water
3 tablespoons butter
1 ½ cups sugar
1 teaspoon salt

1 egg, beaten
2¾ cups sifted flour
1 teaspoon baking soda
1 teaspoon cream of tartar
⅓ teaspoon vanilla
1 cup broken black walnuts

Add water to dates. Mix in butter, sugar and salt. Let cool. Add egg. Sift flour again with soda. Add flour, cream of tartar and vanilla. Mix in walnuts. Grease and flour 2 5 x 9 inch loaf pans. Turn batter into pans. Bake at 350 degrees for 1 hour and 15 minutes. Best second day.

NOTE: For a higher nut bread, use only 1 pan and increase baking time.

LaRue Weber

ORANGE HONEY BREAD

Yields: 1 loaf

2 tablespoons shortening
1 cup honey
1 egg, well-beaten
1 ½ tablespoons grated orange
peel
2½ cups sifted flour

2½ teaspoons baking powder
½ teaspoon baking soda
½ teaspoon salt
¾ cup orange juice
¾ cup chopped nuts

Cream shortening and honey. Add egg and orange peel. Sift dry ingredients together. Alternately add flour mixture and orange juice to creamed mixture. Add nuts. Turn into greased 5 x 9 inch loaf pan. Bake at 325 degrees for 70 minutes.

Fern Jagger

If you run out of superfine sugar, process a bit of granulated sugar in the blender.

ORANGE NUT BREAD

Yields: 1 loaf

1 medium-size orange
1 cup raisins or dates
2 tablespoons shortening, melted
1 teaspoon vanilla
1 egg, beaten
¼ teaspoon salt

1 teaspoon baking powder
½ teaspoon baking soda
1 cup sugar
2 cups sifted flour (Gold Medal general purpose)
½ cup chopped nuts

Extract juice from orange and pour into an 8-ounce liquid measuring cup; add boiling water to fill cup. Remove most of the white membrane from peel. Force peel and dates through food chopper, using coarse blade. Add diluted orange juice. Stir in shortening, vanilla and egg. Sift salt, baking powder, soda and sugar with flour. Add to orange juice mixture. Beat well. Stir in nuts. Line 5 x 9 inch loaf pan with 2 pieces of waxed paper going in opposite directions. Bake at 350 degrees for 1 hour. Cool loaf on wire rack. Slices best the second day.

NOTE: If using glass dish, bake at 325 degrees.

Fern Jagger

PEAR BREAD
(Why make one . . . make a pair)

Yields: 1 loaf

½ cup butter, softened
1 cup sugar
2 eggs
½ teaspoon baking soda
⅛ teaspoon nutmeg
½ teaspoon salt

2 cups flour
1 teaspoon baking powder
¼ cup plain yogurt or buttermilk
1 teaspoon vanilla
1 cup coarsely chopped pears

Cream butter and sugar. Beat in eggs, 1 at a time. Combine dry ingredients. Alternately add dry ingredients and yogurt or buttermilk to egg mixture. Stir in vanilla and pears. Grease loaf pan with butter. Pour batter into pan. Bake at 350 degrees for 1 hour.

Ann Garner

PUMPKIN BREAD

Yields: 2 loaves

3 ½ cups flour
3 cups sugar
2 teaspoons baking soda
1 ½ teaspoons salt
1 teaspoon cinnamon
½ teaspoon nutmeg

½ teaspoon cloves
1 cup oil
3 eggs
⅔ cup water
2 cups pumpkin

Grease and flour 2 5 x 9 inch loaf pans. Sift all dry ingredients together. Make a well in center of flour mixture and add all remaining ingredients. Mix until smooth. Pour into loaf pans. Bake at 350 degrees for 1 hour.

Teresa Meyer

RHUBARB BREAD

Yields: 1 loaf

½ cup milk
½ teaspoon lemon juice
¾ cup brown sugar
⅓ cup oil
1 egg
½ teaspoon vanilla
1 ¼ cups flour

½ teaspoon salt
½ teaspoon baking soda
½ pound rhubarb, diced
¼ cup chopped walnuts
¼ cup sugar
1 ½ teaspoons margarine,
    softened

In a small bowl combine milk and lemon juice and let stand for 5 minutes. In a large bowl combine brown sugar, oil, egg and vanilla. Beat until smooth. Sift together flour, salt and baking soda. Alternately add dry ingredients and soured milk to sugar mixture. Beat mixture after each addition until smooth. Dust rhubarb with flour. Fold in rhubarb and nuts. Grease loaf pan with butter. Pour batter into pan. Combine ¼ cup sugar with margarine. Sprinkle over batter. Bake at 325 degrees for 1 hour. Let bread cool in pan for 10 minutes. Turn onto rack to cool.

Shirley Norman

CARAMEL NUT ROLLS
(Worth the work)

Yields: 2½ to 3 dozen

¼ cup hot water
¼ cup warm milk
1 teaspoon sugar

1 package dry yeast
¾ cup flour

Stir together water and milk. Add sugar and dry yeast. Add flour to make soft batter. Cover with plastic wrap and set in warm place for about 2 hours.

3 cups flour
¼ cup sugar
1½ teaspoons salt

⅓ cup margarine, softened
2 eggs, beaten
1 cup milk

Mix flour, sugar, salt and margarine to a pie crust consistency. Add to yeast mixture. Stir together eggs and milk. Add to flour mixture. Stir until well mixed. Cover. Place in refrigerator for several hours or overnight.

butter or margarine, softened
sugar, brown or white

cinnamon

With floured hands place dough on floured board. Divide dough in half. Roll dough out into rectangle. Spread dough with soft butter or margarine. Sprinkle with sugar and cinnamon. Roll dough up starting from long side of rectangle. Cut into 1 inch slices. Repeat with second half of dough. Makes 24 to 27 slices.

Prepare pans:
8 x 8 inch pan (9 rolls):
½ cup brown sugar
¼ cup butter or margarine
1 tablespoon light corn syrup
chopped nuts

9 x 13 inch pan (15 to 18 rolls):
¾ cup sugar
⅓ cup butter or margarine
2 tablespoons light corn syrup
chopped nuts

Combine ingredients in pan. Heat slowly, stirring until melted. Add chopped nuts to melted mixture. Place rolls into pans. Let rise for 30 minutes. Bake at 400 degrees for 15 minutes, until golden brown. Remove rolls from pans immediately by flipping pans over and lifting pan off rolls slowly.

Sherry Wilson

FRUIT SWIRL COFFEECAKE

Serves: 18

1 ½ cups sugar
½ cup butter or margarine,
　softened
½ cup shortening
1 ½ teaspoons baking powder
1 teaspoon vanilla

1 teaspoon almond extract
4 eggs
3 cups flour
2 21-ounce cans cherry pie filling
　or other pie filling

Glaze:
1 cup confectioners' sugar

2 tablespoons milk

Preheat oven to 350 degrees. Blend sugar, butter, shortening, baking powder, vanilla, almond extract and eggs in a large bowl. Use mixer on low speed. Add flour. Grease jelly roll pan. Spread ⅔ of the batter in jelly roll pan. Spread pie filling over batter. Drop remaining batter by the spoonful over pie filling. Bake at 350 degrees for 45 minutes.

Glaze:
Mix sugar and milk. Drizzle over cake after it is removed from the oven. Cut into 1 ½ inch pieces.

Margaret Goodwin

JEWISH COFFEE CAKE

Serves: 10 to 12

1 cup plus 3 tablespoons butter,
　softened
1 ¼ cups sugar
2 eggs, well beaten
2 cups flour

½ teaspoon baking soda
1 teaspoon baking powder
1 cup sour cream
1 teaspoon vanilla

Nut mixture:
1 cup ground or chopped nuts
½ teaspoon cinnamon

3 tablespoons sugar
1 teaspoon vanilla

Cream butter. Add sugar and eggs. Cream mixture until very smooth. Combine flour, soda, and baking powder. Add flour and sour cream alternately. Add vanilla. Grease bundt pan. Put ½ dough mixture in bundt pan first, then ½ nut mixture. Top with one more layer of dough, then remaining nut mixture. Bake at 350 degrees for 1 hour.

Terri Piatek

COTTAGE CHEESE PANCAKES

Serves: 2 to 3 people

3 eggs, well-beaten
1 cup creamed cottage cheese (a
creamy blend is best)

2 tablespoons butter
¾ cup sifted flour
¼ teaspoon salt

Combine ingredients in blender until well mixed. Drop batter onto well greased grill or frying pan by large spoonfuls. Serve with fresh strawberries, peaches, or any fruit syrup instead of maple syrup.

Bev and Dick Schultz

LIGHT WHOLE WHEAT PANCAKES
(Many whole wheat pancakes are too heavy;
this combination of flours yields a light, delicious pancake.)

Serves: 4

1 cup whole wheat flour
1 cup unbleached white flour
4 teaspoons baking powder
¼ cup oil

2 eggs
1 cup milk
1 cup water

Combine ingredients. Spoon batter onto lightly oiled, hot griddle. Fry until puffy and bubbly. Turn and fry other side.

VARIATIONS:
Fruit pancakes: Spoon batter into pan. Immediately add sliced fruit or stir mashed bananas or applesauce into batter.

Wholesome pancakes: Use 2 cups whole wheat flour omitting white flour or, add ¼ cup wheat germ to batter.

Barbara and Rick Heinze

OVEN-BAKED GERMAN PANCAKE

Serves: 2

3 eggs
½ cup flour, sifted
¼ teaspoon salt

½ cup milk
2 tablespoons butter, melted

Beat eggs with fork. Gradually add flour, beating constantly. Stir in salt, milk and butter. Grease 10 inch skillet or 9 x 13 inch cake pan. Pour batter into pan. Bake at 450 degrees for 10 minutes, then at 350 degrees for 12 minutes. Serve with preserves, syrup or confectioners' sugar.

Pat Krivonak

REPUBLICAN PANKAKKAS
(Swedish Pancakes)

Serves: 12

1 pound bacon, cut in 1 inch
  pieces
3 tablespoons bacon fat
3 eggs

¾ cup sugar
dash of salt
3 cups flour
5 cups milk

Fry bacon. Place in bottom of a 9 x 13 inch cake pan or 2 8 x 8 inch cake pans. Add bacon fat. Mix eggs, sugar, salt, flour and milk in a large mixing bowl. Pour batter over bacon in pan(s). Bake at 500 degrees until bubbly at the edges. Reduce heat to 375 degrees. Bake for 1 hour or until done. Pancakes should rise and look puffy, with a lightly browned crust on top. Cut into squares. Serve with syrup and butter.

Grace H. Pearson

SOUR CREAM PANCAKES

Serves: 4 to 5

2 eggs, well beaten
1 cup sour cream
1 cup milk
1 cup flour

1 tablespoon sugar
1 teaspoon baking soda
pinch of salt

Mix all ingredients together. Fry on greased griddle.

Nancy Conover

WAFFLES
(A Scandinavian treat!)

Serves: 8

4 eggs
3 cups sifted flour
5 teaspoons baking powder
¾ cup sugar
1 teaspoon salt

1 teaspoon grated cardamom
1½ cups milk
1 teaspoon vanilla
6 tablespoons butter, melted

Beat eggs in medium mixing bowl. Sift together flour and baking powder. Place all remaining ingredients in mixing bowl. Stir until smooth. Additional milk may be added to batter if it begins to thicken.

Dorothy Baker

NANNY'S BLINTZES
(Cheese Crepes)

Yields: 12

Filling:
1 pound Ricotta cheese
1 egg, beaten

1 teaspoon sugar
salt to taste
pepper to taste

Crepes:
2 to 3 eggs, beaten
¾ cup flour

1 teaspoon butter
½ cup margarine

Filling:
Mix together cheese, egg, sugar, salt and pepper. Refrigerate while making crepes.

Crepes:
Gradually add flour to beaten eggs, mixing well. Mixture should flow from spoon. Heat pan over medium temperature setting. Melt butter and spread over surface of pan. Pour about 2 tablespoons of batter into pan. Quickly tilt pan around to form a very thin crepe, 6 to 8 inches in diameter. When edges look crisp, flip and lightly brown other side. Remove from pan. Repeat process to make about 12 crepes.

To Assemble:
Lay the crepe flat so that the side that is more yellow is underneath. Place 1 to 2 tablespoons of the filling just above the center of the crepe. Fold sides in toward center. Fold top flap over center and roll tightly towards you. Check tucks for possible leaks.

To Cook:
Melt margarine in a heavy skillet over medium high heat. Brown blintzes on each side. Drain on paper toweling.

NOTE: Serve with a dobble of sour cream. Can be made ahead of time and frozen.

Sue Spagnuolo

GRILLED PEANUT BUTTER AND JELLY
(For an unusual breakfast that's fast and tasty)

Serves: 1

Spread peanut butter and jelly on one slice of bread. Place other slice of bread on top. Fry in butter until brown on both sides.

Barbara and Rick Heinze

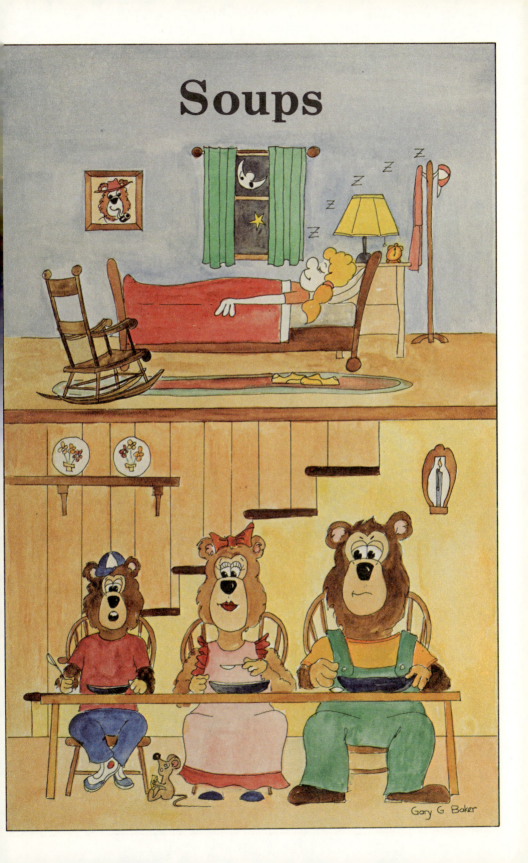

Soups

Gary G. Baker

CHAPTER III

The Three Bears' ... Soups

These bears had good taste, we are sure,
And we didn't have to snoop.
For there in that cottage was Goldilocks' lure,
Waiting warm, slurpy bowls of good soup!

A simmering pot of soup on the back of the stove is always as comforting as a bear hug, and, if you like, making it can be as adventurous as a walk in the woods.

Too hot or too cold, too bland or too boring will never be problems with these.

Soup of the evening or of the morning, the entire bear family will please!

From
Papa
to
Mama
to
Baby.

AMEL'S FAMOUS CREAM OF BROCCOLI SOUP

Yields: 2½ quarts

1 to 2 bunches broccoli
½ cup margarine
1 cup diced onion
¾ cup flour

1 cup half and half (optional)
½ gallon milk
1 heaping tablespoon chicken base
1¼ pounds American cheese

Cook broccoli until tender. Chop, leaving the florets intact. Melt margarine in a large pot. Sauté diced onion in margarine until translucent. Add flour. Cook, stirring constantly with a wire whisk until thickened. Add half and half, milk and chicken base. Heat thoroughly, stirring constantly. Add cheese. Continue stirring until cheese melts and soup thickens. Do not boil. Turn off heat. Add broccoli. Serve piping hot.

Amel's Restaurant

BAKED RIPE OLIVE MINESTRONE

Yields: 3½ quarts

1½ pounds lean stew meat
1 cup coarsely chopped onion
1 teaspoon minced garlic
1 teaspoon salt
¼ teaspoon pepper
2 tablespoons olive oil
3 10½-ounce cans beef broth (4 cups), undiluted
2 10½-ounce cans water (2⅔ cups)
1½ teaspoons Italian herb seasoning

1 16-ounce can tomatoes, undrained
1 15¼-ounce can kidney beans, undrained
1¾ cups pitted ripe olives
1 cup liquid from olives
1½ cups thinly sliced carrots
1 cup small seashell macaroni, uncooked
2 cups sliced zucchini
grated Parmesan cheese

Preheat oven to 400 degrees. Cut meat into 1¼ inch cubes. Mix meat, onion, garlic, salt and pepper together in Dutch oven. Add oil and stir to coat meat evenly. Brown uncovered in preheated oven for about 40 minutes (stirring once or twice). Reduce heat to 350 degrees. Add broth, water and Italian seasoning. Cover and cook 1 hour, until meat is tender. Remove from oven. Stir in tomatoes, beans, olives, olive liquid, carrots and macaroni. Sprinkle sliced zucchini on top. Cover and return to oven. Bake 40 to 45 minutes, until macaroni is tender. Serve with grated Parmesan cheese.

Eleanor Marshall

BEAN SOUP
(A robust lunch for "Baby Bear")

Yields: 5 quarts

1 pound navy beans
1 6-ounce can tomato sauce with bits
4 large potatoes, diced
1 large onion, diced
1 large carrot, diced
3 to 4 stalks of celery, diced

½ teaspoon garlic powder
½ teaspoon marjoram leaves, crushed
salt to taste
pepper to taste
1 pound ham, diced

Place beans in large bowl. Cover with water. Soak beans overnight in the refrigerator. Rinse them twice with cold water. Cover the beans with 5 quarts of hot water. Cook for a few minutes. Add the remaining ingredients. Cook over medium to low heat for 2 hours or until beans are of desired tenderness. This can be frozen.

Vera King

BEEF AND VEGETABLE SOUP

Yields: 4 quarts

1 ½ pounds stewing beef or beef shin
1 soup bone
4 quarts water
1 bay leaf
1 teaspoon salt
½ teaspoon pepper
1 medium cabbage, thinly sliced
2 medium zucchini, sliced
4 to 5 carrots, sliced
1 cup chopped celery

1 cup chopped onion
½ 10-ounce package frozen corn
½ 10-ounce package green beans
2 tablespoons chopped parsley
1 12-ounce can tomatoes, undrained
1 6-ounce can tomato paste
1 teaspoon Worcestershire sauce
1 beef bouillon cube
¾ teaspoon sugar
pinch of oregano

Put beef and soup bone in heavy kettle. Cover with cold water. Add bay leaf, salt and pepper. Cover and bring to a boil. Turn heat to low. Add cabbage, zucchini, carrots, celery and onion. Simmer for 2 hours. Add remaining ingredients. Simmer, covered, for 1 to 1 ½ hours. Remove meat and bone. Cut meat into small pieces and add to soup.

NOTE: Vegetables may be varied - broccoli, lima beans, peas and potatoes are good alternates. This soup freezes well.

Jean Getz

GAZPACHO
(Cold Soup)

Serves: 6

1 ½ cups vegetable juice
2 beef bouillon cubes
2 large tomatoes, chopped
1 medium cucumber, chopped
½ medium green pepper,
  chopped

½ medium onion, chopped
2 tablespoons wine vinegar
2 tablespoons red cooking wine
3 drops Tabasco sauce
1 tablespoon oil
1 teaspoon Worcestershire sauce

Heat vegetable juice to boiling. Add bouillon cubes. Stir until dissolved. Combine remaining ingredients in blender and purée. Add puréed vegetables to vegetable juice. Simmer 15 minutes. Chill several hours. Serve with accompaniments of herbed croutons, chopped tomatoes, unpared cucumber and green pepper.

Susan Ferrell-Berman

VEGETARIAN GAZPACHO

Serves: 4

½ cup diced green pepper
½ cup diced red pepper
¼ cup chopped hot pepper
½ cup chopped onion
½ cup diced cucumber
1 or 2 garlic cloves
3 teaspoons olive oil

½ teaspoon freshly ground
  pepper
1 10¾-ounce can tomato soup,
  undiluted
1 10¾-ounce can water
1 or 2 drops Tabasco sauce

Combine ingredients in blender, purée. Chill. Garnish with croutons. May serve with bread sticks. Keeps in refrigerator for days.

Penny Goldstein

If the soup is too hot for your child, add an ice cube to the bowl. It will cool the soup down quickly.

IRISH CHOWDER
(Delicious and very easy to prepare)

Yields: 1 quart

3 stalks celery, including leaves,
  finely chopped
1 medium onion, chopped
1 tablespoon butter
¾ pound scallops
¾ pound white fish
3 medium potatoes, cubed

1 small bay leaf
salt and pepper to taste
3 to 4 cups water or stock
1 cup instant dry milk
1 tablespoon butter
4 slices cooked bacon, crumbled
dry dill or dill weed

Sauté celery and onions in butter. Put scallops, fish, potatoes, bay leaf, salt and pepper in a heavy pot. Cover with 3 to 4 cups water or stock. Cook over medium heat until potatoes and fish are tender. Cool for a short time. Slowly whisk in dry milk and butter. Reheat if necessary. Garnish with bacon and dill.

Jean Getz

MANHATTAN SUPPER SOUP

Serves: 12

1 pound ground chuck
2 cups chopped cabbage
1 onion, sliced
1 stalk celery, chopped
3 carrots, sliced
1 medium potato, cubed
½ 3-ounce can tomato paste
1 16-ounce can tomatoes

1 10¾-ounce can condensed
  beef broth, undiluted
2 10¾-ounce cans water
1 tablespoon parsley flakes
1 teaspoon salt
¼ teaspoon pepper
1½ teaspoons sugar
1 10-ounce package frozen peas

Brown meat. Add all ingredients except peas to meat. Bring to a boil. Simmer for 50 minutes. Add peas. Cover and cook for 10 minutes.

Shirley Norman

Rubbing lemon juice on your hands will help to remove the smell of onion and garlic, and remove ugly vegetable stains.

ITALIAN WEDDING SOUP

(This recipe has been in the family for many years)

Yields: 4 to 6 quarts

Meatballs:
1 pound ground beef
2 eggs
¼ to ½ cup grated Romano
  cheese

1 tablespoon fresh parsley
½ cup Italian bread crumbs
1 clove garlic, finely chopped
salt to taste
pepper to taste

Soup:
3 pounds escarole
1 3½ to 4½-pound stewing
  chicken
1 onion, chopped

several pieces of celery, diced (if
  desired)
salt to taste
2 eggs, beaten
¼ cup grated Romano cheese

Meatballs:
Mix all ingredients together. Put oil on hands and on cookie sheet. Make
marble-sized meatballs. Bake at 350 degrees until lightly browned.

Soup:
Wash escarole twice. Cut into bite size pieces. Boil until barely tender. Drain.
Put chicken, onion and water into a 4 to 6 quart pot. Boil, then reduce to
simmer until chicken is tender. Strain chicken and onion from broth.
Debone chicken. Discard bones. Add small pieces of chicken, celery, salt
and meatballs to broth. Simmer about 10 minutes. Add escarole. When
serving, bring to a boil and slowly drizzle eggs mixed with cheese into soup
mixture. Stir as the egg mixture cooks. It gives the soup a wonderful flavor.

Judy Oakley

POTATO-ALMOND SOUP

Serves: 4

1 10¾-ounce can cream of
  potato soup, undiluted
1 ½ cups half and half cream
½ cup slivered almonds

1 10¾-ounce can beef
  consommé
dash of pepper
parsley

In a blender place soup, half and half and almonds. Blend until smooth.
Add beef consommé and pepper. Cook over medium heat until
thoroughly heated. Garnish with parsley.

Dorothy Baker

MINESTRONE SOUP

Serves: 8

3 slices bacon, finely chopped
1 cup chopped onion
½ cup chopped celery
2 large cloves garlic, minced
1 teaspoon basil leaves, crushed
1 10½-ounce can beef broth, undiluted
1 11½-ounce can bean and bacon soup, undiluted
1½ 11½-ounce cans water
1 16-ounce can tomatoes, undrained
½ cup uncooked ditalini or macaroni
½ teaspoon salt
1 cup shredded cabbage
1 cup cubed zucchini

Brown bacon in large saucepan. Add onion, celery, garlic and basil. Stir in soups, water, tomatoes, ditalini and salt. Bring to boil. Cover and simmer for 5 minutes. Stir occasionally. Add cabbage and zucchini. Cook for 10 minutes or until done. Stir occasionally.

Marjorie H. Gray

MOM-MOM'S VEGETABLE SOUP

Serves: 12 to 15

1 tablespoon salt
soup bones and/or short ribs
1 onion, chopped
2 carrots, sliced
1 celery stalk, chopped
½ cup barley
1 10¾-ounce can green pea soup, undiluted
1 2½-ounce can mushrooms or ½ cup diced mushrooms
1 sweet potato, diced
½ cup fresh green beans, cut (optional)
1 package of Streits Vegetable Soup Mix (follow instructions on bag)
1 16-ounce can tomatoes
1 10¾-ounce can tomato soup, undiluted
parsley, dill and pepper to taste
1 10-ounce package frozen mixed vegetables

Fill 5 to 6 quart pot, ½ to ¾ full of water. Add salt and bones or ribs to water. Bring to boil, removing fat from top. Add all ingredients except mixed vegetables and seasoning packet of Streits Vegetable Soup Mix. Cook 2 hours on low heat. Add frozen vegetables and Streits Vegetable Soup Mix seasoning packet. Cook ½ hour. Can be frozen.

NOTE: Streits Vegetable Soup Mix is found in the Kosher food section.

Penny Goldstein

MULLIGATAWNY SOUP
(A blend of many flavors, this is a hearty soup
that has filtered down from India through England to the U.S.)

Serves: 4 (generously)

1 3-pound chicken, cut into
  serving pieces
½ cup butter
¼ cup chopped onion
2 teaspoons curry powder
½ cup flour
5 cups hot water
5 chicken bouillon cubes

1 small apple, peeled and
  chopped
1 teaspoon lemon juice
½ cup coconut milk or light
  cream
salt to taste
pepper to taste

Melt butter in heavy skillet. Add chicken, brown lightly and remove from pan. Sauté onions in butter until golden brown. Add curry powder and flour, blending well. Dissolve bouillon cubes in hot water. Add gradually to curry and onion mixture. Bring to a boil. Add chicken and chopped apple. Simmer for approximately 1 hour. Remove chicken from bones. Discard bones. Add lemon juice, coconut milk or cream and chicken pieces to soup. Reheat. Add salt and pepper to taste.

NOTE: Garnish each bowl of soup with slivers of ham, grated fresh coconut, hot rice or chutney.

Anne Austen

MUSHROOM SOUP IN A CLEAR BROTH
(From the Cedar House Restaurant's kitchen)

Yields: 3 quarts

¼ cup diced scallions
½ cup shredded carrots
½ cup chopped celery
½ cup butter

2 pounds mushrooms, quartered
3 quarts chicken stock
⅓ cup chopped parsley
½ teaspoon white pepper

Sauté scallions, carrots and celery in butter until soft. Add mushrooms and a small amount of stock. Cook until mushrooms are barely soft. Add parsley and pepper. Stir. Add remaining stock.

Fran Smetanka

OLD-FASHIONED CHICKEN SOUP WITH DUMPLINGS

Yields: 4 quarts

Soup:
1 small frying chicken
4 celery stalks, diced
2 carrots, diced

1 onion, diced
salt to taste
pepper to taste
fresh chopped parsley

Dumplings:
1 cup farina
3 to 4 eggs, beaten

dash of salt
dash of pepper

Soup:
Wash chicken. Place in a large pot and cover with 4 quarts water. Add vegetables. Cook over medium heat for 45 minutes. Lift chicken from broth. Debone chicken. Cut chicken into small pieces and place in broth with vegetables.

Dumplings:
Mix all ingredients together. Blend thoroughly and allow to sit for 30 minutes. Make teaspoon-size dumplings. Drop into hot soup. Heat for 10 minutes. Serve hot.

Vera King

ONION SOUP
(A perfect start to any meal)

Serves: 6

6 cups beef broth
4 large yellow onions, sliced
2 tablespoons butter
1 tablespoon flour
salt to taste

pepper to taste
French bread or croutons
¾ cup shredded Swiss cheese
¼ cup Parmesan cheese, grated

Simmer beef broth. Sauté sliced onion with butter until soft, not brown. Stir flour into cooked onions. Add onion mixture, salt and pepper to broth. Cover and simmer for 20 minutes over medium heat. Place bread in individual bowls. Pour soup over bread and cover with Swiss and Parmesan cheese. Set under broiler for 3 to 5 minutes.

NOTE: Recommend use of 4 cans Swanson Beef Broth and 1 beef bouillon cube.

Millie McCathren

PEASANT SOUP

(Suitable not only for peasants, but also for ROYALTY.)

Serves: 15 to 20 (6 to 7 quarts)

2 2-pound veal shanks
3 quarts water
4 teaspoons salt
½ teaspoon pepper
¼ cup oil
½ cup chopped celery
½ cup chopped fresh spinach
½ cup chopped green pepper
½ cup chopped onion
½ pound pepperoni, thinly sliced
2 cups diced potatoes
2 cups diced turnips
2 cups diced carrots
2 cups uncooked small macaroni
 shells
1 16-ounce can tomatoes
1 10-ounce package frozen peas
3¾ cups canned beef broth,
 undiluted
1 clove garlic, minced
¼ teaspoon dried basil
grated Parmesan cheese

Place veal shanks in deep kettle. Cover with water. Add 2 teaspoons salt and ¼ teaspoon pepper. Cover and heat until boiling. Reduce heat and simmer approximately 2 hours or until meat is fork tender. Allow meat to cool in broth. Remove bones and meat. Cut meat into bite size pieces. Set aside. Chill broth. Remove fat from surface. Heat oil in skillet. Sauté celery, spinach, green pepper and onion until onion is golden. Heat veal broth until simmering. Add contents of skillet, pepperoni, potatoes, turnips and carrots. Simmer until vegetables are almost tender. Cook macaroni shells according to directions on package. Drain well and add to soup. Add veal, tomatoes, peas and beef broth. Season with remaining salt and pepper, garlic and basil. Serve sprinkled with Parmesan cheese.

NOTE: This soup can be frozen. Freeze before macaroni shells have been added to maintain their firmness. The initial cost of this soup is large, but cost per serving is not.

Anne Austen

A muffin cup with large cups makes an excellent tray for the child who is sick in bed. Each cup will hold food, and a glass will fit in one of them. Children can handle this tray without worry about spills.

SOPADE ZANAHORIA
(Carrot Soup)

Serves: 4

4 medium carrots, sliced
½ cup water
2 teaspoons instant chicken
   bouillon granules
½ teaspoon sugar
¼ teaspoon dried mint, crushed
½ cup chopped onion

1 tablespoon butter or margarine
1 tablespoon flour
2½ cups milk
1 3-ounce package cream
   cheese, cubed
½ teaspoon salt
pepper to taste

Cover carrots with water. Add bouillon granules, sugar and mint. Cook for about 25 minutes or until carrots are very tender. Sauté onion in butter until tender but not brown. Stir flour into cooked onions. Add milk to onion mixture. Cook stirring constantly, until thickened and bubbly. Place cream cheese in large bowl. Gradually add 1 cup of the hot milk and onion mixture to the cream cheese. Beat until smooth. Set aside. Pour carrots and liquid into a blender. Purée carrots until smooth. Add puréed carrot mixture to milk and cream cheese mixture. Cook and stir until soup just comes to a boil. Stir in salt and pepper. Garnish with fresh mint leaves, if desired.

Pat Krivonak

SWISS CHOWDER

Serves: 4

1 ham bone
1 10-ounce package broccoli,
   chopped
½ cup chopped onion
1½ tablespoons butter

1 cup milk
1 cup heavy cream
1 cup shredded Swiss cheese
2 tablespoons flour
¼ cup water

In cooking pot, cover ham bone with water. Cook for 2 hours. Cool. Skim fat from broth. Reserve 2 cups broth. Add broccoli to broth and cook for 5 minutes. In a separate pan, sauté onion in butter. Add sautéed onion, milk, cream and cheese to broth. Stir constantly. Cut ham from bone. Add to soup mixture. Mix flour with water. Add to soup to thicken. Heat.

Nancy Johns

CHAPTER IV

Rapunzel's ... Salads

Rapunzel, Rapunzel, let down your hair,
So the prince may climb the golden stair!

Lettuce
Radish
Cabbage
Potato!

Onions
Celery
Chives
Tomato!

Rampion
and
Greens of Spring

Leeks
and
Mushrooms
for
Seasoning!

Escarole
and
Peppers crunchy,

Dill and Parsley,
Fresh and bunchy!

The prince has saved you! What a blessing!
Don't cry now, dear one. Just pass the dressing!

HAWAIIAN CABBAGE SALAD

Serves: 8 to 10

1 medium head red cabbage,
  chopped
1 medium red onion, diced
2 large carrots, shredded

1 8½-ounce can crushed
  pineapple, drained
1 10-ounce jar Marzetti Original
  Slaw Dressing

Combine vegetables and pineapple. Mix dressing with vegetables. Chill. Serve cold.

Bobbi Snyder

HEALTH SALAD

(Makes a lot and keeps well for a couple weeks in the refrigerator)

Serves: 8

1 cup sugar
1 large head cabbage, thinly sliced
1 onion, thinly sliced
1 green pepper, chopped
3 carrots, grated

1 cup cider vinegar
¾ cup oil
1 teaspoon dry mustard
1 teaspoon salt
1 teaspoon celery seed

Sprinkle sugar over the combined vegetables. In a saucepan, bring vinegar, oil, mustard, salt and celery seed to a boil. Pour over vegetable mixture. Store in glass container with a cover. Refrigerate 6 hours before serving.

Doris DePierre

SAUERKRAUT SALAD

Serves: 6 to 8

1 cup finely chopped celery
½ cup chopped green pepper
3 tablespoons chopped onion
1 pound sauerkraut, drained, not
  rinsed

½ cup cider vinegar
½ teaspoon salt
½ teaspoon pepper
¾ cup sugar
½ cup oil

Mix chopped vegetables with the sauerkraut. Cook vinegar on low heat. Add salt, pepper, sugar and oil. Stir until sugar is dissolved. Cool and pour over vegetables. Chill 24 hours before serving.

Loretta Lucas

THREE BEAN SALAD

Serves: 10

⅔ cup wine vinegar
¼ cup oil
¾ cup sugar
1 teaspoon salt
dash of pepper
1 onion, sliced in rings
1 16-ounce can kidney beans,
   rinsed and drained

1 16-ounce can green beans,
   drained
1 16-ounce can yellow beans,
   drained
1 cup coarsely chopped celery
1 green pepper, cut in strips
   (optional)

Place vinegar, oil, sugar, salt and pepper in large bowl. Mix thoroughly. Add vegetables. Allow to marinate for several hours or overnight.

Debbie and Frank McKenna

GARDEN MACARONI SALAD
(Add everything but the kitchen sink!)

Serves: 12

2 cups elbow macaroni,
   uncooked
1 large green pepper, cut up in
   chunks
1 large cucumber, diced
2 cups chopped celery
6 hard boiled eggs, chopped
3 large firm tomatoes, diced

1 small onion, minced
4 heaping tablespoons sweet
   pickle relish
2 tablespoons mustard
¾ to 1 cup mayonnaise
1 teaspoon Morton's Nature's
   Seasoning
1 teaspoon sugar

Cook macaroni according to directions on package. Rinse in cold water and drain thoroughly. Add remaining ingredients. Mix gently. Garnish with egg slices, olive slices and paprika if desired.

NOTE: It is important to thoroughly drain macaroni. The vegetables should be chunky.

Phyllis Fox

LINGUINI SALAD
(Great for a summer picnic)

Serves: 8

2 pounds linguini, uncooked
½ jar Salad Supreme
2 cucumbers, chopped
4 tomatoes, chopped

1 large onion, chopped
1 8-ounce bottle Wishbone Italian
  Dressing

Cook and drain linguini. Cool to room temperature. Add Salad Supreme, cucumber, tomato and onion. Toss with Wishbone Dressing.

Mary C. Ruffennach

MACARONI SALAD
(Pair this with "Our Artist's Favorite Sloppy Joes")

Serves: 10 to 12

2 cups elbow macaroni,
  uncooked
6 hard boiled eggs, finely
  chopped
2 stalks celery, chopped
2 tablespoons chopped onion

1 tablespoon vinegar
2 tablespoons sugar
salt to taste
pepper to taste
Hellman's mayonnaise

Cook macaroni according to directions on package. Drain and place in large bowl. Add eggs, celery, onion, vinegar, sugar, salt and pepper. Stir in mayonnaise to desired consistency.

NOTE: To freshen salad the day after, stir in fresh mayonnaise.

Elaine Baker

Is your child going for an overnight or weekend visit? Pack an empty pillowcase for your child to put dirty clothes in. This will help you do the sorting when your child comes home.

GERMAN HOT POTATO SALAD

Serves: 10

8 medium potatoes, boiled
½ pound bacon
¼ cup sliced green olives
¼ cup diced onion
½ cup chopped celery
½ cup chopped green pepper
2 tablespoons bacon fat
¾ cup vinegar

¼ cup water
1 tablespoon sugar
3 teaspoons salt
¼ teaspoon paprika
¾ teaspoon dry mustard
¼ teaspoon pepper
2 eggs, beaten
4 hard boiled eggs, diced

Peel potatoes and slice thin while hot. Fry bacon until crisp and crumbly. Sauté olives, onion, celery and green pepper in bacon fat. Heat vinegar, water, sugar, salt, paprika, mustard and pepper to boiling. Add sautéed mixture. Add beaten eggs. Layer potatoes, crumbled bacon and hard boiled eggs in fry pan. Pour mixture over top. Heat, stirring gently.

David Smith

KING'S DEVIL SALAD
(Ham is the extra touch to this potato salad)

Serves: 4 to 6

4 potatoes, cooked, peeled and
    finely diced
4 hard boiled eggs, finely diced
½ cup cooked, shredded carrots
1 large sweet pickle, shredded

1 cup finely diced ham
1 cup mayonnaise
2 tablespoons oil
dash of pepper

Mix all ingredients in bowl. Chill. May serve on crackers or party rye. Decorate top with green or black olives, if desired.

Vera King

SEVEN-LAYER SALAD

Serves: 8 to 10

1 head iceberg lettuce
½ cup chopped green pepper
½ cup thinly sliced red onion
½ cup chopped celery
1 10-ounce package frozen peas,
   thawed

2 cups mayonnaise
2 tablespoons sugar
6 to 8 ounces cheddar cheese,
   grated
crumbled bacon

Fill bowl with lettuce, broken into bite-size pieces. Add remaining ingredients in layers. Do not toss. Cover bowl tightly. Refrigerate for 8 hours.

NOTE: It may be necessary to drain juices from vegetables. The secret of this salad is to have all vegetables as dry as possible.

Eileen Joll

SUPER SPINACH SALAD
(Attractive and unique combination)

Serves: 8

10 ounces fresh spinach
1 pint whole strawberries, rinsed,
   leaving stem intact
¼ cup sugar

juice of 1 large lemon
1 egg yolk
6 tablespoons oil

Rinse spinach and pat dry with paper towel. Place in large salad bowl. Add strawberries. Combine sugar, lemon, egg yolk and oil in a jar. Shake. Toss lightly over strawberries and spinach.

NOTE: This is a beautiful salad to look at, for the egg yolk coats the spinach and makes it shiny. The contrast of the red and green makes it good for a Christmas dinner or brunch.

Mary C. Ruffennach

Storing lettuce and celery in brown paper bags instead of cellophane bags in the refrigerator will aid in retaining their freshness.

ORIENTAL SPINACH SALAD

Serves: 6

1 pound spinach
1 14-ounce can bean sprouts,
  drained

1 cup water chestnuts, drained
  and chopped
6 slices bacon, fried and
  crumbled

Dressing:
1 cup oil
¾ cup sugar
⅓ cup ketchup

2 tablespoons Worcestershire
  sauce
¼ cup vinegar
1 small onion, grated

Tear spinach into bite-size pieces. Add other salad ingredients and toss. Combine all dressing ingredients in blender and mix until smooth. Pour dressing over salad and toss.

NOTE: This keeps well in the refrigerator.

Phyllis Fox

DUTCH SPINACH SALAD

Serves: 6

1 pound spinach
¼ cup chopped onion

6 slices bacon, fried and
  crumbled

Dressing:
¼ cup wine vinegar
1 tablespoon sugar

1 teaspoon salt
¼ teaspoon pepper

Tear spinach into bite-size pieces. Add other salad ingredients and toss. Combine dressing ingredients in a saucepan. Slowly bring the liquid to a boil. While hot, pour dressing over the spinach. Toss until salad is well-coated with hot dressing.

Phyllis Fox

To perk up wilted or blemished vegetables, pick off the brown edges, sprinkle with cool water, wrap in a towel and refrigerate for an hour or so.

TACO SALAD

Serves: 8 to 10

1 pound ground chuck
1 16-ounce can kidney beans,
　drained
1 package taco seasoning
⅓ to ½ cup water
1 head lettuce, torn

3 tomatoes, chopped
1 avocado, chopped
4 ounces cheddar cheese, grated
1 medium onion, finely chopped
1 8-ounce bottle Thousand Island
　dressing

Brown and drain meat. When almost completely browned, add beans and seasoning. Simmer for 15 minutes. In a separate bowl, combine the remaining ingredients. Toss. Add meat mixture, while still warm, to salad greens. Serve immediately.

Judy Tulley

AMEL'S TABOOLEE

Serves: 6 to 8

1 bunch fresh parsley
2 cups bulgar wheat
½ cup diced onion
mint to taste

salt to taste
½ cup lemon
½ cup oil
2 tomatoes, chopped

Pick tops of parsley. Discard stems. Chop parsley by hand or in a food processor. Mix chopped parsley with bulgar wheat. Add onion, mint, salt, lemon, oil and tomatoes. Toss ingredients lightly. Chill. Garnish with a lemon wedge and mint leaf.

Amel's Restaurant

For a quick and easy salad dressing, add a few ingredients to that nearly empty ketchup bottle. Mix together 1 tablespoon vinegar, 2 tablespoons oil, and ⅛ teaspoon Italian seasoning. Pour into the bottle and shake well.

TABOOLEH
(Syrian summer salad to make in a large bowl)

Serves: 10 to 12

2 cups bulgar wheat (buy at foreign food shops and some health food stores)
1 small head lettuce
2 medium tomatoes
1 to 2 bunches green onions, with tops
2 medium cucumbers

2 large bunches of parsley, without large stems
1 large bunch mint (if unable to obtain, use more parsley)
3 to 5 lemons
oil
salt to taste

Soak wheat by covering it with hot water (approximately 3 cups) for about ½ hour or until soft to chew. Chop all vegetables finely, especially the parsley and mint. Place in large bowl. Squeeze excess water out of the wheat by the handful. Add to the vegetables. Squeeze 2 or 3 lemons onto the salad. Add others to your own taste. Add oil to make dressing. Add salt to taste. Mix with your hands to be authentic!

NOTE: The salad should be tart. It should not be greasy and will need salt. The green should dominate and the wheat should be mixed throughout. Serve alone or on a lettuce leaf or raw grape leaf.

Marty Juliano

BROCCOLI SALAD

Serves: 6 to 8

1 large bunch of broccoli
8 to 10 slices of bacon

1 cup raisins

Dressing:
½ cup mayonnaise

¼ cup sugar
1 tablespoon vinegar

Chop broccoli. Dice bacon and cook until crisp. Combine broccoli, bacon and raisins. Mix dressing ingredients. Pour over salad and toss.

VARIATION:
Substitute 1 cup cheddar cheese, cubed and 1 small red onion, chopped, for the raisins.

Phyllis Fox

BLACK CHERRY SALAD

Serves: 8 to 10

1 20-ounce can crushed pineapple, reserve juice
1 16-ounce can pitted, halved black cherries, reserve juice

2 3-ounce packages black cherry Jello
12 ounces cola (1½ cups)
1 cup pecans, chopped
½ cup grated coconut

Combine juices drained from pineapple and cherries. Heat 2 cups of juice and pour over Jello. Stir to dissolve. Slowly add cola. Blend. Refrigerate until slightly thickened. Stir in fruits, nuts and coconut. Pour into a mold and refrigerate until set.

Carolyn Heaton

EMERALD SALAD
(Excellent with pork)

Serves: 6 to 8

1 3-ounce package lime Jello
¾ cup hot water
¾ cup peeled and grated or shredded cucumbers, drained
2 teaspoons grated onion

1 cup cottage cheese
1 cup Miracle Whip or mayonnaise
¼ cup slivered almonds, nuts or ripe olives (optional)

Dissolve Jello in hot water. Cool slightly. Combine cucumber and onion. Add vegetables to Jello. Beat cottage cheese and mayonnaise together until fairly smooth. Fold mayonnaise (with nuts and olives) into cooled Jello. Refrigerate until firm.

Ada Bates

CRIMSON CRANBERRY SALAD

Serves: 10

1 6-ounce package raspberry Jello
2 cups boiling water

2 cups ginger ale or Fresca
2 cans cranberry relish

Stir together Jello, water and ginger ale or Fresca. Refrigerate until thickened. Add cranberry relish. Return to refrigerator until set. Dress with lemon juice, whipped cream or mayonnaise.

Nancy Johns

LEMON SALAD

Serves: 9

1 3-ounce package lemon Jello
1 cup hot water
1 10-ounce jar maraschino
   cherries and juice
1 8½-ounce can crushed
   pineapple, drained

1 envelope Dream Whip
1 8-ounce package cream
   cheese, softened
½ cup nuts

Combine Jello and hot water. Chill until partially set. Add cherries and pineapple to Jello. Whip Dream Whip until very stiff. Mash cream cheese and beat into the Dream Whip. Fold cream cheese mixture into Jello. Add nuts. Pour into mold or 8 x 8 inch pan. Allow to set in refrigerator for several hours until firm.

Elaine Axelson

RED HOT APPLESAUCE JELLO SALAD
(Kids love it with turkey)

Serves: 10 to 12

6 ounces "red hots"
2 cups boiling water
3 3-ounce packages cherry Jello

2 cups cold water
1 20-ounce can applesauce

Dissolve red hots in boiling water. Add Jello and stir thoroughly. Add cold water and applesauce. Stir. Place in large mold. Stir again. Allow to set firmly.

Twyla Jagger

 To give your children practice in cutting on the lines, let them help you cut out your store coupons. If your child is just learning to cut, give him or her the coupons you won't be using.

STRAWBERRY PRETZEL SALAD
(Different and delicious!)

Serves: 12 to 16

2 cups crushed pretzels
3 tablespoons sugar
¾ cup butter, softened
1 8-ounce package cream
cheese, softened
1 cup sugar
1 8-ounce container Cool Whip

1 6-ounce package strawberry
Jello
2 cups boiling water
2 10-ounce packages frozen
strawberries
1 20-ounce can crushed
pineapple, drained

Mix pretzels, 3 tablespoons sugar and butter. Press into a 9 x 13 inch pan. Bake at 400 degrees for 7 minutes. Cool. Blend cream cheese, 1 cup sugar and Cool Whip in mixer. Spread over pretzel mixture. Chill. Dissolve Jello in boiling water. Add strawberries and pineapple. Chill until thickened. Pour over cream cheese mixture. Chill until firm.

Mary Jane Roderick

HEAVENLY RICE

Serves: 6 to 8

1 cup rice, uncooked
1 teaspoon salt
1 cup sugar
2½ cups milk
6 ounces small marshmallows

1 20-ounce can crushed
pineapple, drained
1 cup whipping cream
maraschino cherries, cut in
pieces

Boil rice and salt in water for 3 minutes. Drain and rinse in cold water. Cook rice, sugar and milk in top of double boiler, covered, until all the milk is absorbed. Cool slightly and then add marshmallows. Mix well and chill. Add crushed pineapple. Fold in stiffly whipped cream. Add cherries and a little cherry juice for pink color, if desired.

Sue and Bill Law

ROSA MARINA SALAD
(Takes two days to make)

Serves: 15

¾ cup sugar
2 tablespoons flour
½ teaspoon salt
2 eggs
1 tablespoon lemon juice
1 20-ounce can pineapple
chunks, reserve juice

1 11-ounce can mandarin
oranges, reserve juice
½ pound Rosa Marina macaroni,
uncooked
strawberries, in season
1 12-ounce container Cool Whip

Mix sugar, flour, salt, eggs, lemon juice and juice from pineapple and oranges. Cook slowly until thickened. Set aside to cool. Cook macaroni until soft, not mushy. Add macaroni to cooled sauce and put in refrigerator. Next day, fold in fruit and Cool Whip.

Teresa Meyer

SIMPLE SUMMER SALAD
(A Texas recipe · very refreshing on a hot day)

Serves: 8

1 8-ounce carton cottage cheese,
small curd
½ 3-ounce package Jello, any
flavor

1 8-ounce container Cool Whip
1 8½-ounce can crushed
pineapple, drained

Mix together all ingredients thoroughly. Chill until set.

NOTE: Could use orange Jello with 1 8-ounce can mandarin oranges, drained.

Shirley Rose

BLEU CHEESE DRESSING

Yields: 1½ cups

1 4-ounce package bleu cheese,
crumbled
⅓ cup light cream

1 3-ounce package cream
cheese, softened
½ cup mayonnaise

Reserve ⅓ cup bleu cheese. Blend light cream and cream cheese on low speed in small mixing bowl. Add mayonnaise and remaining bleu cheese until creamy. Stir in reserved bleu cheese. Cover and refrigerate at least 3 hours.

Pat Krivonak

CELERY SEED DRESSING

Yields: 1½ cups

½ cup sugar
1 teaspoon salt, scant
1 teaspoon dry mustard
2 teaspoons grated onion

¼ cup vinegar
¾ cup oil
2 teaspoons celery seed

Mix dry ingredients with grated onion. Add liquid and mix - do not beat. Add celery seed. Mix.

Gerri Bartelme

HOT DRESSING

(For watercress or young dandelion greens)

Yields: 1¼ cups

4 strips bacon, cut in pieces
1 egg
⅔ cup sugar
¼ cup vinegar

¼ cup water
salt to taste
pepper to taste

Cook bacon. Lift bacon pieces from pan, leaving bacon fat in skillet. Beat together egg and sugar. Add all ingredients except bacon to fat. Stir and cook until thick and opaque. Spoon over watercress or dandelion greens. Sprinkle with bacon bits.

Betty Douglass Campbell

PEARSON'S SALAD DRESSING

(Can double as a vegetable sauce)

Yields: 1½ cups

1 cup Bertoulli olive oil
¼ cup kame (rice wine vinegar)
1 teaspoon salt
1 tablespoon sugar

½ tablespoon Italian Seasoning
1 large clove garlic, crushed
juice of ½ lemon
1 teaspoon Dijon mustard

Mix above ingredients into bottle. Shake well.

NOTE: Excellent on chilled asparagus spears, 1 pound of pasta salad, blanched broccoli or blanched cauliflower.

Sandy Pearson

SWEET AND SOUR VEGETABLE SALAD DRESSING

Yields: ¾ cup

½ cup sugar
¼ cup vinegar

1 teaspoon celery seed

Combine ingredients in jar. Shake well. Refrigerate for 24 hours, shaking frequently.

Betty Douglass Campbell

WHITE FRENCH DRESSING

Yields: 1 gallon

2¼ teaspoons cornstarch
4½ cups vinegar
1 cup and 1½ teaspoons salt
3 tablespoons dry mustard
¾ teaspoon white pepper

¼ teaspoon cayenne pepper,
  scant
3⅓ cups sugar
1 egg
8½ cups oil

Add cornstarch to 2 cups vinegar. Mix and boil until clear and free of cornstarch taste. Cool. Combine salt, mustard and peppers. Add cornstarch mixture to make paste. Dissolve sugar in remaining vinegar. Beat egg until thick and lemon colored. Add egg to paste mixture and beat for 5 minutes. Add oil slowly. Add sugar and vinegar mixture. Chill.

Gerri Bartelme

YOGURT SALAD DRESSING
(Lo-cal for spinach)

Yields: 2¼ to 2¾ cups

1 cup mayonnaise
1 to 1½ cups yogurt
1 tablespoon parsley, fresh or
  dried
1 tablespoon basil

1 tablespoon dill
pinch garlic powder
pinch onion powder
salt and pepper to taste

Cut mayonnaise into yogurt. Mix well. Add remaining ingredients and mix.

NOTE: Dressing is best on spinach salad. One tablespoon of dressing contains about 60 calories.

Sue Spagnuolo

Eggs & Cheese

Gary G. Baker

CHAPTER V

Jack and the Beanstalk's ... Eggs and Cheese

"Bring me my golden egg-laying Hen!" roared the Giant.
"Fee, fie, foe, fum!"
But our lad, Jack, did what was wise,
Grabbed that talented hen for his prize,
And climbed down the beanstalk, by gum!

But the giant ran after the boy and the bird,
So Jack took a hatchet and chopped!
With an action so clever
He earned gold eggs forever,
And, crash! That giant was stopped!

There's nothing magic about cooking with eggs and cheese, but each dish here, as you'll see, is worth its weight in gold.

EASY BRUNCH CASSEROLE

Serves: 8

1 pound bacon
6 eggs
2 cups milk
1 teaspoon salt
1 teaspoon dry mustard

4 slices Italian bread, cubed
1 cup shredded sharp cheddar
   cheese
1 medium green pepper, chopped

Cook bacon and crumble. Beat eggs, add milk, salt and mustard. Mix thoroughly. Place a layer of bread cubes in bottom of well-greased 9 x 13 inch casserole dish. Sprinkle crumbled bacon, cheese and green pepper over bread cubes. Pour egg mixture over top. Refrigerate overnight. Bake uncovered at 350 degrees for 45 minutes.

Teresa Meyer

CHEESE SOUFFLÉ
(Serve any time of the day!)

Serves: 4 to 6

3 slices bread, trimmed and
   cubed
½ pound grated cheddar cheese
4 eggs

1 teaspoon salt
1 teaspoon dry mustard
2 cups milk
paprika

Put bread in greased 1½ quart casserole. Sprinkle bread with cheddar cheese. Beat together eggs, salt, mustard and milk. Pour egg mixture over bread. Sprinkle with paprika. Cover casserole and refrigerate overnight. Bake uncovered at 325 degrees for 1 hour.

Barbara Cooledge

Oops! You dropped an egg on the floor. Sprinkle it heavily with salt; let it set for 5 to 10 minutes, sweep the remains into a dustpan.

EGGS & CHEESE

HOLIDAY BRUNCH CASSEROLE

Serves: 8 to 10

4 cups medium white sauce
salt and pepper, to taste
dash of marjoram
2 tablespoons chopped parsley
few drops Worcestershire sauce
½ pound sharp cheddar cheese,
    cut into large chunks
2 tablespoons white wine

3 packages Brown N' Serve
    Sausage, browned and cut into
    pieces
1 dozen hard boiled eggs, cut
    into large chunks
2 2½-ounce cans sliced
    mushrooms, drained
bread crumbs

Add seasonings to white sauce. Add cheese, wine, sausage, eggs and mushrooms to white sauce. Mix well and turn into greased, shallow, oblong baking dish. Top casserole with bread crumbs. Bake at 325 degrees for 35 to 40 minutes.

NOTE: Casserole can be made the day before and refrigerated. If so, cover with foil and heat for 1 hour at 325 degrees.

Doris DePierre

MILLIE'S EGG SOUFFLÉ CASSEROLE
(Great for Christmas breakfast - you make it the night before)

Serves: 10

8 slices white bread, crusts
    removed
½ pound Monterey Jack cheese,
    shredded
½ pound sharp cheddar cheese,
    shredded

⅔ cup ripe olives, sliced and drained
6 eggs
½ teaspoon dry mustard
4 cups milk
ham or bacon (optional)
8 green stuffed olives

Butter a 9 x 13 inch casserole. Layer bread, cheese and ripe olives. Beat eggs. Add mustard and milk. Pour egg mixture over bread and cheese layers. Refrigerate at least 1 hour or overnight. Bake at 350 degrees for 1 hour. Garnish with green olives and serve.

NOTE: Ham or bacon can be added as a layer.

Millie McCathren

ZUCCHINI-CHEESE SOUFFLÉ

Serves: 6 to 8

2 pounds zucchini, sliced
1 onion, sliced
3 tablespoons butter
1 teaspoon salt

1 cup milk
½ pound grated cheese, Swiss or
  cheddar
2 eggs, beaten

Place sliced zucchini and onion, butter and a small amount of water in a fry pan. Cover, and cook over medium to low heat until tender. Add remaining ingredients and mix well. Pour into a greased 1½ quart casserole. Bake at 350 degrees for 1 hour and 15 minutes.

Rosemary Ross

YOGURT HERB CHEESE

(Your favorite herb will make all the difference)

fresh cheese strainer (a large
  plastic mesh berry basket will
  do)
cheese cloth

large container, to hold strainer
1 tablespoon crushed basil (or
  your favorite herb)
2 pounds plain yogurt

Line strainer with cheese cloth and place in larger container so as to support the strainer. Do not let the strainer touch the bottom of container. Crush basil and mix with yogurt. Place yogurt in the strainer and refrigerate. Let yogurt drain in strainer for about 24 hours. Use like cream cheese spread.

Don Polito

HAMBURGER QUICHE

Serves: 8

1 9-inch pie shell, unbaked
½ pound ground beef
½ cup mayonnaise (do not use
  Miracle Whip)
½ cup milk
2 eggs

1 tablespoon cornstarch
1½ cups grated cheese (cheddar
  or Swiss or both combined)
⅓ cup sliced onion
⅓ cup chopped green pepper

Brown beef in skillet over medium heat. Drain fat and set aside. Blend mayonnaise, milk, eggs and cornstarch. Stir in meat, cheese, onion and pepper. Turn into pastry shell. Bake at 350 degrees for 35 to 40 minutes or until golden brown and knife inserted in center comes out clean.

Gail Holsinger

POCATELLO PIE

Serves: 8

Potato mixture:
2 tablespoons butter, softened
3 potatoes, shredded

Egg mixture:
2 eggs
1 cup milk
½ teaspoon salt
½ teaspoon pepper

½ cup chopped onion
1 teaspoon salt
1 cup shredded Swiss cheese

½ teaspoon paprika
¼ teaspoon dry mustard
2 tablespoons chopped parsley
mushrooms, sautéed (optional)
green pepper, sautéed (optional)

Spread softened butter over bottom and sides of 9-inch pie plate. Mix potatoes, onion and salt together and drain well. Spread potato mixture over pie plate to form shell. Sprinkle Swiss cheese over shell. Beat eggs, milk and seasonings together and pour over potato mixture. Add mushrooms and green pepper on top, if desired. Bake at 375 degrees for 50 to 60 minutes or until knife comes out clean. Let pie stand for 5 to 10 minutes before cutting.

Marilyn Hayes

QUICHE PROVINCIAL
(Straight from the Giant's oven)

Serves: 6

1 9-inch pie shell, unbaked
¾ cup grated Parmesan cheese
½ cup finely diced onion
2 large tomatoes, peeled and
    sliced
1 tablespoon flour

½ cup pitted black olives
2 eggs, slightly beaten
1 pint heavy cream or ½ light
    plus ½ whipping cream
½ teaspoon salt
dash of pepper

Sprinkle ½ cup cheese into bottom of pie shell. Sprinkle ½ of the onions over the cheese. Dust sliced tomatoes with flour. Arrange in one layer on pie shell. Sprinkle with more cheese, remaining onion and sliced olives. Mix eggs with cream. Add salt and pepper. Pour over tomatoes. Sprinkle more cheese on top. Bake at 400 degrees for 35 to 45 minutes, until knife comes out clean and quiche is firm.

Carolyn Heaton

QUICK AND EASY QUICHE

Serves: 8

3 eggs
½ cup Bisquick
½ cup melted butter
1 ½ cups milk
¼ teaspoon salt

dash of pepper
chopped onion
1 cup shredded Swiss cheese
½ cup ham, bacon or crabmeat
mushrooms, sliced

Place all ingredients except cheese, meat and mushrooms in blender and blend. Pour mixture into greased 9 or 10-inch pie pan or quiche pan. Sprinkle cheese, meat and mushrooms on mixture and push below the surface of mixture. Bake at 350 degrees for 45 minutes. Let set 10 minutes before cutting.

Millie McCathren

SPINACH CHEESE PIE

Serves: 9

3 pounds fresh spinach
2 cups low-fat cottage cheese
2 eggs, beaten
1 lemon

½ teaspoon salt
½ cup Italian bread crumbs
paprika

Wash spinach thoroughly and remove stems. Chop spinach and cook quickly in heavy pan with no water added, stirring constantly until wilted. Drain spinach well. Beat together cottage cheese, eggs, juice of 1 lemon and salt. Stir 1 cup cottage cheese mixture into spinach and press mixture into greased 8 x 8 inch baking dish. Spread remainder of cottage cheese mixture evenly over top. Sprinkle top with bread crumbs and paprika. Bake in preheated 350 degree oven for 30 minutes or until set.

Nancy Latshaw

After boiling hard boiled eggs, immediately immerse in cold water and crack the shell with a spoon. This will assure easy shell removal.

SPINACH QUICHE

(If you don't know what to do with those "Golden Eggs...")

Serves: 12 to 16

2 pounds fresh spinach, washed,
  cooked and drained
¾ pound canned or fresh
  mushrooms, sliced
2 tablespoons butter
2 cups grated Swiss cheese

8 eggs, beaten
2 cups soft whole wheat bread
  crumbs
1½ teaspoons salt
1 tablespoon Worcestershire sauce
2 cups cottage cheese

Prepare spinach. Sauté mushrooms in butter. In a large bowl mix together drained spinach, mushrooms and all remaining ingredients. Pour into two greased 10-inch pie plates. Bake at 350 degrees for 30 minutes.

Rosemary Ross

TOMATO-CHEESE PIE

(All alone or as a complement to any meal)

Serves: 6 to 8

butter
4 or more bread slices, trimmed
  and buttered on 1 side
4 large ripe tomatoes
salt and pepper to taste

1 teaspoon sugar
1 tablespoon grated onion
4 ounces grated cheddar cheese
2 eggs
1 cup milk

Butter 9-inch square, oven-proof glass pan. Line pan with bread, buttered side down. Slice tomatoes and place on bread. Sprinkle tomatoes with salt, pepper, sugar and grated onion. Cover top with grated cheese. Beat eggs and milk together and pour over cheese. Bake in preheated oven at 350 degrees for 30 minutes.

Marilyn Hayes

Before using eggs in cakes, they should be at least three days old.

ZUCCHINI PIE

Serves: 8

Crust:
1 8-ounce package cream cheese, softened
1 cup butter or margarine, softened
¼ cup whipping cream
3 cups flour
1 teaspoon salt

Filling:
4 cups thinly sliced zucchini
1 cup chopped green onion
2 cloves garlic, minced
3 tablespoons butter or margarine
½ cup snipped parsley
¾ teaspoon dried basil
½ teaspoon salt
½ teaspoon oregano
¼ teaspoon pepper
2 eggs, beaten
1½ cups (6 ounces) shredded Mozzarella cheese
2 teaspoons Dijon mustard

Crust:
Cream together cheese and butter. Beat in whipping cream. Combine flour and salt and stir into butter mixture, kneading until smooth. Chill dough. Divide in half. Roll out and transfer to pie plate. Trim dough to within ½ inch of edge. Roll edge under, do not crimp. To bake, line crust with double layer of heavy foil. Bake at 450 degrees for 5 to 7 minutes. Remove foil and bake, until golden. May be frozen for later use.

Filling:
Cook zucchini, onion and garlic in butter for 10 minutes. Stir in spices. Combine eggs, cheese and mustard in a bowl. Stir in zucchini mixture. Pour into hot crust. Bake at 375 degrees for 20 to 25 minutes, until knife comes out clean.

Sherry Wilson

Every year on your child's birthday save the front page of the newspaper. You can start the day your child is born. As your child grows older it will be interesting to look back at what was going on in the world.

ZUCCHINI MUSHROOM QUICHE

Serves: 8

⅓ cup chopped onion
1 clove garlic, minced
butter
2 medium zucchini, sliced and
   quartered
½ pound sliced mushrooms

½ teaspoon oregano
¼ teaspoon basil
1½ cups cooked brown rice
⅓ cup Parmesan cheese
1 tablespoon butter
4 eggs, lightly beaten

Sauté onion and garlic in butter. Add zucchini, mushrooms and spices. Cook and stir mixture until zucchini is transparent. Add rice and Parmesan cheese to vegetable mixture. Butter a 9-inch pie pan. Add vegetable-rice mixture. Pour slightly beaten eggs over mixture. Dot top of mixture with butter and sprinkle with extra Parmesan cheese. Bake in lower part of oven at 350 degrees for 15 minutes and in upper part of oven at 350 degrees for 15 minutes.

Nancy Latshaw

AKE KAKE
(Swedish Egg Cake)

Serves: 10 to 12

¼ cup butter
3 eggs
2 cups milk

2 tablespoons sugar
1 teaspoon salt
1 cup flour, white or whole wheat

Place butter in 9 x 13 inch pan. Place in oven at 450 degrees until butter melts. In a large bowl, beat eggs. Stir in milk, sugar, salt and flour, in that order. Pour batter into melted butter in pan. Bake at 450 degrees for 20 minutes or until puffy and golden brown. Serve for breakfast with syrup, honey, applesauce, jam or fruit.

Sherry Wilson

If you place a clock in your window, the kids won't have to keep running in and out of the house to check the time.

MOTULENO'S
(A Mexican breakfast dish)

Serves: 2

2 6-inch corn tortillas
2 tablespoons oil
¾ cup refried beans
2 fried eggs
tomato hot sauce to taste

¼ cup chopped ham
¼ cup chopped cheese
green peas
Parmesan cheese, grated
½ banana, fried

Fry tortillas in oil. Spread a layer of refried beans on top of tortilla. Top with fried eggs. Add hot sauce, ham and cheese. Garnish with a few green peas and Parmesan cheese. Fry banana in a small amount of oil over slow heat, and serve with your Motuleno's.

Marsha DeCaria

MOON-OVER-MIAMI
(A favorite of young and old)

Serves: 1

1 slice bread
butter

1 egg

Tear a silver dollar-sized hole out of the middle of the bread. Melt butter in frying pan. When butter is hot, put bread on top of butter. Break the egg into the hole of the bread. Cook until the egg white solidifies through the bread. Turn over and fry until top is the desired texture.

Barbara and Rick Heinze

For clean teeth and a bright smile: Buy a three minute egg timer, and tell your children to brush until the sand runs out. You won't have to watch your kids brush their teeth. Your kids will think it's fun and they won't rush the job.

ORANGE DAYDREAMER
(Orange-Cinnamon French Toast, a Citrus Cook-off winner)

Serves: 4

1 8-ounce package cream cheese, softened
½ cup chopped pecans
1 teaspoon orange juice
½ teaspoon grated orange peel
4 slices raisin-cinnamon bread, sliced 1 inch thick

1 cup unsifted all-purpose flour
2 teaspoons sugar
2 teaspoons baking powder
½ teaspoon salt
1 cup half and half
2 large eggs, beaten
oil for deep-fat frying

Orange Syrup:
2 cups orange juice
2 cups sugar
2 teaspoons grated orange peel

½ to 1 teaspoon ground cinnamon
4 oranges, peeled and sectioned

In a medium mixing bowl, combine cream cheese, pecans, orange juice and orange peel. Blend until smooth. With a sharp knife, make a deep slit in each bread slice to form a pocket. Spoon cream cheese filling into each pocket. In a medium bowl, combine flour, sugar, baking powder and salt. Beat in half and half and beaten eggs to form a smooth batter. Heat 3 to 4 inches of oil in a deep-fat fryer to 375 degrees. Dip filled bread in batter to coat both sides. Fry until lightly brown; turn and fry other side. Remove and drain on paper towel. Serve hot with orange syrup.

Orange Syrup:
In a small saucepan, combine orange juice, sugar, orange peel, and cinnamon. Stir over low heat until sugar dissolves. Remove from heat. Add orange sections.

NOTE: Toast can also be prepared using the regular egg dip and grilled like French toast.

Judy Helman

A bucket of water and an old paint brush will keep small children busy for quite a while. They can "paint" the drive, the front walk, or the back patio. And no stain if there's a spill!

Seafood

Gary G. Baker

CHAPTER VI

The Fisherman and His Wife's ... Seafood

Lobster, scallops, flounder and sole!
Di jon the sauces and butter the bowl!
Peppercorn spice and tarragon oil!
Cook them now. Don't let them spoil!

What nonsense are these
Three
Silly
Wishes!

There's much more promise in
Fresh
Fishy
Dishes!

Try some new ideas for "spicies"
On these fresh and tender Pisces!

CRABMEAT AND SCALLOP QUICHE
(From the Bay to your table)

Serves: 6

1 9-inch pie shell, unbaked
½ cup evaporated milk
4 eggs
2 tablespoons flour

1 ½ cups grated Monterey Jack cheese
¾ cup grated cheddar cheese
1 6½-ounce can crabmeat
½ pound scallops, diced

Pre-bake pie shell for 2 minutes and set aside. Mix milk, eggs, and flour with a whip. Blend cheeses into milk/egg mixture. Add fish. Pour into pie shell. Bake at 400 degrees for 35 to 40 minutes.

Zuzanna K. O'Brien

CRABMEAT CASSEROLE

Serves: 4

1 teaspoon minced onion
2 tablespoons butter
1 10¾-ounce can cream of
    mushroom soup, undiluted
½ cup milk
1 teaspoon A-1 sauce

½ teaspoon celery salt
¼ teaspoon dry mustard
1 cup cooked rice
1 6½-ounce can crabmeat
⅓ cup grated sharp cheese

Sauté onion in butter. Add soup, milk, A-1 sauce, celery salt and mustard. Heat to boiling. Add rice and crabmeat. Pour into 1½ quart casserole. Sprinkle with cheese. Cover and bake at 375 degrees for 30 minutes.

Barbara Cooledge

CRABMEAT LUNCHEON DELIGHT

Serves: 6

2 3-ounce packages cream
    cheese, softened
1 6½-ounce can crabmeat,
    drained
Worcestershire sauce to taste

onion juice to taste
1 lime
6 English muffins, toasted
tomato slices
cheese slices

Mix cream cheese with crabmeat. Add small amounts of Worcestershire sauce and onion juice. Mix in the juice of 1 lime. Spread a thick layer of crabmeat mixture on toasted English muffins. Top with a slice of tomato, then a slice of cheese. Bake at 350 degrees for 20 minutes.

Carolyn Heaton

CRABMEAT QUICHE
(Dieters' "Seafood Special")

Serves: 6 (270 calories each)

1 9-inch deep dish pie crust
1 tablespoon butter
1½ cups sliced mushrooms
¼ cup chopped green pepper
½ cup mayonnaise
½ cup milk (or cream for richer flavor)
2 eggs, lightly beaten

1 tablespoon Dijon mustard
1 tablespoon flour
pinch of garlic powder
salt and white pepper to taste
2 cups grated Swiss cheese
1 6½-ounce can white crabmeat, drained and flaked
paprika

Preheat oven to 350 degrees. Melt butter in skillet at moderate heat. Add mushrooms and green peppers. Simmer slowly. Mix mayonnaise, milk, eggs, mustard, flour, garlic powder, salt and pepper together in a large bowl while peppers and mushrooms are simmering. Reserve enough cheese for topping and add remaining cheese to mayonnaise mixture. Add crabmeat to green peppers and mushrooms when peppers are tender. Add vegetables and crabmeat to mayonnaise mixture and mix well. Pour mixture into pie crust. Sprinkle top with remaining cheese and paprika. Bake at 350 degrees for 40 to 45 minutes until top is golden. Remove and let stand 5 to 10 minutes before serving.

Susan Spagnuolo

CRABMEAT SPAGHETTI CASSEROLE

Serves: 6 to 8

8 ounces thin spaghetti
¼ cup diced onion
½ cup margarine
1 10¾-ounce can cream of mushroom soup, undiluted
1 13-ounce can evaporated milk

2 cups grated, sharp cheese
3 hard-boiled eggs, cut
1 tablespoon chopped pimiento
dash of pepper
½ teaspoon salt
1½ pounds crab meat

Boil spaghetti. Drain thoroughly. Set aside. Sauté onions in margarine until translucent. Stir in soup until smooth. Combine all ingredients, including spaghetti. Pour in 9 x 13 inch casserole dish. Sprinkle additional cheese on top. Bake at 350 degrees for 30 minutes.

Judy and Bill Alexy

CRABMEAT STUFFED RED PEPPER
(Don't miss the shrimp sauce)

Serves: 2

8 ounces lump crabmeat or snow
  crabmeat
1 egg yolk
2 teaspoons diced shallot or
  scallion
1 tablespoon diced green pepper

1 tablespoon fine bread crumbs
salt to taste
white pepper to taste
dash seafood seasoning, optional
1 large red pepper, cut in half
2 pats of butter

Sauce:
1 tablespoon butter
1 tablespoon flour
2 cups half and half

salt to taste
white pepper to taste
1 cup baby shrimp

Clean crabmeat well, removing all cartilage. Mix crab with egg. Add shallot, green pepper, bread crumbs, salt, pepper and seasoning. Blend well. Stuff each half pepper with mixture, mounding it nicely. Top each with a pat of butter and bake at 400 degrees for 20 minutes.

Sauce:
Melt butter over low heat and blend in flour until the mixture is smooth, do not brown. Heat half and half until hot. Add butter and flour mixture to the half and half using a wire whip to incorporate roux into the cream. Add salt and white pepper. Sauce should be smooth and thickened. Add shrimp and stir. Spoon sauce over pepper and garnish with fresh chopped parsley.

Fran Smetanka

CURRIED SHRIMP SALAD
(Great for that backyard get-together)

Serves: 6

1 10-ounce package frozen
  shelled shrimp, cooked
1 6-ounce can sliced
  mushrooms, drained
¼ cup Wishbone Deluxe French
  Dressing
¼ cup mayonnaise

½ teaspoon salt
⅛ teaspoon curry powder
1 cup toasted pecans
1 cup diced celery
8 cups mixed salad greens
  (lettuce, romaine, bibb lettuce,
  etc.)

Place shrimp, mushrooms and dressing in a bowl. Mix thoroughly. Cover and refrigerate for 2 hours. Blend together mayonnaise, salt and curry powder. Add pecans, celery and salad greens to shrimp-mushroom mixture. Add mayonnaise mixture. Toss lightly.

SHRIMP AND OKRA GUMBO
(A Louisianna treat)

Serves: 4 to 6

10 ounces okra
2 tablespoons olive oil
¼ cup margarine
2 cups diced onion
2 green peppers, cut in ½ inch
    pieces
¼ teaspoon minced garlic
¼ cup flour
1 28-ounce can tomatoes

2 10¾-ounce cans chicken broth
2 bay leaves
¼ teaspoon thyme leaves
¼ teaspoon hot pepper sauce
½ teaspoon Worcestershire sauce
1 teaspoon salt
1 pound shrimp, shelled and
    cleaned

Wash and dry okra. Cut in ⅛ inch slices. Heat olive oil and margarine in heavy saucepan over medium heat. Sauté okra, onion, green pepper, and garlic for 3 to 4 minutes, stirring constantly. Sprinkle with flour and continue stirring until flour becomes golden brown. Add next 8 ingredients. Cover, bring to boil. Simmer, uncovered, for 45 minutes.

Judy and Bill Alexy

SHRIMP CASSEROLE

Serves: 6 to 8

1½ pounds frozen shrimp
1 tablespoon lemon juice
3 tablespoons oil
¾ cup uncooked rice
2 tablespoons margarine
¼ cup chopped green pepper
¼ cup minced onion
1 teaspoon salt
⅛ teaspoon pepper

⅛ teaspoon mace
dash cayenne pepper
1 10¾-ounce can tomato soup,
    undiluted
1 cup heavy cream
½ cup slivered almonds
½ cup cooking sherry
paprika

Cook shrimp in boiling, salted water 5 to 8 minutes and drain. Put in a 2 quart casserole. Sprinkle lemon juice and oil over shrimp; chill several hours. Cook rice and drain; chill. About 1 hour and 15 minutes before serving, heat oven to 350 degrees. In margarine, sauté pepper and onion for 5 minutes. Add to shrimp. Add remaining ingredients, except for ¼ cup almonds and paprika. Top casserole with almonds and paprika. Bake at 350 degrees for 55 minutes.

Pat Smetanka

SHRIMP CREOLE
(Hot and spicy)

Serves: 12 to 15

5 pounds shrimp, cleaned and
   deveined
½ cup butter or margarine
⅔ cup flour
2½ cups chopped onion
1 large bell pepper, chopped (1
   cup)
1 cup chopped celery
2 14-ounce cans tomato sauce
3½ cups hot water

1 teaspoon dried thyme
2 bay leaves
4 teaspoons sugar
2 cloves garlic, minced
4 teaspoons salt
2 teaspoons cayenne pepper
dash of Tabasco sauce
¼ cup chopped parsley
hot cooked rice

Clean and devein shrimp. Sauté shrimp in butter in a large Dutch oven for 5 minutes or until pink. Remove shrimp from pan. Brown flour slightly in the leftover butter and juices from shrimp. Add onion, bell pepper and celery and sauté until tender, about 5 minutes. Add tomato sauce, water, thyme, bay leaves, sugar, garlic, salt, pepper and Tabasco sauce. Stir well and simmer, covered, for 30 minutes, stirring occasionally. Add shrimp and cook 10 minutes longer. Add parsley just before serving over hot rice.
NOTE: Can be cut in half for fewer servings.

Gladys Douglas

SHRIMP IN LEMON GARLIC SAUCE

Serves: 6 to 8

1 pound shrimp
1½ cups milk
2 egg yolks
1½ tablespoons lemon juice
1 tablespoon parsley
2 to 3 cloves garlic, crushed
2 teaspoons chopped chives
½ teaspoon salt

½ teaspoon mustard
dash of ground red pepper or a
   dash of Tabasco sauce
½ cup butter, melted
1 cup oil
1 cup flour seasoned with salt
   and pepper

Clean shrimp and soak in refrigerator in milk for 20 minutes. Place egg yolks, lemon juice, parsley, garlic, chives, salt, mustard and pepper in blender or food processor. Blend for 30 seconds. With blender running on low speed, add melted butter and process for 1 minute or until thickened. Set aside. Heat oil in skillet. Drain shrimp and dredge in seasoned flour. Fry shrimp until golden. Arrange shrimp in individual dishes. Top with sauce from blender. Broil for about 30 to 45 seconds until bubbly.

Marjorie H. Gray

SHRIMP CURRY
(Jhinga Kari)

Serves: 4 to 6

16 jumbo shrimp
1 tablespoon vinegar
2 teaspoons salt
1 cup coarsely chopped fresh
  coconut
¼ cup coriander seeds
1¼ cups warm water
5 tablespoons oil
1 tablespoon scraped, fresh
  chopped ginger root

1 tablespoon finely chopped
  garlic
½ cup finely chopped onion
1 teaspoon turmeric
½ teaspoon cumin
¼ teaspoon hot red pepper
¼ teaspoon pepper
coconut milk, reserved from 1
  coconut

Marinate shrimp in vinegar and salt at room temperature for 20 to 30 minutes. Combine coconut, coriander seeds, and water in blender and purée . Pour mixture into double thickness of dampened cheesecloth. Wring all liquid out and set purée aside. Makes 1¼ to 1½ cups. In a large skillet, heat 3 tablespoons oil to a moderate level. Add shrimp and cook until they turn pink. Remove shrimp with slotted spoon and return to marinade. Add remaining oil, ginger, garlic, and onions to skillet. Fry until the onions are brown. Add turmeric, cumin, red pepper, and black pepper. Pour marinade without shrimp, into the skillet and bring to a boil. Return shrimp to skillet and coat with mixture. Pour in reserved coconut milk and bring to a boil over high heat, stirring constantly. Cook for 3 minutes. Serve over hot rice and a chutney.

NOTE: Flake coconut and canned coconut milk can be substituted for the fresh.

Anong Litwin

To open a coconut: With an ice pick puncture the eyes and drain out the coconut milk. Place the coconut in a shallow pan. Bake at 350 degrees for 45 to 60 minutes, until the shell begins to crack. When cool enough to handle, tap with a hammer. The shell will almost spring apart. Pry the meat out with a knife.

SHRIMP STEW
(A meal for a Mardi Gras night)

Serves: 4 to 6

¼ cup margarine
½ cup chopped onion
½ cup chopped celery
1 garlic clove, finely minced
2 tablespoons flour
1 teaspoon salt
1 teaspoon sugar
dash of cayenne

1 teaspoon paprika
½ small bay leaf
4 drops red pepper sauce
½ cup dried green pepper
1 6-ounce can tomato paste
1 pound shrimp, cleaned and
  cooked
rice

Sauté onions, celery and garlic in margarine. Add remaining ingredients except shrimp and rice. Stir until thoroughly blended. Cook for 10 minutes. Add shrimp and heat. Serve over rice.

NOTE: Extra shrimp and hot sauce can be added to taste.

Judy and Bill Alexy

OYSTER PUDDING
(An old, oft-used recipe. Of course, the more oysters, the better the dish!)

Serves: 8

1 large box oyster crackers
1 quart oysters
½ cup butter

salt and pepper to taste
milk

Butter a 2 quart casserole dish. Add in layers crackers, oysters and pieces of butter. Sprinkle with salt and pepper in casserole. Repeat until all ingredients are used. Top with crackers. Pour in enough milk until you can see it around the edges. Bake at 350 degrees for 45 minutes to 1 hour, until it puffs and top is light brown.

Judith Diehl

BAKED SCROD
(For the working woman)

Serves: 3

2 tablespoons white wine
1 pound scrod fish
fresh bread crumbs
parsley

pinch of thyme
3 tablespoons butter
garlic powder

Preheat oven to 400 degrees. Pour wine in shallow baking dish. Add fish. Cover with freshly grated bread crumbs mixed with parsley and thyme. Bake in hot oven at 400 degrees for 12 minutes. While the fish is in the oven, melt butter and garlic powder in a small pan. Pour melted butter/garlic mixture over all. Bake 1 minute. Serve immediately. (Adjust quantity to number to be served.)

Carolyn Graham

BAKED SOLE
(A do-ahead, quick-to-bake entreé)

Serves: 4

4 fillets of sole
Sauterne wine
bread crumbs
1 cup mayonnaise

1 cup sour cream or substitute
⅓ cup chopped onion
bread crumbs
paprika

Marinate sole in wine for 2 hours. Dry and coat with bread crumbs. Place in baking pan. Mix remaining ingredients together. Spread the mixture over the sole. Sprinkle with bread crumbs and paprika. Bake at 500 degrees for 10 minutes.

Dotty France

BAKED SOLE

Serves: 4

½ teaspoon oil
1½ teaspoons flour
½ cup white wine
1½ cups sliced, fresh
   mushrooms

½ cup chopped green onions
¼ cup parsley
1 to 1½ pounds fillet of sole
buttered bread crumbs
grated Swiss cheese

Layer oil, flour and wine in glass baking dish. Spread mushrooms, onions and parsley over mixture. Lay sole on top and cover with buttered bread crumbs. Bake at 350 degrees for 20 minutes or until fish is done. Last few minutes of cooking, sprinkle grated Swiss cheese over top.

Gail Holsinger

SWEET AND SOUR FISH

Serves: 4

Fish:
1 pound fillet of flounder
2 tablespoons wine

3 tablespoons cornstarch
3 tablespoons flour
oil for deep fat frying

Vegetables:
½ 4-ounce can bamboo shoots,
  shredded
3 bell peppers, seeded and
  quartered
1 onion, quartered

1 large carrot, cut in small
  wedges and boiled for 8
  minutes
1 8½-ounce can pineapple
  chunks, drained
5 tablespoons oil

Sauce:
6 tablespoons sugar
4 tablespoons soy sauce
1 tablespoon wine or sherry

2 tablespoons vinegar
4 tablespoons tomato sauce
1 tablespoon cornstarch
½ cup cold water

Cut fish into 1½ inch cubes and mix with other fish ingredients except oil. Deep fat fry fish until golden brown. Drain on paper towel. Heat 5 tablespoons oil and sauté vegetables. Mix sauce ingredients in bowl, except cornstarch and water. Add sauce to sautéed vegetables. Heat over medium heat until mixture boils. Add cornstarch mixture, stirring constantly. Add fried fish and mix well. Serve over hot rice.

Anong Litwin

FILLET AND SHRIMP IN A LIGHT DIJON CREAM SAUCE
(A specialty of the Cedar House Restaurant)

Serves: 2

2 3-ounce fillets, ¾ inch thick
flour
salt
pepper
3 tablespoons butter
1 tablespoon oil

6 raw shrimp, cleaned
1 medium shallot, diced
2 ounces dry white wine
½ cup heavy cream
1 teaspoon Dijon mustard
chopped fresh parsley

Dust fillets with flour, salt and pepper. Heat butter and oil over moderate heat. Add fillets. Cook for 3 minutes, turn and cook 3 to 5 minutes. Add shrimp and shallots. Cook for 3 minutes on each side. Add wine. Stir, scraping the pan. Reduce heat slightly. Add cream and mustard, stirring well to blend. Serve when heated and slightly thickened. Garnish with fresh parsley.

Fran Smetanka

SCALLOPED SALMON PIE

Serves: 6 to 8

1 6-ounce package Stove Top
    Stuffing, chicken flavor
1 egg
½ teaspoon dry mustard

Sauce:
1 ½ tablespoons butter
1 tablespoon cornstarch

1 16-ounce can salmon, flaked
    and drained
1 cup shredded cheddar or
    American cheese

1 cup milk
dash of pepper
1 cup cooked peas

Prepare stuffing mix according to directions on package. Add egg, mustard and salmon. Mix well. Add cheese. Turn into a greased 9-inch pie pan. Bake uncovered at 350 degrees for 35 to 40 minutes or microwave on high for 10 minutes.

Sauce:
Melt butter in saucepan. Blend in cornstarch. Gradually add milk. Cook until bubbly. Stir in pepper and peas. Pour over pie.

NOTE: Can be served with or without sauce.

Barbara and Rick Heinze

POOR MAN'S LOBSTER

Serves: 4

1 pound frozen haddock or
    flounder
1 tablespoon Old Bay Seasoning

1 tablespoon salt
4 tablespoons butter, melted

Place fish in boiling water to cover. Add Old Bay Seasoning and salt. Boil without lid for 20 minutes. Place on platter. Score in sections. Pour melted butter over fish.

LaRue Weber

TUNA CASSEROLE
("Charlie" will love this one!)

Serves: 4

½ cup milk
1 6½-ounce can tuna, flaked
1 ½ cups potato chips, crushed

1 10-ounce package frozen peas
1 10¾-ounce can cream of
    mushroom soup, undiluted

Mix milk, tuna, 1 cup potato chips, peas and soup together. Pour into 1 ½ quart casserole. Sprinkle ½ cup crushed potato chips on top before baking. Bake uncovered at 350 degrees for 20 minutes.

Peggy Osborne

CASSEROLE SAINT JACQUES

Serves: 6

1 pound scallops
1 cup dry white wine
1 small onion, sliced
1 tablespoon parsley, snipped
2 teaspoons lemon juice
salt to taste
4 tablespoons butter or
   margarine
6 tablespoons flour
1 cup light cream

2 ounces Gruyere cheese, cut up
dash of pepper
1 6½-ounce can crabmeat,
   drained or equivalent fresh
   crabmeat
1 4½-ounce can shrimp
1 2½-ounce can sliced
   mushrooms, drained
1½ cups soft bread crumbs
1 tablespoon butter, melted

Combine scallops, wine, onion, parsley, lemon juice and salt. Bring to boil and decrease heat to simmer 5 minutes. Drain, reserving 1 cup liquid and set aside. Melt 4 tablespoons butter in saucepan and stir in flour. Add cream and reserved scallop liquid all at once. Stir and cook over medium heat until mixture thickens and bubbles. Remove from heat. Stir in cheese and dash of pepper until cheese melts. Add scallop mixture, crab, shrimp and mushrooms. Spoon into 6 individual-sized or 1 2-quart casserole. Combine bread crumbs with 1 tablespoon melted butter and spoon over casserole. Bake in preheated 350 degree oven for 25 minutes or until heated through and bubbly. About 420 calories per serving.

Gladys Douglas

To keep garlic for a longer period of time, store it in the freezer. Peel and chop before thawing, when ready to use.

SEAFOOD LASAGNE
(Pasta and fish, a rare combination)

Serves: 12

8 lasagne noodles
1 cup chopped onion
2 tablespoons margarine
1 8-ounce package cream cheese, softened
1½ cups cream-style cottage cheese
1 egg, beaten
2 teaspoons dried basil, crushed
½ teaspoon salt
½ teaspoon pepper
2 10¾-ounce cans cream of mushroom soup, undiluted
⅓ cup milk
⅓ cup dry white wine
1 6½-ounce can crabmeat
1 pound shelled shrimp, cooked and halved
¼ cup grated Parmesan cheese
½ cup shredded sharp cheese

Cook noodles according to package directions, drain. Arrange 4 noodles in bottom of greased 9 x 13 inch pan. Sauté onion in margarine until tender. Blend in cream cheese, cottage cheese, egg, basil, salt and pepper in a bowl and add cooked onions. Spread half of mixture on top of noodles. Combine soup, milk and wine in a bowl and set aside. Drain crabmeat. Remove cartilage and flake crabmeat. Stir shrimp and crabmeat into soup mixture. Spread half over cottage cheese layer. Repeat layers. Sprinkle with Parmesan cheese. Bake uncovered at 350 degrees for 45 minutes. Remove from oven. Top with sharp cheese. Bake 2 to 3 minutes more. Let stand 15 minutes before serving.

Judy and Bill Alexy

SEAFOOD MOLD

Serves: 8 to 10

4 3-ounce packages of cream cheese, softened
2 envelopes unflavored gelatin
⅓ cup cold water
1 10¾-ounce can tomato soup, heated
3 cups lobster (or crab), flaked
½ cup finely chopped celery
1 onion, grated
2 cups mayonnaise
1 tablespoon Worcestershire sauce
1 teaspoon seasoned salt
Tabasco sauce to taste
crackers

Beat cream cheese until fluffy. Soften gelatin in cold water. Dissolve in hot soup. Combine soup mixture with cheese. Beat until smooth. Fold in all other ingredients, except crackers. Pack lightly in oiled mold and chill. Remove from mold and serve with crackers.

Janet Holliday

SEAFOOD ROLL
(Well worth the effort!)

Serves: 6

Sauce:
1 10¾-ounce can cream of celery
   soup, undiluted
½ cup milk

1 10-ounce package frozen mixed
   vegetables, cooked and
   drained

Filling:
¼ cup sour cream
1 6½-ounce can crabmeat,
   drained and flaked

1 5-ounce can shrimp, drained
   and chopped
¼ cup chopped parsley

Dough:
2 cups buttermilk pancake mix
¼ cup shortening

⅔ cup milk

Sauce:
Combine ingredients and heat.

Filling:
Combine ingredients and set aside.

Dough:
Cut shortening into pancake mix and add milk. Turn onto floured board.
Roll into a 12 x 15 inch rectangle. Spread with filling. Roll as for jelly roll. Cut
into 12 1-inch slices. Place on greased cookie sheet. Bake at 400 degrees
for 15 to 20 minutes. Serve with hot sauce.

NOTE: Roll can be made ahead and frozen. Defrost just enough to slice.

Barbara Cooledge

To freeze fish: Fillet and rinse fish in cold water. Place in plastic bags, then
add a mixture of 4 cups cold water and 1 tablespoon of salt to bag.
Release any air from the bag, seal and freeze.

SEAFOOD SOUFFLÉ

Serves: 8

8 slices bread
2 cups crab or shrimp (or both)
½ cup mayonnaise
1 onion, chopped
1 green pepper, chopped
1 cup chopped celery
3 cups milk

4 eggs
1 10¾-ounce can cream of
    mushroom soup, undiluted
grated cheese (as much as you
    would like for topping)
paprika

Cube half of bread and place into buttered 9 x 13 inch pan. Mix crab or shrimp, mayonnaise, onion, pepper and celery in a bowl and spread over bread. Cube remaining bread and place over mixture. Beat milk and eggs well and pour over bread. Refrigerate overnight. Bake at 325 degrees for 15 minutes, then remove from oven and spoon soup over top. Sprinkle with cheese and paprika. Bake at 325 degrees for 1 hour or until raised.

Barbara Cooledge

Poultry

GARY G. BAKER

CHAPTER VII

Henny Penny's ... Poultry

Henny Penny, Henny Penny,
In regard to brains, you haven't any.
Cocky Locky, a fricassee you'll make
AND
Ducky Lucky, in the oven you'll bake.

Goosey Loosey, Goosey Loosey,
As a box of nuggets you'll be juicy.
Turkey Lurkey, run! You're the flock's last try!
It's the fox who'll get you and not the sky!

There's no nonsense about this flock of poultry recipes.
Boneless or brainless, these ideas are painless.
(And your family's praises will hold up the sky!)

ALMOND CHICKEN CASSEROLE

Serves: 8 to 10

4 whole chicken breasts, cooked
and cubed
1 5-ounce package sliced
almonds

2 10¾-ounce cans cream of
celery soup, undiluted
½ cup milk
crushed potato chips

Arrange chicken in greased 9 x 13 inch glass baking dish. Sprinkle with almonds. Blend soup and milk; heat. Pour soup mixture over chicken. Cover with a thin layer of potato chips. Bake at 300 degrees for 20 minutes. Serve over rice or noodles.

Phyllis Fox

APRICOT STUFFED CHICKEN BREASTS

Serves: 12

6 whole chicken breasts, split
1 6-ounce package Pepperidge
Farm Stuffing Mix, prepared
flour
oil

1 8-ounce bottle Seven Seas
Creamy Italian Salad Dressing
2 10½-ounce cans Franco
American Chicken Gravy
1 10-ounce jar apricot preserves
1 package Lipton Onion Soup
Mix

Bone and flatten chicken breasts. Stuff each breast with two tablespoons of prepared stuffing mix. Secure with toothpicks and roll in flour. Brown in oil. At this point, breasts can be frozen. To make sauce, stir together salad dressing, chicken gravy and preserves. Pour over chicken. Sprinkle with onion soup mix. Bake at 350 degrees for 1 hour.

NOTE: Recipe can easily be cut in half.

Gerri Bartelme

ARROZ CON POLLO - "CHICKEN IN RICE"
(Great for a dinner party, but save some for the family the next day)

Serves: 6 to 8

1 4-pound frying chicken, cut into serving pieces
1¼ teaspoons salt
½ teaspoon pepper
⅛ teaspoon paprika
½ teaspoon onion powder
¼ cup olive oil
1 to 2 garlic cloves, finely minced
1 medium onion, chopped
2 green onions, finely chopped
2 cups water

3½ cups canned whole tomatoes
2 chicken bouillon cubes
¼ teaspoon saffron
1 bay leaf
½ teaspoon oregano
½ teaspoon basil
2 cups uncooked rice
1 10-ounce package frozen peas or artichoke hearts, defrosted
3 pimientos, cut in pieces

Preheat oven to 350 degrees. Season chicken with 1 teaspoon of salt, pepper, paprika and onion powder. In a skillet, heat oil. Add chicken and brown on all sides. Remove to a baking dish. To the skillet add garlic, onion and green onion. Sauté until onion is tender. Add water and heat while scraping loose the browned particles. Add the tomatoes, including the liquid, bouillon, remaining seasonings and salt. Bring to a boil and pour over the chicken. Add the rice and stir. Cover tightly. Bake at 350 degrees for 25 minutes. Uncover and toss the rice. Stir in peas or artichokes, and arrange pimientos on top. Cover and cook for 30 minutes, or until chicken is tender.

Penny Goldstein

Poultry Safety Tips: Use care and cleanliness in handling raw poultry or meat. Clean all surfaces and tools after cutting and touching poultry to avoid cross contamination with other foods. Always cook poultry at one time. Do not partially cook and finish at another time.

BAKED CHICKEN PARMESAN
(Easy and different!)

Serves: 4 to 5

¼ cup oil
1 broiler-fryer chicken, cut in
   serving pieces
½ teaspoon oregano

½ teaspoon salt
paprika
1 4-ounce can sliced mushrooms
1 ½ tablespoons grated Parmesan
   cheese

Preheat oven to 425 degrees. Heat oil in 9 x 13 inch pan for about 10 minutes. Remove pan from oven. Place chicken pieces, skin side down, in hot oil. Sprinkle with ¼ teaspoon oregano and ¼ teaspoon salt. Sprinkle lightly with paprika. Return to oven and bake for 30 minutes. Turn chicken pieces. Sprinkle with remaining oregano and salt. Lightly sprinkle with paprika. Bake for 15 minutes longer. Remove from oven. Spoon fat and drippings in pan over chicken. Pour mushrooms, including liquid, over chicken. Sprinkle with Parmesan cheese. Bake for 5 more minutes.

Ada Bates

BAKED PINEAPPLE CHICKEN

Serves: 4

4 boneless chicken breasts
salt
pepper
1 envelope Trim instant chicken
   soup mix

1 15½-ounce can crushed
   pineapple
2 tablespoons white cooking wine
1 tablespoon cornstarch
1 teaspoon water

Place chicken breasts on a large piece of aluminum foil. Sprinkle with salt, pepper, and soup mix. Spoon pineapple and juice on top of chicken. Seal foil tightly. Bake on rack in baking dish at 350 degrees for 1 hour and 15 minutes.

Sauce:
Remove chicken from foil. Pour drippings and pineapple into a small saucepan. Bring to a slow boil. Add wine. Thicken with cornstarch dissolved in water. Serve over chicken with rice.

Barbara Goldsmith

CEDAR HOUSE CHICKEN SALAD

Serves: 2

2 whole chicken breasts
2 celery stalks from the heart,
  finely chopped
2 small scallions, diced
¼ teaspoon salt

¼ teaspoon freshly ground
  pepper
¼ teaspoon curry powder
½ cup mayonnaise
1 hard boiled egg, chopped

Boil chicken breasts for 25 to 30 minutes. Cool and remove skin and bones. Chop chicken into ¼ inch pieces or smaller. Combine all ingredients and mix very well. Serve on a bed of lettuce with tomato, cheese wedges and crackers.

VARIATION: Baby shrimp can be used instead of chicken breasts. Omit egg.

Fran Smetanka

CHICKEN À LA GEORGE

Serves: 6 to 8

½ cup butter
6 tablespoons flour
2 teaspoons salt
½ teaspoon white pepper
2 cups milk, scalded
2 cups light cream, scalded
2 green peppers, cut in 1 inch
  squares

1 cup chopped mushrooms
3 cups diced, cooked chicken
½ pound cooked ham, cut in 1
  inch pieces (optional)
3 pimientos, cut in 1 inch
  squares
¼ cup dry sherry

Melt butter. Set aside 2 tablespoons butter to sauté peppers. Stir in flour, salt and pepper. Gradually add scalded milk and cream. Cook over low heat for 10 minutes. Sauté green pepper in 2 tablespoons butter for 10 minutes. Add mushrooms and continue to sauté until tender. To milk mixture, add chicken and ham. Add remaining ingredients. Cook over low heat until thoroughly heated. Serve with rice or noodles.

Pat Blair

CHICKEN À LA KING
(A quick and easy standby)

Serves: 4 to 6

1 3 to 4-pound chicken, cooked
½ cup frozen peas
2 10¾-ounce cans cream of
chicken soup, undiluted

4 cups water
1 cup milk
3 tablespoons cornstarch

Cut cooked chicken into chunks. Put chicken, peas, soup and water in saucepan. Bring to boil and simmer for 10 minutes. Combine milk and cornstarch. Add to boiling chicken mixture. Simmer 1 to 2 minutes. Serve over rice or toast.

Vera King

CHICKEN A L'ORANGE

Serves: 4

2 whole chicken breasts, split
garlic salt
½ cup orange marmalade

¼ cup A-1 sauce
½ cup ketchup

Sprinkle chicken generously with garlic salt. Place in foil-lined shallow baking dish. Combine marmalade, A-1 sauce and ketchup. Mix well until blended. Baste chicken with mixture. Bake at 375 degrees for 1 to 1¼ hours. Turn and baste chicken while baking.

Joan Clark

CHICKEN AND SCALLOP SAUTÉ
(A Cedar House Restaurant specialty)

Serves: 1

6 ounces boneless chicken
breast
flour
3 tablespoons butter
3 ounces sea scallops
5 mushrooms, sliced

½ red pepper, thinly sliced
1 small shallot, diced
2 ounces Marsala wine
2 ounces chicken stock
½ teaspoon salt
½ teaspoon white pepper

Dust chicken with flour. Sauté on one side in butter for 3 minutes over moderate heat. Turn chicken. Add scallops, mushrooms and red pepper. Cook for 3 to 5 minutes. Add shallots. Turn scallops. Add Marsala wine, scraping any bits from the bottom of the pan. Stir well. Add chicken stock, salt and pepper. Reduce heat, cooking until slightly thickened.

Fran Smetanka

CHICKEN AND SHRIMP IN TARRAGON-CREAM SAUCE
(Straight from the Cedar House Restaurant)

Serves: 1

6 ounces boneless chicken
  breast
flour
salt
pepper

3 tablespoons butter
3 or 4 cleaned raw shrimp
1 small shallot, diced
1 ½ teaspoons tarragon
⅓ cup heavy cream

Dust chicken with flour, salt and pepper. Sauté in butter for 3 minutes over moderate heat. Turn chicken, and add shrimp and shallot to fry pan. After 3 to 5 minutes, turn shrimp. Add tarragon. Stir. Add heavy cream. Cook until slightly thickened.

Fran Smetanka

CHICKEN BREASTS AU PORTO
(Try this with French bread for "sopping" up the wonderful sauce)

Serves: 4

2 whole chicken breasts,
  deboned and flattened
½ cup flour
1 teaspoon salt
¼ teaspoon nutmeg
¼ teaspoon pepper

6 tablespoons butter
1 ½ cups heavy cream or
  evaporated milk
¼ cup Port wine
½ pound fresh mushrooms,
  sliced

Flatten chicken breasts between sheets of waxed paper with bottom of heavy skillet. Combine flour, salt, nutmeg and pepper. Dredge chicken in flour mixture. Brown chicken in 4 tablespoons of butter, then remove from skillet. Add 1 cup cream to skillet, stirring constantly. Bring to a boil and simmer for 2 minutes. Add wine, and return chicken to skillet. Cover and simmer for about 20 minutes. While above ingredients are simmering, cook mushrooms in remaining butter. Add remaining cream and bring to a boil. Pour mushroom mixture over chicken. Salt and pepper to taste. Cover again and simmer 10 more minutes.

Gerri Bartelme

CHICKEN CASSEROLE

Serves: 10

4 cups diced, cooked chicken
2 10¾-ounce cans cream of
   mushroom soup, undiluted
2 cups chicken broth
2 tablespoons chopped onion

1 cup chopped celery
1 5-ounce can Chinese noodles
slivered almonds
crushed potato chips or buttered
   bread crumbs

Stir together all ingredients except potato chips or bread crumbs. Place in a greased 9 x 13 inch pan. Cover with potato chips or bread crumbs. Bake at 300 degrees for 1 hour.

Dorothy Baker

CHICKEN FRICASSEE
(A favorite served at Castle Tavern)

Serves: 6

¼ cup butter or oil
1 cup diced onion
1 cup diced celery
2 pounds mixed giblets (backs,
   necks, hearts, gizzards) cut
   into small pieces

1 teaspoon salt
¼ teaspoon pepper
½ teaspoon garlic powder
4 cups water
¾ cup uncooked rice

Lightly brown onion and celery in butter or oil in frying pan. Add giblets, salt, pepper, and garlic powder. Brown for 5 more minutes. Put into 3 to 4 quart pot. Add water and rice. Bring to a boil. Cover and simmer for 1 hour, until rice and chicken are cooked.

Rose Bloom

For the working mom: Prepare cassettes of your children's favorite stories. Then during the day, the sitter can play back the stories. The kids will be happy to hear your voice.

CHICKEN IN SAUCE
(Recipe from northern Italy)

Serves: 4 to 6

1 2 to 3-pound stewing chicken,
   cut into serving pieces
½ cup oil
1 clove garlic, minced
salt and pepper

1 16-ounce can tomatoes,
   chopped into small pieces
½ cup water
pinch of rosemary

Brown chicken in oil at 350 degrees in an electric frypan or over medium heat in a regular fry pan. Add garlic, salt and pepper while browning. After chicken is browned, cook for 1 hour in frypan, adding small amounts of water when necessary. Drain off excess grease. Add tomatoes, water, and rosemary. Cook until tender for ½ to 1 hour.

Jo Ann Pulcini

CHICKEN SALAD PIE

Serves: 6 to 8

1 Pillsbury Pie Crust stick
⅓ cup grated sharp cheese
⅔ cup mayonnaise
1 cup sour cream
2 cups cubed, cooked chicken

1 cup chopped nuts
1 15¼-ounce can pineapple
   tidbits, drained
½ cup chopped celery

Combine pie crust stick and sharp cheese. Bake as directed in a 9-inch pie pan. Blend mayonnaise and sour cream. Combine chicken, nuts, pineapple and celery. Add ⅔ of sour cream mixture to the chicken mixture. Spead in pie shell. Frost with remaining cream mixture. Refrigerate overnight. Serve in wedges.

Shirley Norman

CHICKEN SALAD SUPREME
(For that hot summer day)

Serves: 8

3 pounds boneless chicken
   breasts
1 cup white seedless grapes,
   halved or 1 cup drained
   pineapple chunks

½ cup slivered almonds
1 teaspoon salt
1 cup mayonnaise
½ cup whipped cream or Cool
   Whip

Wash and cook chicken. Cool. Cut into chunks. Mix all ingredients with the chicken. Refrigerate. Serve on lettuce.

Deb and Ron Wilcher

CHICKEN SALAD WITH STUFFING

Serves: 6

2 whole chicken breasts, cooked
  and cubed
1 tablespoon chopped onion
1½ teaspoons salt
1 cup diced celery
3 hard-cooked eggs, chopped
1 cup cooked rice

3 tablespoons lemon juice
¾ cup mayonnaise
½ cup blanched slivered almonds
1 cup cream of chicken soup,
  undiluted
1 6-ounce package Pepperidge
  Farm stuffing, unprepared

Butter a 2 quart casserole. Mix all ingredients, except stuffing, together thoroughly. Place in casserole and cover with stuffing. Refrigerate overnight. Bake at 375 degrees for 45 minutes to 1 hour.

Millie McCathren

CHICKEN SCALLOPINI

Serves: 6

6 boneless chicken breasts
salt
pepper
½ cup flour
6 tablespoons margarine

½ pound mushrooms, sliced
1 cup beef bouillon
1 cup sherry
⅛ cup flour

Quarter each chicken breast and pound meat until about ¼ inch thick. Season meat with salt and pepper. Coat with flour. Melt margarine in large skillet. Brown chicken in melted margarine. Remove chicken. Add mushrooms to pan and sauté until tender. Add ½ cup of the bouillon and the sherry. Boil about 3 minutes. Return chicken to the skillet. Reduce heat, cover and simmer for 30 to 35 minutes. Baste often. Remove meat. Pour remaining bouillon in pan. Mix flour with enough water to make a thin paste. Add to skillet. Bring to a boil. Cook until thickened. Pour over meat. Serve immediately. Buttered noodles make a delicious side dish.

Jean Getz

CHICKEN SPAGHETTI
(Take to a covered dish dinner)

Serves: 12

1 cup chopped onion
1 green pepper, chopped
½ cup butter
1 16-ounce package spaghetti
1 10¾-ounce can cream of
  mushroom soup, undiluted

1 4-ounce jar pimientos, chopped
2 to 3 cups diced, cooked
  chicken
½ cup sliced black olives
½ pound cheddar cheese, grated

Sauté onion and green pepper in butter in a medium saucepan. In a separate pot, cook spaghetti according to directions on package. Add soup and pimientos to onion-green pepper mixture. Remove from heat and stir in chicken, olives and some of the grated cheese. Stir in cooked, drained spaghetti. Pour into a greased 9 x 13 inch pan. Top with remaining cheese. Bake at 375 degrees for 20 minutes.

Joan Fullwood

CHICKEN STRATA

Serves: 12

16 slices bread
butter or margarine, softened
4 cups cubed, cooked chicken
1 cup chopped onion
1 medium green pepper, finely
  chopped
1 cup mayonnaise
1 cup finely chopped celery

½ tablespoon salt
⅛ teaspoon pepper
3 eggs, beaten
3 cups milk
2 10¾-ounce cans cream of
  mushroom soup, undiluted
1 cup grated sharp cheese

Butter 4 slices of bread and cut in 12 1-inch cubes. Set aside for topping. Cut remaining bread in 1-inch cubes. Place ½ of the bread cubes in the bottom of a 9 x 13 inch pan. Combine cubed chicken, chopped onion, green pepper, mayonnaise, celery, salt and pepper. Spoon evenly over bread cubes. Top with remaining unbuttered bread cubes. Mix eggs with milk and pour over bread cubes and chicken mixture. Cover and chill at least one hour or preferably overnight. Before baking, spread soup over top of dish. Top with reserved buttered bread cubes. Bake at 325 degrees for 50 to 60 minutes. During the last 15 minutes, sprinkle with cheese.

Katie Van Hoozer

CHICKEN STROGANOFF
(Easy and deliciously different!)

Serves: 6

4 cups diced, cooked chicken
fresh mushrooms, sliced
¼ to ½ cup chopped green
   pepper
¼ cup butter
2 tablespoons chopped pimiento
¼ cup water or chicken broth

1 10¾-ounce can cream of
   chicken soup, undiluted
¾ teaspoon salt
⅛ teaspoon pepper
1¼ teaspoons paprika
1 cup sour cream

Sauté mushrooms and green pepper in melted butter. Slowly stir in pimiento, chicken broth and soup. Add spices. Stir in chicken and cook for 5 minutes. Add sour cream. Serve over parsley rice or noodles.

Diana Smith

CHOW MEIN CHICKEN

Serves: 4 to 6

1 frying chicken, cut into serving
   pieces
1 cup sour cream
3 tablespoons dried onion soup
   mix

1 10¾-ounce can cream of
   mushrom soup, undiluted
⅛ teaspoon pepper
1 5-ounce can chow mein
   noodles

Place chicken in shallow baking dish. Mix sour cream, onion soup mix, mushroom soup, and pepper. Spread over chicken. Sprinkle with chow mein noodles. Bake at 375 degrees for 1 hour, or until chicken is thoroughly cooked. Good served with rice.

Judy Douglass

Heating the frying pan before adding oil or butter will keep things from sticking to the pan.

CREAM OF CHICKEN
(Henny Penny's buffet for a crowd)

Serves: 15 to 18

2 10¾-ounce cans cream of chicken soup, undiluted
1 tablespoon Worcestershire sauce
1 cup Parmesan cheese

9 whole chicken breasts, cooked and skinned
½ cup heavy cream, whipped
¾ cup mayonnaise

Pour 1 can of soup in casserole dish. Add Worcestershire sauce. Cover with ⅓ cup cheese. Place chicken on cheese layer, then cover with remaining soup and ⅓ cup of cheese. Mix cream and mayonnaise. Spread over chicken. Sprinkle with remaining cheese. Bake at 400 degrees for 25 to 30 minutes.

NOTE: Browning chicken prior to baking increases the flavor.

Gladys Douglas

DIET CHICKEN
(For the calorie counter)

Serves: 4

1 3 to 4-pound broiler chicken
salt
pepper
¼ cup grated cheese
1 tablespoon chopped parsley
1 teaspoon oregano

¼ cup olive oil
juice of 1 lemon
garlic powder or fresh chopped garlic
2 8-ounce cans tomato sauce

Clean chicken and cut into serving pieces. Sprinkle lightly with salt and pepper. Place chicken in 9 x 13 inch pan. Mix remaining ingredients in bowl. Pour over chicken. Cover with aluminum foil. Bake at 350 degrees for 1 hour.

NOTE: To assume "diet" quality, chicken should be skinned.

Elizabeth Pasquantonio

GARLIC CHICKEN

Serves: 4

1 3 to 4-pound chicken, cut into serving pieces
salt
pepper
flour

oil
garlic powder
¼ cup margarine
½ cup water

Sprinkle chicken pieces with salt and pepper. Dredge in flour. Heat oil in skillet, fry chicken until golden brown. Sprinkle each piece of chicken with garlic powder. Place chicken pieces in square baking pan; add margarine and water. Cover with aluminum foil. Bake at 350 degrees for 40 to 60 minutes.

NOTE: To brown and crisp chicken remove foil for last 15 minutes of baking time.

Bill Kasavage

GLORIOUS CHICKEN SALAD

Serves: 6 to 8

3½ cups diced, cooked chicken
¾ cup oil
2 tablespoons sugar
1 teaspoon salt
⅓ cup honey
⅓ cup lemon juice
1 teaspoon dry mustard

1 teaspoon celery seed
2 ounces pecans
1 tablespoon butter
1⅔ cups chopped celery
1 cup seedless grapes
1 cup pineapple
1 scant cup mayonnaise

Marinate chicken overnight in sauce of oil, sugar, salt, honey, lemon juice, dry mustard and celery seed. Drain chicken. Toast pecans in butter; salt. Add celery, grapes, pineapple and pecans to chicken. Toss with mayonnaise. Serve on lettuce.

Pat Blair

HAWAIIAN CHICKEN

Serves: 10

2 frying chickens, cut into serving
pieces
1 cup flour
1½ teaspoons seasoned salt
½ teaspoon garlic powder
½ teaspoon onion powder
½ teaspoon pepper
1½ cups margarine
2 cups orange juice

2 tablespoons lemon juice
1 cup brown sugar
2 tablespoons corn starch
2 tablespoons soy sauce
1 20-ounce can pineapple
chunks, drained
1 8-ounce can water chestnuts,
drained
¼ cup dry white wine

Shake chicken pieces in flour and seasonings until evenly coated. Place chicken in baking pan. Melt margarine and pour over chicken. In a saucepan, combine orange juice, lemon juice, brown sugar, cornstarch, soy sauce, pineapple, water chestnuts and wine. Bring to a boil, stirring constantly. Pour over chicken. Bake at 350 degrees for 50 minutes.

Penny Goldstein

HENNY PENNY SALAD

Serves: 4

2 cups cubed, cooked chicken
1½ cups finely chopped celery
1 cup Miracle Whip
1 teaspoon salt

2 teaspoons lemon juice
2 teaspoons grated onion
½ cup grated American cheese
1 cup crushed potato chips

Mix chicken, celery, Miracle Whip, salt, lemon juice and onion. Put in large cake pan. Sprinkle cheese and potato chips on chicken mixture. Bake at 450 degrees for 10 minutes. Serve on lettuce leaves.

Jean Getz

Roll chicken in powdered milk instead of flour for golden-brown fried chicken.

HERBED CHICKEN

Serves: 6

1 6-ounce package wild rice
3 whole chicken breasts, split and deboned
4 tablespoons butter
1 10¾-ounce can cream of chicken soup, undiluted

¾ cup Sauterne wine
½ cup sliced celery
1 4-ounce can whole mushrooms
1 8-ounce can sliced water chestnuts

Prepare rice according to directions on package. Place rice in large casserole dish. Brown chicken breasts in butter. Place on top of rice. Add soup to skillet. Add Sauterne, celery, mushrooms and water chestnuts. Stir together. Pour over chicken. Bake covered at 350 degrees for 25 minutes. Remove cover and bake for 15 to 20 minutes.

Nancy Morgan

HONEY-CURRIED CHICKEN
(Don't miss that dip in the sauce!)

Serves: 4

2 whole chicken breasts, split
¼ cup spicy mustard
½ cup honey

1 tablespoon curry powder
1 tablespoon butter or margarine
dash of salt

Clean and pat dry chicken breasts. Arrange in baking dish. Melt butter or margarine. Mix together all ingredients. Pour mixture over chicken. Refrigerate 1 hour or more. Cook at 350 degrees for 1 hour. Baste frequently. Pour sauce over chicken when serving.

NOTE: This dish is best if marinated overnight.

Sandy Simpson

No bread crumbs in the house? Use crushed corn or wheat flakes, or other dry cereal.

HOT CHICKEN SALAD

Serves: 10

2 cups diced, cooked chicken
1 small onion, chopped
4 hard cooked eggs, chopped
1 cup mayonnaise
2 cups cooked rice
1 package slivered almonds

1 teaspoon salt
2 10¾-ounce cans cream of
  mushroom soup, undiluted
2 tablespoons lemon juice
½ cup bread crumbs
2 tablespoons butter

Mix all ingredients except bread crumbs and butter. Pour into 9 x 13 inch baking dish. Toss bread crumbs in melted butter. Sprinkle on top of chicken mixture. Cover and store overnight in refrigerator. Remove from refrigerator 1 hour before baking. Bake at 325 degrees for 45 minutes. Allow to cool 15 minutes before serving.

Frances Dortenza

MARIE'S CHICKEN AND BROCCOLI CASSEROLE

Serves: 4

1 10-ounce frozen package
  broccoli
4 boneless chicken breasts
1 10¾-ounce can cream of
  chicken soup, undiluted
½ cup mayonnaise

½ teaspoon lemon juice
½ teaspoon curry powder
2 tablespoons butter, melted
½ cup shredded cheddar cheese
¼ cup soft bread crumbs

Cook broccoli according to directions on package. In a separate pot, simmer chicken in water for 35 minutes. Drain broccoli, and arrange in an 9 x 9 inch pan. Arrange chicken over broccoli. Mix together soup, mayonnaise, lemon juice and curry powder in a bowl. Spread evenly over the chicken and broccoli. Melt butter in a saucepan. Stir in cheese and bread crumbs until covered with butter. Sprinkle over soup-mayonnaise mixture. Bake at 350 degrees for 25 minutes.

Dorothy Baker

MEXICAN CHICKEN CASSEROLE

Serves: 8

4 whole chicken breasts
salt
bay leaf
peppercorns
8 corn tortillas
1 10¾-ounce can cream of
  chicken soup, undiluted

1 13-ounce can evaporated milk
1 4-ounce can green chili
  peppers, drained and chopped
1 teaspoon chili powder
1 teaspoon Mexican hot sauce
2 cups grated sharp cheddar
  cheese

Place chicken breasts, salt, bay leaf, and peppercorns in large pot. Cover with water. Cook until chicken is tender. Remove chicken from bones, and cut into large pieces. Break tortillas into pieces. Mix together soup, milk, chili peppers, chili powder and hot sauce. In 3 quart ungreased casserole, alternate layers of tortillas, chicken, cheese and soup mixture. Repeat layers ending with cheese and soup mixture. Bake at 350 degrees for 45 minutes to 1 hour. If the top looks dry while baking, sprinkle top with water.

Elaine Cretekos

ORANGE CHICKEN
(An appealing company dish)

Serves: 4

1 3-pound chicken, cut into
  serving pieces
1 teaspoon curry powder
salt to taste
½ cup reconstituted frozen
  orange juice

¼ cup brown sugar
¼ cup honey
3 tablespoons mustard
1 tablespoon flour mixed with 2
  tablespoons water
2 oranges, peeled and sliced

Preheat oven to 375 degrees. Rub chicken pieces with curry powder. Sprinkle with salt. In a saucepan, combine orange juice, brown sugar, honey, mustard and flour mixture. Simmer for 5 minutes, stirring constantly. Place chicken pieces in a baking pan. Pour sauce over chicken and bake for 30 minutes. Turn chicken and baste with sauce. Bake for another 20 to 25 minutes. Add orange slices. Heat for 3 to 4 minutes longer and serve.

Rosemary Ross

PRIZE WINNING CHICKEN

Serves: 4 to 6

3 whole chicken breasts, split
1 teaspoon salt
3 tablespoons flour
1 cup sour cream
1 10¾-ounce can cream of
  mushroom soup, undiluted

½ cup Sauterne wine
½ cup unblanched sliced
  almonds
1 4-ounce jar pimientos, chopped
1 teaspoon paprika

Place chicken in flat baking dish. Sprinkle with ½ teaspoon salt. Combine flour with ½ cup sour cream. Stir and add remaining salt, sour cream, soup and wine. Pour over chicken. Sprinkle chicken with almonds, pimientos and paprika. Bake at 325 degrees for 1½ hours or until chicken is tender.

LaRue Weber

SHEILA'S CHICKEN
(Get out the crock pot!)

Serves: 4 to 5

1 frying chicken, cut into serving
  pieces
2 tablespoons butter or
  margarine, melted
salt
pepper
2 tablespoons dry Good Season's
  Italian salad dressing mix

1 10¾-ounce can cream of
  mushroom soup, undiluted
2 3-ounce packages cream
  cheese, cubed
½ cup Sauterne wine or sherry
1 tablespoon chopped onion

Wash chicken and pat dry. Brush with butter or margarine. Sprinkle with salt and pepper. Place in crock pot. Sprinkle with dry salad dressing mix. Cover. Cook on low for 5 to 6 hours. Forty-five minutes before serving, mix soup, cream cheese, wine and onion in small saucepan. Cook until smooth. Pour over chicken in crock pot. Cover and cook for 30 minutes on low heat. Serve with rice or noodles.

Sheila and Bob Pasquantonio

SMOTHERED CHICKEN
(Chicken and gravy all in one)

Serves: 4

1 frying chicken, cut into serving
   pieces
4 tablespoons flour
1 tablespoon salt

¼ teaspoon pepper
½ cup shortening
2 cups milk
1 2½-ounce can mushrooms

Place flour, salt and pepper in a stout paper bag. Shake chicken in the bag until all pieces are well coated. Reserve flour mixture. Heat shortening in large chicken fryer or Dutch oven. Brown pieces in hot fat. Remove chicken and a little fat from pot. Stir reserved flour into pot, blending it well. Stir in milk, add chicken and mushrooms. Cover pot. Bake at 325 degrees for 1 hour, or until milk is absorbed and gravy results.

Dotty France

STIR FRIED CHICKEN WITH WALNUTS

Serves: 4

4 tablespoons soy sauce
½ teaspoon water
2 tablespoons cornstarch
1 teaspoon grated ginger
3 tablespoons sherry
½ teaspoon sugar
½ teaspoon dry crushed red
   pepper

½ teaspoon salt
2 tablespoons oil
2 cups pea pods
5 green onions, cut on the bias in
   1 ½ inch pieces
1 cup walnuts, shelled and halved
1 ½ pounds boneless chicken
   breast, cut in 1 inch pieces

Blend soy sauce, water and cornstarch. Add ginger, sherry, sugar, red pepper and salt. Heat skillet or wok over medium high heat. Add oil. Stir fry pea pods and onions for 1 ½ minutes, turning frequently. Remove from pan and set aside. Stir fry walnuts for 1 minute, remove and set aside. Add chicken and more oil if necessary to wok or pan. Cook for 3 to 5 minutes, until done. Move chicken to the sides of the wok or pan to form a well in the center. Stir chicken with walnuts. Pour soy sauce into the well. Cook until thick and bubbly. Stir into chicken. Add vegetables and stir until coated. Cover and cook for 1 minute. Serve immediately.

Jean Getz

TEMPTING CURRIED CHICKEN SALAD
(An East Indian aroma)

Serves: 8

1 ½ cups cooked rice
¼ cup minced onion
1 teaspoon curry powder
2 tablespoons vinegar
1 cup diced celery
½ cup finely chopped green
   pepper

¾ cup mayonnaise
½ teaspoon salt
½ teaspoon pepper
½ cup blanched sliced almonds
2 cups diced, cooked chicken,
   chilled

Mix rice, onions, curry powder, and vinegar. Chill well. Toss remaining ingredients with rice mixture. Serve on lettuce leaves.

NOTE: Some people like a little more curry powder. Suit your taste!

Vivian Pennington

TRUDY'S CHICKEN PIE

Serves: 6 to 8

pastry for double crust pie
1 ½ cups chicken broth
2 chicken flavored bouillon cubes
⅓ cup flour
½ cup milk

salt and pepper to taste
3 cups cooked, cubed chicken
1 to 1 ½ cups shredded cheddar
   cheese
1 egg, beaten

In a medium pot bring chicken broth and bouillon cubes to a boil. Mix flour, milk, salt and pepper together well. Stirring constantly mix flour mixture into chicken broth. Simmer till smooth and thickened. Stir in chicken and cheese. Place in bottom half of pie crust. Cover with top crust, fluting the edges. Brush crust with egg. Bake at 425 degrees for 30 minutes.

Zuzanna K. O'Brien

VEAL OR CHICKEN FRICASSEE

Serves: 4 to 6

2 pounds veal or 4 whole chicken breasts
1 medium onion, chopped
3 tablespoons chopped green pepper
salt and pepper

2 tablespoons meat fat or butter
2 tablespoons flour
1 cup veal or chicken broth
1 cup milk
½ pound mushrooms, sliced
3 tablespoons chopped pimiento

In a skillet cook meat with onion, green pepper, salt and pepper, until meat is tender. Cool and cube meat. Melt fat in pan. Add flour, broth and milk, and bring to a boil. Pour gravy, mushrooms and pimiento over the meat. Heat thoroughly. Serve in patty shells, on rice or noodles. Decorate with fresh parsley.

Doris DePierre

TURKEY OR CHICKEN CROQUETTES

(Make a bunch . . . Have a party!)

Yields: 30 croquettes

2 cups thick white sauce (recipe below)
3½ cups cooked turkey or chicken, ground
1½ teaspoons lemon juice

1½ teaspoons sage
½ cup grated onion
fine bread crumbs
1 egg

Mix together white sauce, meat, lemon juice, sage and onion. Chill at least 4 hours. Using 3 tablespoons of mixture, form a 3 inch long by 1½ inch thick patty. Roll patty in fine bread crumbs, egg and again in bread crumbs, until completely covered. Fry in hot fat, 380 degrees for 3 to 5 minutes.

NOTE: These can be frozen. First fry the patty, wrap and freeze. Heat in 350 degree oven for 20 minutes. Serve with leftover gravy.

White Sauce:
2 tablespoons margarine

2 tablespoons flour
2 cups milk

Melt margarine over medium heat. Blend in flour. Stir until smooth. Add milk. Stir over low heat until thick.

NOTE: Recipe makes 2 cups of medium white sauce. To make a thicker white sauce, double the amount of margarine and flour per 2 cups of milk. For a thinner sauce, halve the amount of margarine and flour per 2 cups of milk.

Eleanor Towers

TURKEY OR CHICKEN ROLL-UPS

Serves: 4

1 ½ cups chopped, cooked turkey or chicken
½ cup chopped stuffed olives
⅓ cup mayonnaise

8 slices sandwich bread, crust removed
¼ cup butter, melted

Mix turkey or chicken, olives and mayonnaise. Brush one side of bread with melted butter. Place turkey mixture on plain side of bread and roll as you would a jelly roll. Secure with toothpicks. Arrange on a cookie sheet. Brush again with butter. Bake at 425 degrees for 12 minutes.

Mary Benson

TURKEY AND WILD RICE CASSEROLE

Serves: 4

½ cup butter
½ cup finely chopped onion
2 cups sliced mushrooms
1 cup uncooked wild rice

3 cups chicken broth
2 cups cubed, cooked turkey
1 teaspoon salt
½ teaspoon pepper

Melt butter in skillet. Sauté onions and mushrooms in butter until soft and lightly browned. Butter a 1 ½ quart casserole. Put onions and mushrooms with remaining ingredients into the casserole. Cover and bake at 325 degrees for 1 hour. The broth will be absorbed and the rice will be tender.

Teresa Meyer

Meats & Sauces

CHAPTER VIII

The Three Little Pigs' ... Meats and Sauces

Roast suckling pig and fruit-stuffed bacon,
The wolf was planning to be takin'!

His dreams of pork chops and ragoût,
Were never intended to come true.

For it took the three of them, so it did,
To pot the wolf and hold down the lid!

No matter if your house is made of
Straw
    or
        Sticks
           or
              Bricks.

Any one of these meat recipes will give
a
firm foundation
to a
nourishing meal.

MARINATED FLANK STEAK

Serves: 4

2 pounds flank steak
¾ cup oil
¼ cup soy sauce
¼ cup honey

2 tablespoons vinegar
2 tablespoons diced green onion
1 clove garlic, minced
⅛ teaspoon ginger

Combine oil, soy sauce, honey, vinegar, onion, garlic and ginger. Score the flank steak on both sides. Pour the marinade mixture over the flank steak. Cover, and refrigerate for 24 hours, occasionally turning the meat to coat evenly. Broil the flank steak 4 inches from the heat for 5 minutes; turn and broil for 5 more minutes. To serve, slice very thinly, on diagonal, across the grain.

NOTE: Recipe requires 24 hours advance preparation. The flank steak can also be grilled on a barbecue and is delicious.

Pat Kuehn

PEPPER STEAK
(An ancient Chinese delight)

Serves: 4 to 5

1 ½ pounds round steak, cut in
   strips
flour
salt
pepper
oil
1 16-ounce can tomatoes
1 ¾ cups water
½ cup chopped onion

1 clove garlic, minced
1 tablespoon beef flavored gravy
   base
1 ½ teaspoons Worcestershire
   sauce
2 large green peppers, sliced
2 tablespoons flour mixed with ¼
   cup water

Roll strips of steak in flour, salt and pepper. Brown in oil. Add liquid of can of tomatoes to pan. Add water, onion, garlic and gravy base. Cover and simmer for 1 hour and 15 minutes. Add Worcestershire sauce and peppers. Cover and simmer for 5 more minutes. Thicken the gravy with flour and add tomatoes. Cook for 5 more minutes.

NOTE: Best served over rice.

Nancy Johns

WHITE'S MARINATED FLANK STEAK

Serves: 4

1 flank steak
1 large onion, chopped
½ teaspoon pepper

½ cup wine vinegar
1 cup oil
2 tablespoons garlic salt

Combine all ingredients except steak. Place flank steak in shallow glass pan and pour marinade over the meat. Refrigerate (preferably overnight). Turn steak several times during marinating process. Broil 3 inches from heat to desired "doneness" on each side. Slice steak diagonally across grain in thin slices. Heat remaining marinade if desired and serve with steak.

NOTE: This marinade works very well for rib steaks, chuck steaks or beef cubes for shish-ka-bobs.

Janet White

BEEF BRISKET IN BEER
(Great on a cold day!)

Serves: 8 to 10

3 to 4 pound beef brisket
salt and pepper
1 onion, sliced
¼ cup chili sauce
2 tablespoons brown sugar

1 clove garlic, minced
1 12-ounce can beer (1 ½ cups)
2 tablespoons flour
½ cup water

Trim excess fat from beef. Season with salt and pepper. Place in 9 x 13 inch baking dish. Cover with onion slices. Combine chili sauce, brown sugar, garlic and beer in bowl. Pour over meat. Cover with foil. Bake in oven at 350 degrees for 3½ hours. Uncover and bake 30 minutes more, basting occasionally with juices. Remove meat to platter. Skim excess fat from drippings. Measure liquid and add water to make 1 cup.

Gravy:
Blend flour and water. Combine with drippings in saucepan. Cook, stirring constantly, over medium heat until thick and bubbly. Cut meat across grain.

NOTE: Can be assembled day before or early in day and kept covered with foil in refrigerator.

Anne Austen

SOUR CREAM BRISKET

Serves: 8

4 pound brisket of beef (first cut-
   not corned)
1 quart water
4 packages M.B.T. Beef Broth
2 packages brown gravy mix

1 cup sour cream (or more, if
   desired)
salt and pepper to taste
1 clove garlic, pressed

Brown meat thoroughly in Dutch oven. Cover with water. Add packages of beef broth. Lower heat and simmer until tender, several hours. Remove meat, let cool, then slice thin on diagonal. Add packages of brown gravy mix to remaining liquid. Add sour cream, salt, pepper and garlic. Mix thoroughly. Place meat in shallow 3-quart casserole. Cover with sauce. (May be frozen at this point.) Cover with foil and bake at 350 degrees for 30 minutes. Serve with noodles.

Nancy Johns

SHORT RIBS

Serves: 4

3 to 4 pounds beef short ribs
½ teaspoon salt
½ teaspoon pepper
2 tablespoons molasses

2 tablespoons cider vinegar
1 8-ounce can tomato sauce
1 teaspoon liquid smoke
1 tablespoon minced onion

Salt and pepper all sides of short ribs. Place in roasting pan. Combine remaining ingredients in small saucepan. Bring to boil. Simmer for 5 minutes. Pour over short ribs in roasting pan. Cover and bake at 275 degrees for 3 hours or until tender. Spoon off excess fat before serving.

Margaret and John Koltick

EASY BEEF STROGANOFF

Serves: 4 to 5

1 pound round steak or
   stroganoff beef
oil
1 package Lipton Instant Onion
   Soup

⅔ cup water
1 2½-ounce can mushrooms,
   drained
2 tablespoons flour
1 cup sour cream

Sear meat in oil and drain. Add onion soup, water and drained mushrooms and bring to a boil. Mix flour and sour cream and add to the pan. Cook on low heat until mixture thickens, about 30 minutes. Serve over noodles.

Gail Holsinger

BEEF STROGANOFF
(Stroganoff - A great way to start off!)

Serves: 4

1 to 1¼ pounds sirloin steak, cut ¼ inch thick
flour
salt and pepper
½ cup butter or margarine

¼ cup minced onion
1 10¾-ounce can chicken broth
1 4-ounce jar button mushrooms
1 cup sour cream

Cut meat into 1 or 2 inch strips. Put flour seasoned with salt and pepper in a plastic bag. Shake strips of meat in flour mixture and set aside. Melt half the butter in frying pan. Brown onions, set aside. Add remaining butter, then meat and brown well. Simmer 15 minutes with 1 cup water. Add broth. Return onions to pan and add mushrooms. Cover and simmer until tender - about 45 minutes to an hour. Add sour cream just before serving. Liquid should be minimal at this point to make a nice gravy. Serve over rice and/or Chinese noodles.

Bev Schultz

PLAYDOUGH:

1 cup flour
½ cup salt
2 teaspoons cream of tartar

1 cup water
1 tablespoon oil

Mix all ingredients in a heavy saucepan; cook over medium heat for 2 to 3 minutes or until mixture forms a ball. Stir constantly to prevent scorching. Turn onto counter top. When cool enough to handle, knead for about 1 minute. A few drops of food coloring may be added to water for colored dough. Or, put 2 to 3 drops into finished mixture and work in. Divide dough into 2 or 3 parts before adding coloring to make different colors.

This mixture feels wonderful, and although it is not meant to be eaten, should your child taste it, it will not hurt him or her. Keeps for a long time in a covered container.

LASAGNA

Serves: 12 to 16

1 1-pound box lasagna noodles
2 pounds ground beef
1 onion, sliced
1 teaspoon oregano
1 teaspoon basil
garlic salt to taste
pepper to taste
1 15½-ounce jar Prego spaghetti sauce
1 teaspoon cinnamon
½ teaspoon nutmeg
1 16-ounce container Ricotta cheese
2 eggs, beaten
2 tablespoons parsley
1 8-ounce container small curd cottage cheese
3 cups shredded Mozzarella cheese
Parmesan cheese, grated

Cook noodles according to directions on package. While noodles are cooking, brown ground beef and onion. Drain fat. Sprinkle with oregano, basil, garlic salt, and pepper. Stir in spaghetti sauce, cinnamon and nutmeg. Remove from heat and set aside. In a bowl combine Ricotta cheese, eggs and parsley. Lay lasagna ingredients in a 9 x 13 inch pan as follows. Cover bottom of pan with some of the sauce mixture. Cover with noodles. Add another layer of sauce, then a quarter of the Ricotta cheese mixture, cottage cheese and Mozzarella cheese. Repeat layers 3 more times. Sprinkle the top with Parmesan cheese. Bake in a 350 degree oven for 30 to 40 minutes. Allow a few minutes cooling time before cutting.

Dorothy Baker

CHILDREN'S STEW:

Many children announce that they "hate" carrots or onions or beans ... and every child has eaten at least one serving of stew, and sometimes as many as four servings. Their stew will have much more interest if you let your children help wash, scrape, snap, peel and chop fresh carrots, onions, potatoes, and green beans. Add water, salt and a liberal amount of bacon grease to the vegetables. Bring to a boil, then turn down the heat and simmer for at least one hour. You'll all enjoy the results.

BEEF STEW
(A heartwarming dish)

Serves: 6 to 8

1 ½ pounds stewing meat
⅓ cup flour seasoned with salt
and pepper
2 tablespoons bacon fat
1 8-ounce can tomato sauce
1 10¾-ounce can onion soup,
undiluted

½ to 1 teaspoon horseradish
1 teaspoon Worcestershire sauce
1 teaspoon A-1 sauce
3 stalks celery, chopped
potatoes, diced
4 onions, sliced
10 small carrots, diced

Brown meat and flour in bacon fat. Add tomato sauce, onion soup, horseradish, Worcestershire sauce and A-1 sauce. Cook about 3 hours. Add celery, potatoes, onions and carrots during last 30 minutes.

Marjorie H. Gray

BEEFY MUSHROOM DISH

Serves 4 to 5

1 pound ground beef
1 10¾-ounce can golden mushroom soup, undiluted
1 10¾-ounce can water
1 small onion, chopped

mushrooms, sliced
½ teaspoon basil
½ teaspoon thyme
noodles or rice

Brown ground beef in large skillet. Drain grease. Combine soup, water, onion, mushrooms and spices. Cook until heated. Serve over noodles or rice.

Debbie and Frank McKenna

 Spray your children's shoelaces with laundry starch to keep them from coming untied.

KING RANCH CASSEROLE
(A meal sure to appeal to your "King")

Serves: 6 to 8

1 10¾-ounce can cream of mushroom soup, undiluted
1 10¾-ounce can cream of celery or cream of chicken soup, undiluted
1 16-ounce can tomatoes
1 cup beef broth
1 4-ounce can chopped green chilies
1 pound ground chuck, browned
1 package corn tortillas, quartered
1 onion, chopped
1 cup grated cheddar cheese

Mix soups, tomatoes, broth and chilies together in a bowl. In a casserole, layer browned ground meat, quartered tortillas and onion. Top with soup mixture, then grated cheese. Cover. Bake at 350 degrees for 1 hour. Let stand awhile before serving.

Shirley Rose

SIX IN ONE CASSEROLE
(Take to a covered dish dinner)

Serves: 6 to 8

1 ½ pounds ground chuck, browned
salt and pepper to taste
2 large carrots, sliced
2 large potatoes, sliced
2 large onions, sliced
1 cup peas
1 cup green beans
1 8-ounce can tomato sauce

Grease casserole dish with butter. Add ground meat, lining bottom and sides of dish. Add remaining ingredients in layers. Cover with tomato sauce. Cover with lid or foil. Bake at 350 degrees for 2 hours.

Debbie and Frank McKenna

METZGER MACARONI
(Makes dynamite leftovers)

Serves: 4 to 6

1 cup macaroni
1 pound hamburger
salt and pepper to taste
1 16-ounce can whole tomatoes
1 2½-ounce can mushrooms
1 pound sharp cheese

Cook macaroni according to directions on package in a 4-quart pot. Brown and drain hamburger. Season to taste. Add tomatoes and mushrooms. Simmer for 10 minutes. Meanwhile cut cheese into 1 inch cubes. When macaroni is cooked and drained, put all ingredients back in pot and mix well. Do not allow cheese to melt completely. Serve immediately.

Bill Metzger

133

BARBECUPS

Serves: 6

1 pound ground beef
½ cup barbecue sauce
1 tablespoon instant minced
   onion

2 tablespoons brown sugar
1 8-ounce can baking powder
   biscuits
¾ cup shredded cheddar cheese

Brown beef in large skillet. Drain. Add barbecue sauce, onion and brown sugar. Separate biscuits. Place 1 in each of 12 ungreased muffin cups, pressing dough up sides to edge of cups. Spoon meat mixture into cups. Sprinkle with cheese. Bake at 400 degrees for 10 to 12 minutes until golden brown.

Ruth Miller

BEEF BARBECUE
(Freezes nicely, great for crowds, and men love it!)

Serves: 20

6 pounds chuck roast
1 bunch celery, chopped
3 large onions, chopped coarsely
1 14-ounce bottle ketchup
1 large green pepper, chopped
   coarsely
2 tablespoons salt

2 tablespoons barbecue sauce
3 tablespoons vinegar
1 teaspoon Tabasco sauce
2 tablespoons chili powder
1 teaspoon pepper
1 ½ cups water
sandwich rolls

Put roast in the bottom of a roaster pan. Cover with remaining ingredients. Cover. Roast at 300 degrees for 6 hours. Uncover the last hour. Remove from oven. Pull meat apart until shredded. Remove fat and bones. Serve on rolls.

Teresa Meyer

 For stews, cook tough meat in strong tea rather than water to tenderize.

HOT SANDWICH HAMBURGER LOAF

Serves: 8

1 loaf French bread
⅔ cup evaporated milk
1½ pounds lean ground beef,
    browned and drained
½ cup cracker meal
1 egg
½ cup chopped onion

1 tablespoon mustard
1½ teaspoons salt
¾ teaspoon Accent
⅛ teaspoon pepper
2 cups grated Velvetta or American cheese

Cut entire French bread loaf in half lengthwise. Combine all remaining ingredients in a large bowl. Spread mixture on cut sides of both pieces of bread. Wrap heavy duty foil around crusty part of bread. Place on cookie sheet. Bake at 350 degrees for 25 minutes.

Carolyn Heaton

OUR ARTIST'S FAVORITE SLOPPY JOES

Yields: 6 to 8 sandwiches

1 pound ground beef
1 to 2 onions, chopped
2 stalks celery, chopped
1½ teaspoons Worcestershire
    sauce

½ cup ketchup
1 tablespoon vinegar
1 teaspoon mustard
2 tablespoons sugar
6 to 8 hamburger buns

Brown ground beef, onion and celery in skillet. Remove excess fat from pan. Stir in remaining ingredients. Cook over low heat for 45 minutes to 1 hour, adding water when necessary. Serve on hamburger buns.

Elaine Baker

If you need frozen meat in a hurry, seal it in a plastic bag and place it in a bowl of very warm water. Or, put it in a bag and place it under cold running water for an hour or so.

QUICK BEEF SANDWICH

Serves: 4

1 pound ground beef
¼ cup dried onions
¾ cup barbecue sauce
2 8-ounce cans Crescent dinner
  rolls

¼ cup sliced banana peppers
8 ounces shredded cheddar
  cheese

Brown meat and onions, drain well. Mix meat, onions and barbecue sauce together in bowl and set aside. Arrange dough into 4 long rectangles on cookie sheet. Firmly press perforated edges to seal. Pat firmly together to form long rectangle. Spread meat mixture in center of dough. Arrange peppers on top. Sprinkle cheese on top of peppers. Fold up edges to contain mixture and cheese forming a shallow shell. Bake at 375 degrees for 15 to 20 minutes, or until golden brown. Let stand for 5 minutes before serving.

Sandy Simpson

SATURDAY NIGHT SPECIAL
(This recipe is especially good for a busy family when everyone wants to eat at a different time)

Serves: 6

1 pound ground beef, browned
  and drained
1 10¾-ounce can vegetable beef
  soup (or chicken gumbo),
  undiluted

1 8-ounce can tomato sauce
1 tablespoon dried, minced onion
1 tablespoon Worcestershire
  sauce
½ cup wine (optional)

Combine all ingredients and simmer until thick · about 45 minutes. The longer the mixture simmers, the better. Can be reheated. Good for a crockpot. Serve as a filling for pita bread, hoagie bun or sandwich bun.

Ruth Miller

SAUERBRAUTEN
(If you have the time . . . it's worth the wait!)

Serves: 6 to 8

3 to 4 pounds eye of round roast
1 cup beef broth
½ cup red wine vinegar
½ teaspoon pepper
1 teaspoon salt

1 tablespoon dry mustard
1 teaspoon poultry seasoning
1 bay leaf
1 clove garlic, minced

Combine all ingredients except meat in saucepan. Place over medium temperature until thoroughly heated. Place meat in a bowl. Pour mixture over meat. Cover and refrigerate for 24 to 48 hours. Roast the beef at 350 degrees for 2½ to 3 hours or until desired doneness. Drippings can be used to make gravy and are tasty served with egg noodles.

Pat Kuehn

ROLLED CABBAGE

Serves: 4 to 6

1 medium head of cabbage
1 pound ground chuck
1 medium onion, chopped
1 onion, sliced
1 16-ounce can whole tomatoes

*brown sugar
*lemon juice
raisins (optional)
salt

*(You have to use your own judgement and taste as to how much sugar and lemon you wish to add. Frequent tasting and smelling is necessary.)

Boil cabbage until soft - 15 minutes to ½ hour. Cool and remove leaves carefully. This is best accomplished by first removing core. Combine ground chuck and chopped onion and mix thoroughly. Place small amount of meat in leaf (depending on size of leaf) and roll. Place cabbage rolls in pot. Add sliced onion, tomatoes, sugar, lemon juice, raisins and salt. Simmer, covered, very slowly for 2 hours. When ready to serve, place rolls in shallow pan in 350 degree oven for ½ hour. Baste often and brown well. Adjust seasoning if necessary.

Anne Austen

BAKED PORK CHOPS
(Very easy and good)

Serves: 4

4 pork chops
1 lemon, sliced

1 onion, sliced
½ to 1 cup ketchup or chili sauce

Place pork chops in covered baking dish. Top with slices of lemon and onion rings. Pour ketchup or chili sauce to thoroughly cover meat. Bake at 350 degrees for 1 hour.

Joan Clark

OVEN BARBECUE RIBS

country style pork ribs
flour seasoned with salt and
  pepper

oil
barbecue sauce
liquid smoke

Dust ribs in flour. Brown in hot oil in skillet (preferably an iron skillet) until golden brown on all sides. Remove to shallow casserole. Sprinkle with your favorite barbecue sauce and liquid smoke. Bake covered at 325 degrees for 2 to 2½ hours depending on size and amount of ribs. If necessary add a cup of water after an hour or so.

Dotty France

PORK CHOP AND MACARONI DINNER
(There are no specific amounts given in this recipe because
the whole recipe is a matter of taste)

pork chops
macaroni
ketchup

onion, chopped
green pepper, chopped

In a skillet, cover pork chops with water and cook until water is absorbed and chops brown, or bake chops in oven until water is absorbed. Cook macaroni according to directions on package; drain. Mix macaroni with ketchup until moist and add onion and pepper. Add macaroni mixture to pork chops. Bake at 350 degrees for about 30 minutes. If dish appears to be drying out, cover pan.

NOTE: This can also be cooked on top of stove, but seems to taste better if baked in the oven.

Doris DePierre

PORK CHOPS WITH CURRIED APPLES AND RAISINS

Serves: 4

4 pork loin or rib chops, about ¾ inch thick
1 cube chicken bouillon
¾ cup boiling water
1 to 2 teaspoons curry powder
¼ teaspoon cinnamon
celery, chopped

1 medium cooking apple, cored and chopped
1 small onion, chopped
¼ cup raisins
1 tablespoon cornstarch
2 tablespoons water
brown or wild rice, cooked

Trim fat from pork chops. Dissolve bouillon in boiling water. Stir in curry and cinnamon. Set aside. Combine celery, apple, onion and raisins in 8 x 8 inch baking dish. Top with pork chops. Pour bouillon mixture over the meat. Cover with foil and bake at 350 degrees for 45 minutes. Remove chops to a warm platter. Pour meat sauce and fruit in medium saucepan. Blend cornstarch with 2 tablespoons water in a small dish until smooth. Gradually stir cornstarch mixture into sauce mixture and cook over medium heat, stirring constantly, until gravy thickens. Serve sauce with meat and brown or wild rice.

Sherry Wilson

SWEET AND SOUR PORK CHOPS
(A happy ending to the Three Little Pigs)

Serves: 6

6 pork chops
¼ cup flour
1 teaspoon salt
½ teaspoon pepper
1 teaspoon ginger

1 teaspoon paprika
1 tablespoon butter
1 cup pineapple juice
2 tablespoons vinegar
3 teaspoons brown sugar

Combine flour, salt, pepper, ginger and paprika. Coat both sides of pork chops with dry mixture. Melt butter in a skillet. Brown pork chops on both sides in butter. Pour pineapple juice and vinegar over the pork chops. Sprinkle with brown sugar. Cover and cook over low heat for 40 minutes or until chops are tender.

Rosemary Ross

BOTTLE-CHILI BARBECUE
(Something different for a summer picnic)

Yields: 1½ pints

1 12-ounce bottle chili sauce
12 ounces water (1½ cups)
1 to 1½ cups brown sugar
1 tablespoon margarine or butter

½ teaspoon mustard
⅓ cup ginger ale
chipped ham
buns

Mix together chili sauce, water, brown sugar, margarine and mustard in a medium pot. Bring to a boil. Simmer for 30 minutes. Add ginger ale. Add chipped ham. Simmer until ham is hot. Serve on buns.

NOTE: This will keep in the refrigerator. It can be used again.

Caroline O'Brien

HAM BALLS
(Also makes a delicious appetizer)

Yields: 10 to 15

Ham Balls:
1 pound ground pork
1 pound ground ham
1 cup bran flakes

¼ teaspoon salt
dash of pepper
2 tablespoons chopped onion
1½ cups evaporated milk

Syrup:
½ cup brown sugar
½ cup dark Karo syrup

3 teaspoons vinegar
1 teaspoon prepared mustard

Mix together pork, ham, bran flakes, salt, pepper, onion and milk. Form into balls about 2 inches in diameter. Bake at 350 degrees for 20 minutes. While ham balls are baking, mix syrup ingredients in a saucepan and heat until blended. Pour syrup over meat balls. Bake another 20 minutes at 350 degrees.

NOTE: These freeze well. Approximate preparation time is 20 minutes.

Bonnie Emerick

HAM BARBECUE

Serves: 8 to 10

2 cups vinegar
2 cups brown sugar
2 cups ketchup
1 cup chili sauce
⅔ cup Worcestershire sauce
2½ tablespoons dry mustard

4½ tablespoons lemon juice
½ cup grated onion
4 to 5 garlic cloves, crushed
¼ cup pickle relish
2 pounds ham, chopped or sliced
1 8-ounce can tomato sauce

Mix vinegar, brown sugar, ketchup, chili sauce, Worcestershire sauce, mustard, lemon, onion, garlic and relish in a large saucepan. Simmer for 2 to 3 hours over low heat. The sauce should become thick. Add chipped ham and tomato sauce to barbecue sauce. Cook over low heat for 45 more minutes. Serve on buns.

Eleanor Towers

QUICK HAM ROLLS

Serves: 6

¼ pound mushrooms, chopped
1 garlic clove, chopped
2 tablespoons butter

1 cup cooked rice
salt and pepper to taste
12 thin slices boiled ham

Sauté mushrooms and garlic in butter. Stir in rice, salt and pepper. (If mixture is too dry, add a little melted butter.) Spread stuffing mixture on slices of boiled ham. Fold or roll slices and wrap in aluminum foil. Bake rolls in 350 degree oven for 15 to 20 minutes. Can be prepared ahead of time.

Ruth Miller

If you run out of ketchup, combine 1 cup of tomato sauce, 1½ cups brown sugar, 2 tablespoons vinegar, ¼ teaspoon cinnamon, a dash of ground clove, and a dash of allspice.

HAM LOAF
(A great idea for left-over ham)

Serves: 12 to 15

3 pounds ground ham
1 pound ground pork
2 cups graham cracker crumbs

3 eggs
½ cup milk

Sauce:
1 10¾-ounce can tomato soup,
   undiluted
1 cup brown sugar

½ cup water
1 tablespoon dry mustard
½ cup vinegar

Thoroughly mix meats, cracker crumbs, eggs, and milk. Place in a 9 x 13 inch pan. Score the top and partially cut into serving pieces. Blend sauce ingredients. Pour over meat. Refrigerate overnight. Bake at 350 degrees for 1½ to 2 hours.

Delores Helm

CHEESY ITALIAN SAUSAGE CASSEROLE

Serves: 8

1½ pounds sweet Italian sausage
   (bulk)
16 slices white bread, crusts
   trimmed off
1 6-ounce can Italian tomato
   paste
1 tablespoon Italian seasoning

8 ounces shredded Provolone
   cheese
8 ounces shredded Mozzarella
   cheese
⅓ cup grated Parmesan cheese
3 eggs, slightly beaten
3 cups milk
salt to taste

Cook sausage in a skillet for 20 to 25 minutes or until desired tenderness. Set aside. Place 8 slices of bread on bottom of greased 9 x 13 inch baking dish. Spread tomato paste over bread slices. Sprinkle Italian seasoning and Provolone cheese over paste. Spoon all of sausage over cheese. Sprinkle with Mozzarella and Parmesan cheeses. Place remaining bread slices over cheeses. Set aside. Blend eggs, milk and salt together and pour over bread. Refrigerate overnight. Bake, uncovered, at 350 degrees for 45 minutes.

NOTE: Overnight refrigeration is required.

Sandy Simpson

HOT POKER SAUSAGE
(Having a "poker" party?)

Serves: 4

2 8-ounce cans tomato sauce
2 6-ounce cans tomato paste
3½ cups water
1 teaspoon garlic salt
1 teaspoon onion salt
1 teaspoon oregano

1 teaspoon Italian seasoning
3 teaspoons sugar
1 pound hot Italian sausage, cased
1 to 2 green peppers, sliced in strips

In a 4 quart pot, mix thoroughly tomato sauce, paste, water and seasonings. Stir. Bring the sauce to a boil; reduce to a simmer. After the sauce has simmered for 2 hours, cook hot sausage and green peppers in a skillet. Cut sausage into equal lengths. Add sausage and peppers to sauce and continue to simmer for 1 hour. Serve on sausage rolls.

Dan Findley

ITALIAN SAUSAGE BREAD
(From appetizer to entrée)

Yields: 2 rings of 10 to 12 servings

2 1-pound loaves frozen white bread dough
1 pound mild Italian sausage
2 tablespoons barbecue sauce
1 egg

1½ cups shredded Mozzarella cheese
1 tablespoon Parmesan cheese, sesame seed or caraway seed
1 egg, beaten with fork

Defrost bread according to package directions. Remove casing from sausage. Cook over medium heat until crumbly and brown. Remove from heat. Drain off fat. When cooled, add barbecue sauce, 1 egg and Mozzarella cheese. Stir to blend. On a lightly floured board, roll and stretch 1 loaf of bread dough into a 6 x 15 inch rectangle. Spoon half the sausage mixture over rectangle to within ½ inch of the edges. Moisten edges of bread with water. Roll up dough from long side and pinch edges to seal. Gently place on cookie sheet and form into ring. Pinch ends together to seal. Using scissors, cut the top about 1 inch deep at 1½ inch intervals. Beat remaining egg and brush over ring. Sprinkle with Parmesan cheese or seeds. Repeat procedure for the second ring. Place on separate cookie sheet. Allow to rise until double in bulk. Bake at 350 degrees for 30 minutes or until golden brown. Serve warm or cool. May be frozen.

NOTE: Can be served as an appetizer, breakfast dish or an accompaniment to soup or salad.

Sherry Wilson

143

BAKED LAMB CHOPS AND RICE

Serves: 4

4 shoulder or loin lamb chops
salt
pepper
flour
2 tablespoons oil
½ cup uncooked long grain rice
4 medium onions, halved

1 beef bouillon cube, dissolved in
  1 cup boiling water
½ cup sherry
1 teaspoon rosemary
¼ teaspoon curry powder
1 clove garlic
½ cup chopped parsley

Dredge lamb chops in salt, pepper and flour. Brown slowly in hot oil. Turn lamb chops over and add uncooked rice to skillet. Brown meat and rice, turning often. Remove meat and rice to baking pan. Lay onion halves on rice. Mix dissolved bouillon, sherry, rosemary, curry powder, garlic and parsley and pour over chops. Cover and bake at 325 degrees for 50 minutes. Add boiling water if necessary.

Margaret and John Koltick

VERY QUICK ONE
(For the liver lover)

Serves: 3

1 pound beef liver
sherry (cocktail style - inexpensive
  brand)
seasoned bread crumbs

Parmesan cheese mixed with
  flour
butter

Put small amount of sherry in pie pan or shallow pan. Put liver in sherry and let soak a few minutes. Roll in crumbs and Parmesan mixture (dip in beaten eggs before crumbs if desired.) Pan broil in butter.

Anne Austen

CORNED BEEF NOODLE CASSEROLE

Serves: 8 to 10

1 8-ounce package noodles
1 12-ounce can corned beef
  slices
¼ pound American cheese, diced
1 cup milk

1 10¾-ounce can condensed
  cream of chicken soup,
  undiluted
½ cup chopped onion
½ cup buttered bread crumbs

Cook noodles in boiling, salted water until tender. Drain. Add corned beef, cheese, milk, soup and onion. Pour into greased 2 quart casserole. Top with buttered bread crumbs. Bake at 350 degrees for 45 minutes.

Millie McCathren

CORNED BEEF SANDWICHES
(A great late night snack)

Serves: 8

2 12-ounce cans corned beef
6 tablespoons chopped onion
3 tablespoons mustard
4 tablespoons horseradish

6 tablespoons mayonnaise
16 slices American cheese
sandwich buns

Mix first 5 ingredients together and spread on sandwich buns. Place 1 slice of cheese on each bun. Wrap in foil. Bake at 350 degrees for 25 minutes. Serve while hot.

NOTE: Approximate preparation time is 20 minutes.

Bonnie Emerick

Need help in identifying meats? Look at the bones. Long bones such as T-bones or ribs are usually tender cuts of meat while round bones like chuck are less tender.

REUBEN CASSEROLE

Serves: 10

1 27-ounce can sauerkraut, drained
1 large or 2 small fresh tomatoes, sliced
2 tablespoons butter
2 tablespoons Thousand Island Dressing
¾ pound corn beef, shredded
½ pound Swiss cheese, shredded
1 can of 10 buttermilk biscuits (Hungry Jack)
2 Rye Crisp crackers, crumbled
½ teaspoon caraway seeds

In a 9 x 13 inch ungreased baking dish place sauerkraut. Cover with tomatoes. Dot with butter and sprinkle dressing on top. Layer corn beef, then Swiss cheese over tomatoes and dressing. Place in oven and bake at 425 degrees for 15 minutes. Remove from oven. Separate biscuits into 30 pieces. Place 3 rows of dough over cheese. Sprinkle with cracker crumbs and seeds. Bake at 425 degrees for another 15 to 20 minutes.

NOTE: Two cups fresh rye bread crumbs may be used instead of biscuit dough. Omit crackers and dot bread crumbs with 1 tablespoon butter.

Nancy McCloskey

VEAL PAPRIKA
(Veal paprika is similar to beef stroganoff, but you may even like it better! Great for a buffet dinner.)

Serves: 6 to 8

4 tablespoons shortening
½ cup ground or chopped onion
¾ teaspoon paprika
1 or 2 teaspoons sugar
2 pounds veal (shoulder or other inexpensive cuts) cut into 2 inch pieces
2 cups water or beef broth
3 tablespoons flour
sautéed or canned mushrooms, optional
½ cup sour cream

Melt shortening in large frypan. Brown onions. Stir in paprika and sugar. Add veal pieces, brown for 5 minutes. Add water or broth, simmer gently until tender. Mix flour with a small amount of water, stir into veal to thicken. Add mushrooms if desired. Gradually stir in sour cream. Serve over rice or noodles.

Judy Douglass

VEAL AND PEPPERS
(A romantic meal for two)

Serves: 2

2 tablespoons butter
1 pound veal, diced
salt to taste
pepper to taste
pinch of oregano

½ cup chicken or beef stock
2 green peppers, sliced
1 tablespoon flour
2 tablespoons water

Sauté diced veal, salt, pepper and oregano in butter. Add chicken or beef stock. Simmer over low heat. In separate pan, sauté sliced green pepper. Stir together flour and water. Add to the peppers. Stir to thicken, over medium heat. Mix pepper-flour mixture with the veal mixture. Serve over noodles or rice.

Mike Kmiecik

SAUSAGE STUFFED VEAL

Serves: 12

1 pound hot Italian sausage links
¼ cup water
2 eggs
¾ cup fresh bread crumbs
1 4-ounce jar diced pimientos,
   drained

¼ pound fresh green beans
salt
1 4-pound rolled boneless veal leg
   sirloin roast
1 8-ounce package thick sliced
   bacon

In 10-inch skillet heat sausages and water to boiling. Cover and simmer 5 minutes. Cook uncovered for 20 minutes, until water evaporates. Drain sausage links on towel. Finely chop sausage and combine with eggs, bread crumbs and pimientos. Cook green beans. Untie veal roast. Place fat side of roast down on work surface. Slice meat horizontally to form a 1 x 10 x 12 inch rectangle. If necessary, pound meat to attain 1 inch thickness. Spoon sausage onto veal. Place green beans along 1 shorter end of rectangle. Starting at the end with the green beans, roll veal like a jelly roll. Fasten with skewers. Place seam side down. Wrap meat with bacon slices. Tie with string at 2 inch intervals. Place meat on rack in open roaster. Insert meat thermometer. Roast at 325 degrees for approximately 2 hours - until 170 degrees. Gravy can be made with the drippings.

Sherry Wilson

MEAT BALL STEW

Serves: 4 to 6

½ pound ground meat
¼ cup bread crumbs
1 egg
1 8-ounce can tomato sauce
½ teaspoon salt
⅛ teaspoon onion salt
⅛ teaspoon pepper

⅛ teaspoon allspice or nutmeg
4 cups water
½ package onion soup mix
1 cup sliced carrots
4 potatoes, diced
1 16-ounce can green beans, drained

Combine ground meat, bread crumbs, egg, 2 tablespoons tomato sauce, salt, onion salt, pepper and allspice in bowl. Form into meat balls. Mix water, remaining tomato sauce, onion soup mix, carrots and potatoes. Add meat balls and cook slowly until vegetables are tender, about 1½ hours. Add 1 can drained green beans. Heat until beans are warm.

Debbie and Frank McKenna

STUFFED CABBAGE
(A Polish tradition)

Serves: 10

1 head of cabbage
2 cups uncooked River rice
1¼ pounds ground beef
1¼ pounds ground pork
2 eggs
salt and pepper to taste

1 onion, chopped and sautéed
parsley (optional)
2 10¾-ounce cans tomato soup, undiluted
½ to ¾ cup water
1 tablespoon sugar

Cook cabbage in small amount of water until leaves can be separated. Core the cabbage - do not overcook. Scrape some of the veins off larger leaves. Cook rice. Mix rice, meats, eggs, salt, pepper, onion and parsley (optional) with hands. Place a generous tablespoon of meat mixture on each cabbage leaf and roll - folding sides in first. Place in a casserole dish close together. Mix tomato soup with water, salt and sugar. Pour over cabbage rolls - cover. Cook at 350 degrees for 45 minutes to 1 hour.

Zuzanna K. O'Brien

SWEDISH MEAT BALLS
(A sweetheart pleaser)

Yields: 30 to 40

4 to 5 pounds ground meat
 (combined beef, veal and pork)
1 ½ cups bread crumbs
1 10¾ ounce can tomato soup,
 undiluted
2 eggs

3 tablespoons minced onion
 flakes
½ teaspoon allspice
4 teaspoons Season All
1 teaspoon pepper
1 teaspoon garlic salt

Combine all ingredients. Form into meat balls 1 inch in diameter. Brown in skillet. Remove to a baking pan. Bake at 350 degrees for 20 minutes.

Elaine Axelson

SWEDISH MEATBALLS AND SAUCE

Yields: 60

Meatballs:
½ cup chopped onion
3 tablespoons butter
1 egg, beaten
1 cup light cream
½ cup bread crumbs
¼ cup chopped, fresh parsley

Sauce:
2 tablespoons flour
1 teaspoon instant beef bouillon

1 ½ teaspoons salt
dash of pepper
dash of ground nutmeg
dash of ginger
1 ½ pounds ground beef or
 mixture of ground beef, pork,
 veal
½ teaspoon instant coffee
1 ¼ cups water

Meatballs:
Cook onion in 1 tablespoon butter until tender. Combine beaten egg and cream in mixing bowl. Stir in bread crumbs, cooked onion, parsley, salt, pepper, nutmeg and ginger. Add meat and mix well by hand. Shape into ¾ or 1 inch balls. Mixture will be soft. For easier shaping, wet hands or chill mixture overnight in refrigerator. Brown meatballs in remaining 2 table-spoons butter and remove from skillet.

Sauce:
Stir flour, bouillon and coffee into pan juices. Add water and stir until mixture is thickened and bubbly. Add meatballs, cover and simmer 30 minutes, basting occasionally.

Vera King

PIZZA

Yields: 2 12 x 18 inch pizzas

Basic dough:
2 cups warm water
1 package dry yeast

1 tablespoon sugar
2½ teaspoons salt
4 to 5 cups flour

Sauce:
1 16-ounce can pizza sauce
1 8-ounce can tomato sauce

½ teaspoon oregano
½ teaspoon garlic salt
cheese, grated

Put warm water in large bowl. Add yeast and stir to dissolve. Add sugar, salt and 3 cups flour. Beat mixture 1 to 2 minutes, until smooth. Add enough flour to make a nice smooth dough (too much flour causes dough to be tough). Mix with spoon. Place dough on well floured surface and knead until smooth - about 8 minutes. Shape dough into ball and place in well greased bowl. Cover with towel and set in warm place for 1 hour. Punch dough down. Divide in half and shape into smooth balls. Cover and let stand for 5 minutes. Roll dough out thin and place on cookie sheet. Oil hands and work dough to fit cookie sheet. Mix pizza sauce, tomato sauce, oregano and garlic salt in bowl. Spread sauce evenly on dough with spoon. Top with cheese. If desired, can also top with pepperoni, sausage, meatball slices, fried chopped pepper, fried chopped onion or sliced mushrooms. Bake pizza at 400 degrees for 25 minutes.

Eleanor Towers

BARBECUE SAUCE

(This sauce is not only good for barbecuing, but is great for doctoring up baked beans or making ham barbecues. Make it in the spring, freeze it - then use all summer.)

Yields: 1½ to 2 quarts

2 cups vinegar
2 cups brown sugar
2 cups ketchup
1 cup chili sauce
⅔ cup Worcestershire sauce

2½ tablespoons dry mustard
4½ tablespoons lemon juice
½ cup grated onion
4 to 5 garlic cloves, crushed
¼ cup pickle relish

Mix all ingredients together in a large saucepan. Simmer for 2 to 3 hours over low heat. The sauce should become thick.

NOTE: To make delicious baked beans, add ¼ to ½ cup of sauce to baked beans.

Eleanor Towers

LONDON BROIL MARINADE

5 tablespoons dry mustard
5 tablespoons soy sauce
1 tablespoon oil

1 tablespoon Worcestershire
   sauce
salt and pepper to taste
garlic salt to taste

Combine mustard, soy sauce, oil, and Worcestershire sauce. Mix well. Apply to flank steak which has been lightly scored diagonally on both sides. Sprinkle with salt, pepper and garlic salt to taste.

NOTE: This is best when cooked over open fire and is not as good in conventional ovens. It may be used to marinate meat overnight or within a few minutes after applying.

Fern Jagger

MARINADE
(Great for London Broil)

⅓ cup vinegar
¼ cup ketchup
2 tablespoons oil
2 tablespoons Worcestershire
   sauce

2 tablespoons soy sauce
1 teaspoon mustard
1 teaspoon salt
¼ teaspoon pepper
¼ teaspoon garlic powder

Mix ingredients with wire whip and pour over meat. Marinate overnight. Baste meat with marinade while cooking.

Bonnie Emerick

SNAPPY BARBECUE SAUCE

Yields: 1½ cups

1 cup ketchup
1 cup water
¼ cup vinegar
1 tablespoon sugar
1 teaspoon salt

1 tablespoon Worcestershire
   sauce
1 teaspoon celery seeds
2 dashes hot pepper sauce

Combine all ingredients. Bring to boil, reduce heat and simmer uncovered for 30 minutes. Baste meat last 15 to 20 minutes of cooking time.

Doe Clark

SECRET SAUCE FOR BARBECUE

(The easiest and most unusual ingredients make a perfect barbecue sauce for pork, beef or chicken. Leftover sauce freezes well.)

2 cans beef bouillon
1 8-ounce jar orange marmalade
   (or other citrus marmalade)
1 tablespoon whole cloves

3 to 4 large, fresh garlic cloves, minced
4 cups ketchup (32 ounces)
1 15½-ounce can pineapple chunks and juice

Mix all ingredients, except pineapple in a large saucepan. Heat to boiling. Reduce heat and simmer ½ hour, stirring occasionally. Pour enough sauce over raw meat to cover and marinate several hours or overnight. Bake meat in sauce, uncovered until meat is done and sauce absorbed. Add pineapple chunks and juice during last hour of baking.

NOTE: This sauce is easily prepared in the microwave oven and keeps exceptionally well.

Lora T. Spence

SUNDAY SPAGHETTI SAUCE

(A heavenly way to start your week)

Serves: 4

1 pound ground sirloin
2 8-ounce cans tomato sauce
2 6-ounce cans tomato paste
3½ cups water
1 teaspoon garlic salt

1 teaspoon onion salt
1 teaspoon oregano
1 teaspoon Italian seasoning
3 teaspoons sugar

Brown ground sirloin in a 4 quart pot. Drain grease thoroughly. Add tomato sauce, paste and water. Stir until smooth. Add remaining ingredients and stir until blended. Slowly bring to a boil. Reduce heat and cover, allowing the steam to escape. Simmer for 3 hours or until desired thickness, stirring frequently. Serve over spaghetti.

Dan Findley

Vegetables

CHAPTER IX

The Princess and the Pea's ... Vegetables

Twenty mattresses and a pea
Helped the prince determine her pedigree.
And the dear dainty damsel who lost her sleep
Got bruises,
   A husband,
      And
        A castle to keep!

Cook's Note: Of all the great garden vegetables, the pea is not the only versatile vegi. The suggestions here will confirm that and will give your family as much contentment as a good night's sleep.

SICILIAN STUFFED ARTICHOKES

Serves: 6

6 artichokes
1 ½ cups seasoned Italian bread
crumbs

water
½ cup oil

Strip artichokes of outer leaves. Cut about 1 ½ inches off the tops of the artichokes. Remove the stem. Rinse with warm water. Turn upside down to drain. Spread open the artichoke leaves and sprinkle bread crumbs inside. Arrange in a tight circle in a large pot. Sprinkle with water. Pour ¼ cup oil over the artichokes. Pour the remaining oil into the pot. Add an additional ⅓ cup water to the pot. Cover. Cook on stove over medium heat for 35 to 40 minutes. Do not allow the artichokes to dry while cooking. Check pot and add water when necessary.

Jo Ann Pulcini

STUFFED ARTICHOKES

Yields: 3 to 4

3 to 4 artichokes
1 pound ground meat
¼ pound ground pork
2 eggs
¼ cup Parmesan cheese
garlic powder to taste

salt to taste
pepper to taste
Italian seasonings
1 ½ cups bread crumbs
¼ cup olive oil
¼ cup grated Romano cheese

Strip outer leaves of artichokes. Remove 1 ½ inches from top and stem from artichokes. Rinse and drain. Mix together meats, eggs, Parmesan cheese, seasonings, and bread crumbs. Add more bread crumbs if necessary, so that stuffing is not too meaty. Stuff meat mixture between each artichoke leaf. At top of artichoke, spread inner leaves apart and stuff meat inside. Place artichokes in large pot. Cover with water to just below the top of the pot. Pour olive oil on top of water. Sprinkle Romano cheese over the oil. Simmer for 2 to 2½ hours. Artichokes are done when tender.

Joan and Gilbert Iacono

BEAN CASSEROLE
(All it needs is a salad and hot rolls for a winter meal)

Serves: 4 to 6

½ pound ground meat
½ pound bacon, cut in pieces
½ cup ketchup
½ cup chopped onions
½ cup sugar
¾ cup brown sugar
1 teaspoon dry mustard
1 teaspoon salt
2 teaspoons vinegar

1 16-ounce can green beans, drained
1 16-ounce can butter beans, drained
1 16-ounce can kidney beans, drained
1 16-ounce can pork and beans, undrained

Brown and drain ground meat and bacon. Stir in remaining ingredients. Pour into crock pot and cook slowly all day or bake in the oven at 350 degrees for about 40 minutes.

Deb and Ron Wilcher

THE BEST BAKED BEANS
(A good, old stand-by for the Fourth of July)

Serves: 12

2 pounds navy or lima beans
1 teaspoon baking soda
1 pound dark brown sugar
1 cup ketchup

1 medium onion, chopped
1 pound bacon, diced
salt and pepper to taste

Soak beans overnight. The following day, drain water from beans. Put beans into a 4 quart pot. Cover beans with fresh water, add baking soda and bring to a boil. Drain beans. Cover beans with cold water and simmer until tender, but not mushy. Transfer into a 3 quart casserole. Add remaining ingredients to beans. Bake at 300 degrees for 4 to 5 hours.

Sally Joiner

LENTIL BAKE

Serves: 4 to 6

2 cups cooked lentils, puréed
1 cup tomato purée
1 small onion, chopped
2 stalks celery, chopped

1 cup whole wheat bread crumbs
¼ teaspoon cayenne pepper
1 clove garlic, chopped
pinch of salt (optional)

In mixing bowl, combine all the ingredients. Turn into an oiled 5 x 9 inch loaf pan and cover. Bake at 350 degrees for 40 minutes.

Linda Polito

LIMA BEAN CASSEROLE
(When ol' baked beans just don't seem right)

Serves: 6 to 8

1 pound baby lima beans, dry
1 teaspoon salt
½ cup butter or margarine
¾ cup dark or light brown sugar

1 ½ teaspoons salt
1 tablespoon dry mustard
1 tablespoon dark molasses
1 cup sour cream

Soak lima beans overnight. The following day, drain lima beans. Add fresh water and 1 teaspoon salt. Cook lima beans until tender. Place lima beans in buttered 2-quart casserole. Add butter to beans. Mix together brown sugar, salt and dry mustard. Sprinkle seasonings on top of beans. Add dark molasses and sour cream to beans. Stir gently. Bake at 350 degrees for about 1 hour. Mixture thickens as it sets.

Gerri Bartelme

PINTO BEANS

Serves: 4 to 6

2 16-ounce cans pinto beans, drained
1 small onion, diced
1 4½-ounce can whole peeled tomatoes, chopped

1 4-ounce jar taco sauce (hot, if desired)
3 hot green chili peppers, diced
1 cup grated cheddar cheese

Mix all ingredients and place in a 2½ quart casserole. Bake at 375 degrees for 50 to 55 minutes.

Pat Smetanka

ORANGE SPICE HARVARD BEETS

Serves: 4

1 16-ounce can cut red beets	dash of cloves
¼ cup sugar	dash of allspice
1 tablespoon cornstarch	1 orange rind, grated
¼ teaspoon salt	1 tablespoon butter
2 tablespoons vinegar	

Drain beets, reserving 2 to 4 tablespoons beet liquid. In a saucepan mix sugar, cornstarch and salt. Add vinegar and beet liquid. Cook, stirring constantly, until thick and clear. Add a dash of cloves and allspice, more, if desired. Add grated orange rind and butter. Stir well. Add beets. Heat beets thoroughly.

Fern Jagger

BROCCOLI AND ONION CASSEROLE

Serves: 6 to 8

2 10-ounce packages frozen broccoli	dash of pepper
	¼ cup water, if needed
1 10-ounce package frozen creamed onions	2 tablespoons butter, melted
	1 cup bread crumbs
1 3-ounce package cream cheese	¼ cup Parmesan cheese

Cook frozen vegetables as directed on package. Add cream cheese, pepper and water, if needed. Pour into a greased 2 quart casserole. Bake at 350 degrees for 20 minutes. Toss bread crumbs and cheese in melted butter. Sprinkle on top of casserole. Return casserole to oven for 10 more minutes.

Gerri Bartelme

Add a wedge of lemon to the water when you're cooking cabbage or onions to prevent the usual unpleasant odor.

BROCCOLI PUFF
(Crackers add a special touch)

Serves: 6

2 10-ounce packages frozen
  broccoli
1 10¾-ounce can cream of
  mushroom soup, undiluted
¼ cup milk
1 egg, beaten

½ cup grated cheddar cheese
¼ cup mayonnaise
1 ½ stacks or 50 loose Ritz
  crackers, finely crushed
½ cup butter, melted

Cook broccoli according to directions on package. Place in a greased 8 x 8 inch baking dish. Mix soup, milk, egg, cheese and mayonnaise in a large bowl. Spread soup mixture over broccoli. Mix crushed crackers and butter together. Sprinkle over soup mixture. Bake at 350 degrees for 45 minutes.

Dorothy Baker

CURRIED BROCCOLI WITH TOFU
(Serve with rice or stuff into pita pockets to complete protein configuration
of tofu or use 4 ounces of cheese melted over dish)

Serves: 4

1 pound firm tofu, cut in ½ inch
  cubes
¼ cup whole wheat flour
¼ cup oil
2 medium onions, finely chopped
2 cloves garlic, finely chopped
1 large bunch broccoli, separate
  heads, finely chop stalks

2 carrots, finely chopped
¼ cup lemon juice
1 teaspoon curry powder (up to 1
  tablespoon, if desired)
1 teaspoon soy sauce (up to 1
  tablespoon, if desired)
¼ cup boiling water

Place cubed tofu in a large plastic bag. Add flour to bag and shake bag gently to evenly coat tofu. Brown tofu in a little oil. Sauté onion and garlic with broccoli stalks in a wok with a little oil. When onion and garlic start to brown, add carrots, broccoli heads, and remaining oil and stir fry. Add lemon juice, curry powder, and soy sauce. Stir fry. Add water and browned tofu. Stir fry.

Don Polito

SWEDISH CABBAGE

Serves: 8

1 medium head cabbage, sliced
4 apples, peeled and cut
3 tablespoons butter

½ cup vinegar
⅔ cup sugar
salt and pepper to taste

Cook cabbage and apples for 15 to 20 minutes, or until tender, in small amount of slightly salted boiling water. Drain. Melt butter. Add vinegar, sugar, salt and pepper. Heat for several minutes. Pour over cabbage and apples. Allow to stand for several hours until properly flavored.

Marilyn Hayes

CARROTS
(Good accompaniment for Chicken Divan)

Serves: 4

¼ cup margarine
1 small onion, diced
6 to 8 carrots, cut in rounds

1½ cups chicken broth
½ cup white cooking wine
2 to 3 bay leaves

Brown onion in margarine. Add carrots and brown for 1 minute. Add chicken broth, wine and bay leaves. Simmer until carrots are tender, about 40 minutes.

Teresa Meyer

MARINATED CARROTS

Serves: 8

2 pounds carrots, pared and
thinly sliced
1 10½-ounce can tomato soup,
undiluted
½ cup oil
½ cup sugar

½ cup white vinegar
1 small onion, thinly sliced into
rings
1 green pepper, thinly sliced into
rings

Cook carrots in water for about 8 minutes. Carrots should retain some crispness after cooking. Drain and set aside. Combine tomato soup, oil, sugar and vinegar. Bring to a boil. In a casserole dish, layer the carrots, onion and pepper. The carrots should end up on the top layer. Pour the soup mixture over the vegetables. Refrigerate 24 hours before serving.

NOTE: For a variation, add 1 whole cauliflower broken into florets.

Loretta Lucas

MOLDED CARROT PUDDING WITH ORANGES AND RAISINS
(A memorable and creative vegi dish)

Serves: 8 to 10

2 eggs
½ cup brown sugar
¼ cup sugar
½ cup butter, softened
1 cup flour
1 teaspoon baking powder
½ teaspoon baking soda

¼ teaspoon salt
1 teaspoon nutmeg
1 ½ cups grated carrots
½ orange, grated (juice, pulp, zest)
½ cup yellow raisins
1 tablespoon lemon juice
1 teaspoon vanilla

Beat together eggs, sugars and butter for 2 minutes at high speed. Beat in dry ingredients and beat for another minute until blended. Add remaining ingredients and mix well. Butter and flour a 2 quart ring mold, tube pan, or flan pan. Pour in mixture and spread evenly. Bake at 350 degrees for about 50 minutes or until cake tester comes out clean. Remove from oven, loosen edges, and carefully invert on platter. Fill center with spiced fruit, cranberry sauce or creamed peas.

Lora T. Spence

BAKED CORN
(Quick to make but long to bake)

Serves: 6

4 eggs
4 tablespoons sugar
4 tablespoons flour
1 teaspoon salt

1 cup milk
2 10-ounce packages frozen corn
2 tablespoons oil

Grease 1 quart baking dish. Put eggs into blender and blend. Add sugar, flour, salt. Blend well. Add milk, then blend again. Add corn and oil. Blend until mixed but corn is still in pieces. Mixture should be thick. Pour in baking dish. Bake at 325 degrees for 1 hour and 15 minutes or until firm.

Teresa Meyer

MEXICAN SPOON BREAD

Serves: 12 to 16

1 cup yellow corn meal
¾ teaspoon salt
½ teaspoon baking soda
¾ cup milk
⅓ cup oil

2 eggs, well beaten
1 16-ounce can creamed style corn
1 4-ounce can chopped green
  chilies, drained
1½ cups shredded cheddar
  cheese

Combine ingredients in order given, except chilies and cheese. Stir between additions. Grease a 9 x 13 inch baking pan. Spoon half the mixture into pan. Sprinkle with half the chilies, then half cheese. Repeat. Bake uncovered at 350 degrees for 45 minutes or until toothpick comes out clean. Serve with a spoon, eat with a fork. Leftovers keep for days.

Dotty France

SCALLOPED CORN AND CHEESE

Serves: 6 to 8

3 cups bread cubes
butter or margarine
½ cup chopped onion
¼ cup chopped green pepper
3 tablespoons flour

1 teaspoon salt
1½ cups milk
3 cups cooked corn (2 12-ounce
  cans)
8 ounces American cheese slices

Sauté bread cubes in butter. Set aside. Sauté onion and pepper. Stir in flour and salt. Add milk. Cook until thick and smooth. Add corn. Layer ½ the corn mixture, cheese and bread in a greased 8 x 8 inch pan. Repeat layers. Bake at 350 degrees for 35 to 40 minutes.

Sherry Wilson

 To retain the freshness of your tomatoes, keep them in storage with the stems pointed downward.

SOUTHERN FRIED CORN
(Serve as a side dish with any meal)

Serves: 4

6 ears sweet white corn or 1 16-
   ounce can white corn, drained
2 slices bacon
dash of salt
1 teaspoon pepper

1 tablespoon sugar
¼ cup diced green pepper
1 tablespoon cornstarch
⅓ cup water

Remove corn from cob. Fry bacon in pan. Add corn to bacon and drippings in pan. Cook over medium heat for 10 minutes, stirring constantly. Add salt, pepper, and sugar to corn mixture. Add peppers for flavoring, if desired. Mix together cornstarch and water in bowl and beat until smooth. Add to mixture in pan. Cook over low heat, stirring constantly until thickened.

Sandy Simpson

STUFFED EGGPLANT

Serves: 4

1 medium eggplant, peeled and
   cut into quarters
1 cup chopped celery
1 cup chopped onion
oil
1 pound ground meat

garlic powder
salt
pepper
Parmesan cheese
Italian bread crumbs
butter

Cook eggplant, in enough water to cover, until tender. Mash eggplant. Sauté celery and onions in oil. Add ground meat and cook until meat is brown - stir to keep from sticking together. Add eggplant and stir well into meat mixture. Add garlic powder, salt and pepper to taste. Cook for 15 minutes and then turn mixture into 2 quart casserole dish. Sprinkle top with Parmesan cheese. Top with Italian bread crumbs and dot with butter. Bake at 350 degrees for 15 to 20 minutes.

Gladys Douglas

ITALIAN STUFFED EGGPLANT

Serves: 8

Egg Dip:
3 eggs
2 cups flour (reserve 1 cup)
salt

pepper
parsley
2 medium eggplants, peeled
1 cup oil

Stuffing:
3 pounds ground meat
1 cup Italian bread crumbs
1 4½-ounce can ripe pitted olives,
   chopped
2 eggs
½ cup milk

1 tablespoon parsley
1 teaspoon basil
½ teaspoon oregano
½ teaspoon garlic powder
spaghetti sauce
Romano cheese, grated

Egg Dip:
Mix together eggs, 1 cup flour, and seasonings to taste. Slice eggplant lengthwise in ¼ inch slices. Salt eggplant slices lightly and place in colander to drain. Pat slices dry on paper towels. Heat oil in pan. Dip eggplant slices in egg dip and then in flour. Fry slices on both sides; slices do not need to be browned. Drain slices on paper towels.

Stuffing:
Put all ingredients, except spaghetti sauce and cheese, in mixing bowl. Mix ingredients by hand until of spreading consistency. Add more milk if mixture becomes too stiff. Spread each eggplant slice with stuffing mixture. Roll each slice and place in baking dish, placing end of roll down. Cover with spaghetti sauce. Sprinkle with Romano cheese. Cover baking dish with foil. Bake at 350 degrees for 40 to 50 minutes. Serve hot.

Elizabeth Pasquantonio

 Try to keep the vitamins in vegetables by putting them in the water after it boils, not before. Also, do not overcook vegetables as nutrients are lost if you do.

STUFFED GREEN PEPPERS
(These are especially good with spicy tomato sauce)

Serves: 6

1 ½ cups chopped onion
3 cloves garlic, crushed
2 teaspoons ground cumin
1 ½ teaspoons salt
3 tablespoons oil

½ cup chopped green pepper
4 cups kidney or pinto beans, cooked and mashed
¼ teaspoon pepper
6 green peppers, possibly more

Sauté onions, garlic, cumin, and ½ teaspoon salt in oil until onions are translucent. Add green pepper and simmer, covered, for 5 minutes. Add beans and black pepper. Add salt, to taste. Mix well. Cut tops off green peppers and remove seeds. Steam green peppers for 5 to 7 minutes, or until barely tender. Fill green peppers with bean mixture. Bake at 350 degrees for 20 minutes.

Nancy Latshaw

SLEET
(A mid-Eastern vegi)

Serves: 4 to 6

½ cup wheat bulgar (available at health food stores or co-op)
½ cup boiling water
1 or 2 cloves garlic, minced, to taste
1 or 2 medium onions, diced, to taste

¼ to ½ cup oil
1 to 1 ½ pounds fresh kale, finely chopped
1 cup black eye peas, cooked
¼ to ½ cup lemon juice
salt and pepper to taste

Pre-soak bulgar in boiling water. Set aside for 15 minutes. Using a wok, sauté garlic and onion in a small amount of oil. Add kale, peas, bulgar and remaining oil. Stir fry. Add lemon juice. Add more oil, if needed. The amount of oil and lemon juice will vary according to taste, but keep proportions equal. Use salt and pepper, if desired.

Don Polito

SPINACH BROCCOLI CASSEROLE

Serves: 6 to 8

1 10-ounce package chopped
   spinach, cooked and drained
1 10-ounce package chopped
   broccoli, cooked and drained
¾ cup water from drained
   vegetables

1 teaspoon flour
1 teaspoon mayonnaise
3 teaspoons Goodman's onion
   soup
3 eggs, lightly beaten
3 to 4 cups crushed corn flakes

Mix together spinach, broccoli, vegetable juice, flour, mayonnaise, onion soup mix, and eggs. Grease an 8 x 8 inch pan. Line the bottom with ½ of the crushed corn flakes. Add vegetable mixture. Top with remaining corn flakes. Bake at 350 degrees for 45 minutes.

Penny Goldstein

TOMATO ZUCCHINI

Serves: 12

8 to 10 zucchini, peeled
butter
¼ pound mushrooms
⅔ cup chopped onions
1 3-ounce can or ⅔ cup
   Parmesan cheese

2 6-ounce cans tomato paste
1 teaspoon salt
½ teaspoon garlic salt or 1 clove
   garlic, crushed
⅛ teaspoon pepper

Slice zucchini and sauté in butter. In a separate pan, sauté mushrooms and onions for 10 minutes. Combine zucchini, mushrooms, and onions. Add ½ of the Parmesan cheese to zucchini mixture. Stir tomato paste, salt, garlic salt and pepper into zucchini mixture. Blend ingredients together lightly. Pour mixture into a greased 3 quart casserole. Sprinkle remaining cheese on top of casserole. Bake at 350 degrees for 30 minutes.

Margaret and John Koltick

To freshen up your disposal, drop in a lemon slice, and grind it up.

TOFU-BURGERS
(A healthy way to have a hamburger)

Serves: 4

½ cup bulgar (available at health food stores or co-ops)
1 cup water
1 small onion, finely minced
¼ to ½ pound mushrooms, chopped
3 tablespoons oil

½ pound tofu (available at health food stores, some grocery stores and co-ops)
1 egg, beaten
small bunch parsley, finely minced
tahini and tamari to taste
¾ to 1 cup whole wheat flour
oil

Add bulgar to boiling water and simmer for 10 minutes or until all water is absorbed. Sauté onions and mushrooms in oil. Mash tofu. Mix mashed tofu, egg, and parsley into sautéed onions and mushrooms. Add tahini and tamari, to taste. Mix cooked bulgar with tofu mixture. When mixture is cool enough to handle, add flour to form patties. Brown in skillet with brushed oil and tamari.

Linda Polito

CREAMED ZUCCHINI
(Sooo . . . easy)

Serves: 4 to 6

4 cups zucchini, peeled
2 eggs
1 cup mayonnaise
1 onion, chopped

¼ teaspoon pepper
1 cup grated cheese
1 tablespoon butter
2 tablespoons bread crumbs

Slice zucchini and place in a large saucepan. Cover with water. Cook zucchini until tender and drain. Mix eggs, mayonnaise, onion, pepper, and grated cheese with zucchini. Put zucchini mixture in a greased 1½ quart casserole. Melt butter into bread crumbs. Pour buttered bread crumbs on top of casserole. Bake for 30 minutes at 350 degrees.

Margaret and John Koltick

ITALIAN ZUCCHINI STEW

Serves: 8

2 medium zucchini
1 tablespoon oil
1 16-ounce can stewed tomatoes
1 8-ounce can tomato sauce
1 4-ounce can sliced mushrooms

1 small onion, chopped
oregano to taste
garlic salt to taste
Parmesan cheese
1 large green pepper, cut in chunks

Cut zucchini in pieces. Sauté zucchini in oil for 5 minutes until translucent. Add tomatoes, tomato sauce, mushrooms, onion, oregano, and garlic salt. Sprinkle cheese over mixture while cooking. Add green pepper and cook for 15 to 20 minutes over low heat. Serve hot. Top with extra Parmesan cheese.

Teresa Meyer

JUDY'S ZUCCHINI BAKE

Serves: 4

2 green peppers or carrots,
   chopped
1 medium onion, chopped
2 medium zucchini, sliced

2 medium tomatoes, sliced
4 to 6 slices American cheese
bread crumbs
butter

Sauté peppers and onion in butter. In a buttered 1½ quart casserole layer zucchini, pepper and onion mixture, sliced tomatoes and American cheese slices. Top with bread crumbs dotted with butter. Bake at 350 degrees for 1 hour. Cover for the last 15 minutes.

Eileen Joll

ZUCCHINI CASSEROLE
(Nutritious and delicious)

Serves: 6 to 8

3 small zucchini, chopped
3 tablespoons chopped onion
2 eggs, beaten
1 cup mushroom soup, undiluted

¼ cup margarine, melted
1 cup crushed saltine crackers
1 cup Parmesan cheese

Boil zucchini and onion in salted water for 8 minutes. Drain. Mix eggs and soup and add to zucchini. Mix margarine, cracker crumbs and cheese. Add ½ crumb mixture to zucchini. Pour into a greased 2 quart casserole. Spread remaining crumb mixture on top. Bake at 375 degrees for 45 minutes.

Millie McCathren

ZUCCHINI AND CHEESE
(Too much zucchini? Cheese it!)

Serves: 4 to 6

1 pound zucchini (or other
   summer squash)
1 small onion, thinly sliced
4 eggs
1 ½ to 2 cups grated cheese

½ teaspoon basil
½ teaspoon oregano
½ teaspoon thyme
½ teaspoon garlic powder

Steam zucchini and onion until tender. Beat eggs and add grated cheese. Mash the zucchini-onion mixture. Stir zucchini mixture and spices into egg mixture. Bake in a covered 2 quart casserole at 325 degrees for 30 to 40 minutes.

Linda Polito

ZUCCHINI SOUFFLÉ

Serves: 4 to 6

2 cups grated zucchini
1 cup chopped onion
1 cup grated cheddar cheese

2 eggs, beaten
½ teaspoon salt

Combine all ingredients. Pour into a greased 8 x 8 inch pan. Bake at 375 degrees for 25 to 30 minutes.

NOTE: Nuts, tomatoes, or eggplant can be added for a different flavor.

Sherry Wilson

When the snow is too wet to make a snowman, let the children paint the snow. Save and wash out plastic spray bottles with the hand grip on them. The pump sprays are too hard to control with mittens on. Fill the bottles with liquid food coloring and water, about 1 teaspoon food coloring to a pint of water. The children will enjoy spraying designs on the snow.

TRIPLE VEGETABLE BAKE
(Three times the taste of scalloped potatoes)

Serves: 10

3 large white potatoes, pared and cut into ¾ inch cubes
1 pound pearl onions
¼ cup margarine
¼ cup flour
1 envelope instant chicken broth

2 cups evaporated skim milk
2 2½-ounce cans sliced mushrooms
⅔ cup bread crumbs
1 pound fresh broccoli, florets only

Cook potatoes and onions, covered, in boiling water for 15 minutes, or until tender. Drain and return to pan. Melt margarine in a separate saucepan. Stir in flour and chicken broth. Cook, stirring constantly, just until bubbly. Add milk and continue cooking and stirring until the sauce thickens. Drain mushrooms and stir the liquid into the sauce. Combine mushrooms with potatoes and onions. Fold in the sauce. Place in a 1½-quart casserole. Sprinkle bread crumbs in the center. Bake at 375 degrees for 30 minutes or until bubbly and crumbs are toasted. While casserole bakes, steam broccoli florets for 5 minutes, or just until crisp and tender. Drain, and arrange in a ring around the top of the casserole. Serve hot.

Eileen Joll

VEGETABLES AU GRATIN

Serves: 6 to 8

¼ cup butter
¾ cup chopped green pepper
1 clove garlic, peeled and crushed
¼ cup flour
⅔ cup milk
¾ teaspoon salt
⅛ teaspoon pepper
⅛ teaspoon basil
⅛ teaspoon oregano

¼ teaspoon sugar
1 cup grated cheddar cheese
1 cup drained solid pack canned tomatoes
1 10-ounce package frozen corn, thawed
2 16-ounce cans boiled pearl onions, drained

Melt butter in saucepan. Add green pepper and garlic. Cook until tender. Stir in flour, milk, and seasonings. Heat and stir until thickened. Remove from heat. Stir in ½ cup cheddar cheese until melted. Add tomatoes and heat gently. Pour into a greased 3 quart casserole. Add corn and onions. Sprinkle top with ½ cup cheddar cheese. Bake uncovered at 350 degrees for 50 minutes.

NOTE: This may be prepared ahead of time. Store in the refrigerator. Return to room temperature before baking.

Carolyn Heaton

BREAD AND BUTTER PICKLES

Yields: About 6 pints

8 cups peeled, sliced cucumbers
2 cups sliced onions
salt
2 cups cider vinegar

3 cups sugar
1 ½ teaspoons celery seed
1 ½ teaspoons turmeric

Salt cucumbers and onions and let stand for 1 hour. Combine remaining ingredients in a saucepan and bring to a boil. Add cucumbers and onions. Boil 20 minutes. Pack in jars or bags. Refrigerate or freeze.

Doe Clark

REFRIGERATOR PICKLES
(Delicious, home-made pickles with no cooking)

Yields: 5 pint jars

4 cups sugar
4 cups dark vinegar
1 teaspoon celery seed
1 teaspoon mustard seed
1 ½ teaspoons turmeric
½ cup non-iodized salt

4 small onions, thinly sliced
enough thin cucumbers to fill 5
    pint jars (the smaller the
    cucumber, the better the
    pickles)

Sterilize pint jars and lids. Mix sugar, vinegar, celery seed, mustard seed, turmeric and salt. Set aside. Line bottom of each jar with sliced onions. Wash and slice cucumber. Fill jars as full as possible with cucumbers. Stir the first 6 ingredients again; then fill each jar to the brim with the mixture. Screw the lids on very tight. Refrigerate. Turn jars upside down for best results. Shake jars every day, for the first 5 days to distribute the spices evenly. After 5 days, the pickles can be eaten. Keep the jars refrigerated at all times. The pickles will retain their crispness as long as they are refrigerated. They will keep as long as store pickles if kept refrigerated.

Loretta Lucas

APRICOT CASSEROLE
(Good side dish with roast beef or pork)

Serves: 4 to 6

2 16-ounce cans peeled apricot
  halves
1 cup sugar
½ cup butter
pinch of salt

½ cup flour
2 tablespoons orange liqueur
grated orange peel (optional)
handful of "Grapenuts" cereal

Drain fruit, reserving juice. Place cut side of apricot up in a buttered casserole. Mix sugar, butter, salt and flour. Place over fruit. Sprinkle with a couple tablespoons of reserved juice and the orange liqueur. Grate a little orange peel over top if desired. Top with "Grapenuts". Bake at 250 degrees for about 1½ hours until bubbly.

Sue and Bill Law

CHUNKY APPLESAUCE

Yields: 6 quarts

6 peeled apples, cut into ½ inch
  cubes
1 20-ounce can sweetened
  applesauce

cinnamon
nutmeg

Cook apples for 20 minutes. Mash slightly if firm. Add applesauce and mix together. Sprinkle liberally with cinnamon and with a small amount of nutmeg. Serve warm or cold.

Doris DePierre

PINEAPPLE CASSEROLE
(Serve with ham)

Serves: 8

½ cup sugar
3 tablespoons flour
3 eggs

1 20-ounce can unsweetened
  crushed pineapple
4 slices white bread, cubed
½ cup butter, melted

Beat sugar, flour and eggs with a spoon. Add pineapple with juice. Pour into a buttered 1½ quart casserole. Stir melted butter into bread cubes. Sprinkle cubes on top of casserole. Bake at 350 degrees for 1 hour.

Joan Clark

Pasta, Rice, Potatoes

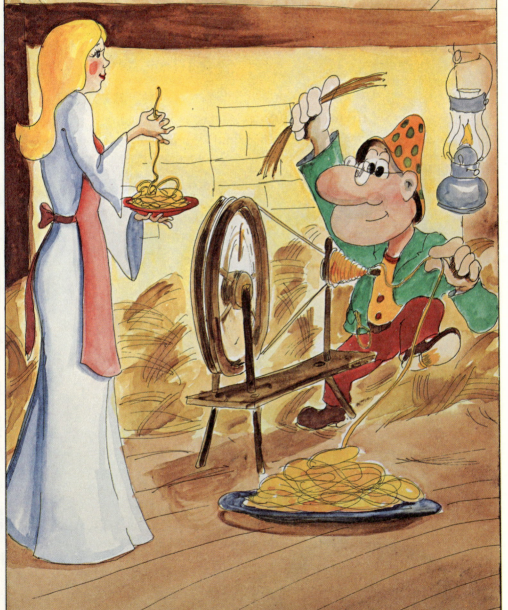

Gary G. Baker

CHAPTER X

Rumpelstiltskin's ... Pasta, Rice and Potatoes

The miller's daughter spun straw into gold,
So Rumplestiltskin her secret would hold.

"This is the way to do it," said he,
As the stuff twirled into golden spaghetti.

"I've shown you the method, but that is all,
For you'll have to make your own meatball!"

Cook's Note: This flourish with food is found quite sparsely,
But you'll do just as well with parsley!

BROCCOLI KUGEL

Serves: 8

½ pound fine noodles
1 10-ounce box frozen, chopped
   broccoli
3 eggs, beaten

1 package onion soup mix
1 cup Coffee Rich
½ cup margarine, melted

Prepare noodles according to package directions and drain. Cook broccoli according to package directions and drain. Mix all ingredients in a large bowl. Pour into greased 8 x 8 inch pan and bake for 350 degrees for 30 minutes or until brown on top.

NOTE: Chopped spinach can be substituted for broccoli.

Penny Goldstein

BROWNED CABBAGE NOODLES

Serves: 6 to 8

1 pound broad noodles
4 cups finely shredded cabbage
1 tablespoon salt
½ cup butter or margarine

½ teaspoon sugar
¼ teaspoon pepper
6 strips crisp bacon, crumbled

Cook noodles according to directions on package and drain. Sprinkle salt on the cabbage and allow to stand 20 minutes in water to cover. Drain thoroughly. Melt butter or margarine in deep skillet. Mix in cabbage, sugar and pepper. Cook over very low heat for 45 minutes, stirring frequently. Add noodles, toss lightly, and cook for 3 minutes. Add crumbled bacon.

Barbara Fisher

Dusting can be fun: Creating hand puppets from old white cotton socks can encourage your youngster to help with the household chores. Just take a sock and draw a face with colored marking pens, then watch your child have a great time dusting.

CHERRY KUGEL
(Castle Tavern's tasty pasta dessert)

Serves: 12 to 16

1 pound medium noodles
8 eggs, well beaten
1½ cups sugar
2 teaspoons vanilla
8 tablespoons margarine, melted
½ cup Cherry Herring or other
    Liqueur (Crème de Cacao,
    Kahlua, etc.)

2 14½-ounce cans sour cherries,
    drained
½ cup chopped walnuts
1 handful baked coconut
cinnamon
sugar
coconut
margarine

Cook noodles in salted water. Drain. Rinse with cold water. Add eggs, sugar and vanilla. Mix well. Add margarine, liqueur and cherries. Mix in nuts and coconut. Pour into a greased 9 x 13 inch pan. Sprinkle top with cinnamon, sugar and coconut. Dot with margarine. Bake at 350 degrees for 2 hours or until browned.

Rose Bloom

CHINESE SPAGHETTI
(Marco Polo would have loved it!)

Serves: 4 to 6

1 pound ground beef
1 10¾-ounce can cream of
    mushroom soup, undiluted
1 10-ounce package frozen
    Chinese stir-fry vegetables

1 8-ounce can water chestnuts
8 medium mushrooms, sliced
2 cups grated longhorn cheese
pasta

Brown ground beef and drain. Add mushroom soup, Chinese vegetables, water chestnuts and sliced mushrooms. Sprinkle frozen vegetable season-ing over mixture. Simmer until vegetables are tender. Top with grated cheese. Serve over pasta.

Peggy Osborne

FETTUCINE VERDÉ

Serves: 4 to 6

1 pound green fettucine
½ cup butter
2 cloves garlic, minced

1 pound mushrooms, cleaned
  and quartered
Romano cheese

Cook noodles in salted water; drain. Sauté garlic in butter. Add noodles. Toss. Add mushrooms. Heat until mushrooms are soft. Garnish with Romano cheese.

Pat Smetanka

HOLIDAY SPAGHETTI
(Stash in the freezer and use in a pinch!)

Serves: 8

1 pound thin spaghetti
3 tablespoons bacon drippings
1 cup minced onion
¾ cup minced green pepper
1 cup sliced mushrooms
1 pound ground beef

2 teaspoons salt
1 teaspoon sugar
3½ cups cooked tomatoes
2 cups grated sharp cheese
bacon
parsley

Cook spaghetti according to package directions. Drain and rinse. Set aside. Sauté onions, green pepper, and mushrooms in bacon drippings. Add ground beef and cook until browned. Add salt, sugar and tomatoes. Heat thoroughly. Mix tomato sauce with cooked spaghetti. Pour into well-greased 2½ quart casserole. Sprinkle with grated cheese. Bake at 350 degrees for 30 minutes. Serve hot and garnish with crisp bacon and parsley.

Teresa Meyer

For a fun craft on a rainy day: Supply the kids with macaroni, white glue and paper. See the creative designs they come up with.

MACARONI AND CHEESE
(Cheese variation on an old standard)

Serves: 6

3 cups uncooked macaroni
oil
4 teaspoons salt
6 cups water
1 tablespoon butter or margarine

1 10¾-ounce can cream of
mushroom soup, undiluted
⅓ cup hot water
2 cups shredded Monterey Jack
cheese
1 tablespoon minced onion

Drop macaroni into 6 cups boiling, salted water to which a small amount of oil has been added. Cook for 3 minutes, stirring constantly. Cover, remove from heat and let stand for 10 minutes. Drain. Add remaining ingredients. Place in greased 1½ quart casserole. Bake at 350 degrees for 30 minutes.

Mary Ellen Weaver

NOODLE PUDDING
(A substitute for potatoes; especially good with corned beef)

Serves: 8

8 ounces egg noodles
3 eggs
½ cup sugar
½ cup margarine, melted
½ teaspoon salt

1¼ teaspoons cinnamon
⅓ cup Grapenuts cereal
⅓ cup raisins
16 ounces cottage cheese (1
pint)

Cook noodles in 3 quarts boiling, salted water. Drain under hot water. Mix remaining ingredients. Toss with noodles. Bake uncovered at 350 degrees for 1 hour.

Sally Joiner

PASTA DEL CARBONARO
(Tired of tomato sauce . . . try this!)

Serves: 3 to 4

3 to 4 slices smoked bacon
3 to 4 slices Proscuitto
3 to 4 slices Capocola

1 large clove garlic, minced
oil
½ pound spaghetti

Cut bacon, Proscuitto, and Capocola into pieces. Fry in oil with garlic. Cook spaghetti according to directions on package. Drain. Mix together noodles and meat mixture. Serve hot.

Marsha DeCaria

RICOTTA GNOCCHI
(An easy home-made pasta)

Serves: 6 to 8

2 tablespoons grated Romano
  cheese
1 pound Ricotta cheese
1 egg

1 egg yolk
salt to taste
2 cups flour

Mix all ingredients, gradually adding flour last. Knead until a smooth, manageable dough is obtained. If necessary, add more flour. Roll dough into long rope-like strips about ¾ inch thick. Cut into ½ inch pieces. Dip in flour. Use thumb to make dented design in each piece. Cook in salted water for about 10 minutes. Serve with a tomato sauce.

Marsha DeCaria

MILLET FIESTA
(Unusual but delicious)

Serves: 8

Tomato Juice Layer:
2 cups millet
4 cups tomato juice

1 teaspoon salt
½ teaspoon pepper

Chicken Broth Layer:
2 cups millet
4 cups chicken broth

1 teaspoon salt
½ teaspoon pepper
cheddar cheese, grated

Sauce:
4 cups whole tomatoes
2 cups tomato purée
½ cup diced celery
½ cup diced onion
1 tablespoon basil

2 tablespoons marjoram
1 teaspoon garlic powder
1 teaspoon Worcestershire sauce
dash of Tabasco sauce
2 green peppers, sliced

Stir together ingredients for tomato juice layer. Cook until millet is soft and some liquid is absorbed. In a separate pan stir together all chicken broth layer ingredients, except cheese. Cook millet same as above. Place tomato juice layer in greased 9 x 13 inch pan. Cover with grated cheddar cheese. Add chicken broth layer and top with more cheese. Bake at 350 degrees for 30 minutes. Place all sauce ingredients, except green pepper, in saucepan. Simmer sauce for 30 minutes. Top casserole with 2 sliced green peppers and pour sauce over top. Bake at 350 degrees for 20 minutes.

Sherry Wilson

CHICKEN NUTTY RICE

Serves: 4

1 ½ cups chicken broth
⅛ teaspoon poultry seasoning
2 tablespoons butter
¼ cup pistachios, chopped

¼ cup chopped parsley
½ tablespoon chopped onion
2 cups cooked rice

Combine all ingredients in a 1 ½ quart greased casserole. Cover and bake at 375 degrees for 25 to 30 minutes.

Barbara Cooledge

ITALIAN/SPANISH RICE

Serves: 8

4 cups Minute Rice, uncooked
2 tablespoons butter or oil
2 medium green peppers, diced
12 medium mushrooms, sliced

8 ounces pepperoni, sliced thin
1 32-ounce jar Ragu spaghetti
   sauce

Prepare rice according to directions on box. Sauté peppers and mushrooms in butter or oil until tender. Combine peppers, mushrooms, pepperoni and spaghetti sauce. Bring to a boil. Add rice and simmer for 30 minutes

Peggy Osborne

 The Heats Off: Here is a fuel-saving way to cook pasta, without heating up your kitchen. First boil the water, then add the pasta. When the water returns to a boil, cover the pot and turn off the heat. Leave the pot on the burner for the remainder of the cooking time, as recommended on the package. Pasta will be cooked to perfection.

OLD FASHIONED RICE PUDDING

Serves: 12 to 15

1 cup uncooked rice
1 cup sugar, white or brown
¾ cup raisins

½ cup water
8 cups milk

Combine rice, sugar, raisins, and water and bring to a boil. Remove from heat and put into a 4-quart casserole. Add milk. Bake in a 275 to 300 degree oven until milk is absorbed - 2½ to 3 hours.

NOTE: Sprinkle with nutmeg if desired.

Millie McCathren

RICE PILAF

¾ to 1 cup butter
1 4-ounce can mushrooms
½ medium onion, diced
2 cups uncooked rice

2 rounded tablespoons oregano
3 cups consommé
2 scant cups water

Combine butter, mushrooms, onion, rice and oregano in saucepan. Simmer for 20 minutes, stirring occasionally. Add consommé and water. Bake in a covered 2½-quart casserole at 400 degrees for 1 hour or until moisture is absorbed.

Marty Matthews

Rice should never be washed. If rice is washed before or after cooking the nutrients will be washed away. This is true for all types of rice.

Brown rice, which retains most of its natural bran, needs a longer cooking time than other rice. It will last on the shelf for six months or longer in the refrigerator.

After cooking, long-grain rice seems to stand apart making it good to use for fried rice or curries. Medium grain-rice becomes sticky after cooking and therefore is tender and moist and good to use for puddings and molds.

RICE AND LENTILS WITH TOFU
(A healthy combination)

Serves: 6 to 8

4-quart pressure cooker
1 cup lentils
1 pound firm Tofu, cubed
¼ cup whole wheat flour
oil
2 medium onions, finely chopped
2 cloves garlic, finely chopped

3 cups uncooked brown rice
¼ cup lemon juice
2 quarts boiling water
1 tablespoon miso*
¼ cup hot water
mushrooms (optional)

Soak lentils overnight in water to cover. Put cubed tofu in large, plastic bag with flour, and shake until tofu is evenly coated. Brown tofu in small amount of oil and set aside. Sauté onions and garlic in oil and add to tofu. Place rice, lentils and lemon juice in pressure cooker. Add boiling water to cover ½ to ¾ inch above food. Cook for 20 minutes at 15 pounds pressure. Add miso that has been mixed with ¼ cup hot water. Fold tofu, onions and garlic into rice and lentil mixture.

*Miso is a fermented paste of brown rice available at health food stores.

NOTE: Rice and lentils can be cooked according to package directions in covered saucepan.

Don Polito

BAKED CHEESE GRITS

Serves: 4 to 6

1 cup grits
4 cups boiling water
½ teaspoon salt
1¾ cups shredded cheddar
cheese

1 clove garlic, minced
½ cup butter or margarine
2 eggs, well beaten
½ cup milk

Preheat oven to 350 degrees. Cook grits in boiling water and salt for 4½ minutes. Stir occasionally, turning heat down so grits do not scorch. Add cheese, garlic, butter or margarine, eggs and milk. Mix thoroughly until cheese is melted. Pour into a greased 2 quart casserole. Bake at 350 degrees for 50 to 60 minutes.

Holly Raulston

FLUFFY POTATO CASSEROLE
(Jazz up those holiday leftovers)

Serves: 6 to 8

1 8-ounce package cream cheese, softened
2 cups leftover mashed potatoes, cold or hot
1 small onion, chopped
2 eggs
2 tablespoons flour
salt to taste
pepper to taste
1 3-ounce can French fried onion rings

Place all ingredients in large mixing bowl except onion rings. Beat until all ingredients are well blended using an electric mixer. Beat on high until potato mixture is light and fluffy. Turn into a greased 9 x 9 inch baking dish. Sprinkle top with onion rings. Bake at 300 degrees for 35 minutes.

Dorothy Baker

BAKED STUFFED POTATOES

Serves: 4

4 large Idaho potatoes
salt to taste
pepper to taste
¼ cup butter
shredded cheddar cheese

Bake potatoes. When cool enough to handle, cut an oval-shaped skin section from top and scoop out the potato. Set skins aside. To the potato add salt and pepper. Cut in butter and cheese. Mixture will be chunky. Put mixture back into potato skins and top with a spoonful of cheese. Return to oven and heat.

NOTE: Can be fixed ahead of time and heated when ready to be used.

Millie McCathren

Too much salt in the stew? Add raw cut potatoes. Once they have cooked and absorbed the salt, discard them. If there are no potatoes in the house, add a teaspoon each of sugar and cider vinegar.

MASHED POTATO CASSEROLE

Serves: 6 to 8

8 medium potatoes, peeled and cubed
¼ cup milk
¼ cup sour cream, optional
2 tablespoons butter
salt
pepper
1 cup grated cheddar or American cheese
paprika

Cook potatoes until tender. Whip potatoes with a mixer. Whisk in milk, sour cream, butter, salt and pepper to taste. Put in ungreased casserole. Top with cheese. Sprinkle mixture with paprika. Bake at 400 degrees for 8 to 10 minutes.

Jean Getz

PARMESAN POTATOES
(Try them with barbecued chicken)

Serves: 4

4 large potatoes, peeled and thinly sliced
1 cup butter or margarine, melted
⅓ cup Parmesan cheese, grated
salt
pepper

Line cookie sheet or broiler pan with aluminum foil. Pour in small amount of butter. Alternate layers of potatoes, butter, cheese, salt and pepper until all ingredients are used. Cover with foil and seal. Bake at 375 degrees for 1 hour and 15 minutes.

Sandy Simpson

POTATO BAKE
(Great with turkey)

Serves: 8

4 cups potatoes, cooked and mashed
1 cup sour cream
1 cup cottage cheese
1 small onion, finely chopped
2 eggs
2 tablespoons butter, melted
¾ teaspoon salt
¼ teaspoon pepper

Cook and mash potatoes. Fold in sour cream and cottage cheese. Add remaining ingredients and mix well. May use an electric mixer. Pour into a buttered casserole. Bake at 350 degrees for 1 hour.

NOTE: Can be made ahead of time and refrigerated until baked.

Mary Benson

POTATO PANCAKES

Serves: 4

6 medium potatoes, coarsely
   grated
2 medium onions, coarsely
   grated

1 egg, beaten
¼ cup milk
2 tablespoons flour
oil

Combine potatoes and onions. Mix in egg, milk and flour as soon as possible to prevent potatoes from turning black. Using ½ cup measure, scoop potato mixture into a skillet containing ½ inch hot cooking oil. Cook pancakes on high heat for 3 to 4 minutes on each side. Top pancakes with sour cream or applesauce, if desired.

Susan Ferrell-Berman

POTATOES ROMANOFF

Serves: 6 to 8

5 cups cooked potatoes, diced (7
   or 8)
2 teaspoons salt
2 cups cottage cheese
1 cup sour cream

¼ cup finely minced green onions
garlic salt to taste
½ cup grated cheddar cheese
paprika

Sprinkle potatoes with 1 teaspoon salt. Combine cottage cheese, sour cream, onions and garlic salt with remaining 1 teaspoon salt. Fold in potato cubes. Pour into a buttered 2½ quart casserole. Top with grated cheese and paprika. Bake at 350 degrees for 40 to 45 minutes. Can be prepared ahead of time and baked at the last minute.

Shirley Rose

If you've peeled too many potatoes, cover them with cold water which has been mixed with a few drops of vinegar. Keep them refrigerated and they'll last a few days.

PIEROGI

Yields: 50 pierogi

Potato Filling:
4 potatoes, cooked and cut up
¾ cup shredded sharp cheddar
  cheese

butter
milk
salt
pepper

Prune Filling:

prunes, cut up

Dough:
3 cups flour
1 teaspoon salt
1 large or 2 small eggs

water
onion
butter

Potato Filling:
Add cheese to hot, cut up potatoes and allow to melt. Add butter, milk, salt and pepper to make a smooth, mashed-potato consistency.

Prune Filling:
Boil cut-up prunes until very soft. Drain and mash.

Dough:
Mix flour and salt in a large bowl. Make a well and drop in egg. Add ½ cup water and scramble with egg. Keep adding flour from around well. Add more water, if needed, but do not allow dough to become too thin or too sticky to roll. Separate dough into 2 parts. Wrap one part in plastic wrap and set aside. Roll dough on liberally-floured board. Roll dough thin and cut in rectangles with zig-zag cutting wheel. Fill, fold over, and seal edges. Boil pierogi gently in salted water for 12 to 15 minutes. Drain. Fry in onions and butter.

Pat Krivonak

Have your children thread Cheerios or Fruit Loops onto string using a toothpick needle. It will keep them busy and provide them with a fun snack.

WHIPPING CREAM CASSEROLE POTATOES
(Adding the cream at the last minute is the final touch)

Serves: 6 to 8

5 to 6 medium red potatoes
salt and pepper to taste

¼ cup butter
1 cup whipping cream

Boil unpared potatoes (not well done) the day before using. Refrigerate overnight. Remove 1 potato at a time from refrigerator; remove skin, grate to "cole slaw" consistency. Butter 1½ quart casserole. Place potatoes, a layer at a time, in the casserole, alternating with salt, pepper and dots of butter until full. Pour unwhipped cream over potatoes, and shake so cream filters through. Bake at 425 degrees for 30 to 40 minutes, until well browned and cream is well absorbed.

NOTE: This may be prepared ahead of time and refrigerated until time to bake; however, do not add cream until just prior to baking.

Janet White

SCALLOPED APPLES AND SWEET POTATOES

Serves: 4 to 6

6 small or 4 large sweet potatoes
  or yams
2 apples
3 tablespoons butter or
  margarine

½ cup honey or brown sugar
dash of salt
dash of cinnamon
¼ cup water

Peel cooked potatoes and cut in slices. Peel apples and cut into slices. Arrange in baking dish. Dot with butter or margarine. Add honey or brown sugar. Add salt and cinnamon. Add water. Cover and bake at 350 degrees for 35 minutes. Uncover for last 5 minutes.

Jean Getz

SWEET POTATO CASSEROLE

(From the deep south - an extra special treat with turkey or ham)

Serves: 6

3 cups cooked and mashed
sweet potatoes
½ cup sugar
2 eggs, beaten

1 teaspoon vanilla
½ cup evaporated milk
2 tablespoons margarine
1 teaspoon salt

Topping:
1 cup brown sugar
½ teaspoon margarine

⅓ cup flour
1 cup flaked coconut
1 cup chopped nuts

Mix ingredients together. Put in greased casserole. Mix topping ingredients together. Sprinkle over potato mixture. Bake at 350 degrees for 30 minutes.

Nancy McCloskey

SWEET POTATOES AND FRUIT

Serves: 10 to 12

1 8-ounce can pear halves, drained
1 8-ounce can peach halves,
drained
1 8-ounce can pineapple slices,
drained

1 8-ounce can apricot halves,
drained
2 16-ounce cans sweet potatoes,
drained

Topping:
⅓ cup brown sugar

2 teaspoons curry powder
⅓ cup butter, melted

Arrange fruit and sweet potatoes in a 9 x 13 inch baking dish. Stir together brown sugar, curry powder and butter. Pour topping mixture over fruit. Cover and bake at 400 degrees for 1 hour.

Deb and Ron Wilcher

Cakes

Gary G. Baker

CHAPTER XI

The Elves and the Shoemaker's ... Cakes

When the elves arrived at midnight,
They tapped and pounded and fixed.
So the shoemaker's wife surprised them
With chocolate cakes that she mixed.

She sewed little jackets and trousers,
Then whipped up a jellyroll.
Cried the elves as they claimed their surprises,
"Your kindness is food for the **sole!**"

Cook's Note: Wearing out shoe leather will help you work off these
calories!

MOIST DEVIL DOG CAKE
(Well worth the calories)

Serves: 12

2 cups flour
2 cups sugar
¾ teaspoon salt
1 teaspoon baking powder
2 teaspoons baking soda

⅓ cup cocoa
1 cup oil
1 cup hot brewed coffee
1 cup milk
2 eggs

Filling:
1 cup shortening
1 cup sugar

6 tablespoons flour
⅔ cup warm milk
1½ teaspoons vanilla

Sift first 6 ingredients together. Add oil, coffee and milk. Beat at medium speed for 2 minutes. Add eggs. Beat for 2 more minutes. Grease and flour bundt pan. Bake at 325 degrees for 40 minutes. Check with toothpick for doneness. Cool in pan on wire rack for 5 minutes. Remove from pan. Can be served plain or with filling (below).

Filling:
Beat shortening and sugar at high speed in mixer until light. Add flour to milk. Blend well. Add flour and milk to shortening and sugar mixture. Beat until thick. Add vanilla. Beat for 1 minute. Refrigerate until ready to use.

Cut cooled cake with a piece of thread into 3 layers. Start at back of cake and pull toward front. Spread filling between layers and on top. Serve.

Eleanor Towers

AUNT MILDRED'S CHOCOLATE CAKE

Serves: 12

4 unsweetened chocolate squares
1 cup boiling water
½ cup butter
½ cup shortening
2 cups sugar
2 eggs

½ teaspoon vanilla
½ cup sour milk
1¼ teaspoons baking soda
¼ teaspoon salt
2 cups flour

Melt chocolate in double boiler. Add boiling water, butter and shortening. Stir until melted. Add sugar, stirring until melted. Beat eggs slightly. Add vanilla to eggs. Slowly pour hot mixture into eggs. Add sour milk and dry ingredients, alternately. Grease and flour 9 x 13 inch pan. Pour batter into pan. Bake at 350 degrees for 40 to 45 minutes.

NOTE: This cake can also be made into a layered cake.

Judith Diehl

BLACK CHOCOLATE CAKE

Serves: 12 to 16

2 cups flour
2 teaspoons baking soda
1 teaspoon baking powder
¾ cup cocoa
1 teaspoon salt
2 cups sugar

1 cup milk
1½ cups oil
2 eggs
1 teaspoon vanilla
1 cup hot brewed coffee

Sift together flour, baking soda, baking powder, cocoa and salt in a large mixing bowl. Stir in remaining ingredients. Beat with an electric mixer for 2 minutes. Pour into a greased 9 x 13 inch pan. Bake at 350 degrees for 35 to 45 minutes or until toothpick inserted into center of cake comes out clean. Ice cake with white frosting.

Elaine Baker

MISSISSIPPI MUD CAKE

Serves: 16 to 20

1 cup butter, softened
4 eggs
1 cup coconut
2 cups sugar
1½ cups flour

Frosting:
½ cup butter, softened
6 tablespoons milk
⅓ cup cocoa

⅓ cup cocoa
1 teaspoon vanilla
1 cup chopped pecans or walnuts
1 13-ounce jar marshmallow cream

1 16-ounce box confectioners' sugar
1 cup chopped pecans or walnuts

In a large bowl, mix butter and eggs until creamy. Add coconut, sugar, flour, cocoa, vanilla and nuts. Mix well with a spoon. Pour into a greased 9 x 13 inch pan. Bake at 350 degrees for 45 minutes. As soon as cake is taken from the oven, spread with marshmallow cream. Let stand for 20 minutes. Make the frosting. In a mixing bowl blend together butter, milk, cocoa, and confectioners' sugar. Beat until smooth. Stir in ½ cup chopped nuts. Spread frosting on cake, swirling through the marshmallow cream. Sprinkle the remaining nuts on top.

Joan Fullwood

OATMEAL CAKE
(A moist cake with an irresistible topping)

Serves: 20

½ cup butter
1 ¼ cups boiling water
1 cup oatmeal
1 cup sugar
1 cup brown sugar, firmly packed

2 eggs
1 teaspoon baking soda
1 ¼ cups flour
¼ teaspoon cinnamon

Topping:
½ cup butter or margarine
¼ cup evaporated milk
¾ cup sugar

½ teaspoon vanilla
1 cup coconut
1 cup chopped pecans

Put butter in bowl. Pour water and oatmeal on top. Let stand for 20 minutes. Add remaining cake ingredients. Mix thoroughly. Pour into greased and floured 9 x 13 inch pan. Bake at 350 degrees for 35 minutes.

Topping:
While cake is cooling, heat together butter, milk, sugar and vanilla. Add coconut and pecans. Let mixture come to a boil. Cover baked cake with topping. Put the cake under broiler for a few minutes to brown.

Teresa Meyer

GRAHAM NUT CAKE

Serves: 20

⅓ cup shortening
1 cup sugar
3 egg yolks
1 13-ounce can evaporated milk
2 cups crushed graham crackers

1 teaspoon baking powder
2 tablespoons flour
¼ teaspoon salt
1 teaspoon vanilla
1 cup chopped nuts

Frosting:
6 tablespoons shortening
1 cup confectioners' sugar

3 tablespoons sour cream or sour
  milk
1 teaspoon vanilla

Combine ingredients in the order given. Pour into greased and floured 9 x 13 inch pan. Bake at 350 degrees for 35 minutes.

Frosting:
Mix all ingredients together. Spread over cooled cake. Keep cake refrigerated.

Gerri Bartelme

PENNSYLVANIA DUTCH CHRISTMAS CAKE

Serves: 12 to 16

1 cup rolled oats
1 ½ cups boiling water
½ teaspoon salt
½ cup butter or margarine,
    softened
1 cup sugar

Topping:
6 tablespoons margarine or butter
¾ cup brown sugar

1 cup brown sugar
2 eggs, beaten
1 ½ cups flour
1 teaspoon cinnamon
1 teaspoon baking soda
1 cup nuts

1 cup coconut
1 cup walnuts
1 teaspoon vanilla

Mix oats, water and salt together. Let cool. Cream butter and sugars until smooth. Blend eggs and cooled oats into creamed mixture. Add flour, cinnamon, baking soda and nuts and stir. Pour into a greased and floured 9 x 13 inch pan.

Topping:
Melt butter. Add sugar. Add the rest of the ingredients. Mix well. Sprinkle on top of cake mixture. Bake at 350 degrees for 40 to 50 minutes.

Millie McCathren

MERINGUE CAKE

Serves: 12

½ cup butter, softened
½ cup sugar
4 egg yolks, beaten
1 teaspoon vanilla
1 cup sifted flour, sift flour 2
    times before measuring

1 teaspoon baking powder
dash of salt
5 tablespoons milk
4 egg whites
1 cup sugar
chopped walnuts

Cream together butter and ½ cup sugar with electric mixer until very smooth. Beat in egg yolks and vanilla. Sift together flour, baking powder and salt. Add to egg mixture alternating with milk. Mix until smooth. Set aside. Beat egg whites until stiff. Gradually add 1 cup sugar. Beat well. Spread first mixture in 2 greased and floured 9-inch round cake pans. Spread egg white mixture on top, leaving a 2 inch margin around the edge of the pans. Sprinkle with chopped nuts. Bake at 325 degrees for 30 minutes.

NOTE: Cake should be served as a layer cake. It is recommended that the first layer be topped with strawberries or pineapple chunks and whipped cream before the second layer is placed on top.

Dorothy E. Christiansen

CHEESE CAKE

Serves: 10

Crust:

1⅓ cups graham cracker crumbs
(about 16 crackers)

3 tablespoons sugar

¼ cup butter or margarine,
melted

1 teaspoon cinnamon

Mix crust ingredients together. Grease 9 or 10-inch spring form pan. Place ¾ of mixture into pan. Pat down. Save extra to sprinkle on top. Do not bake.

Filling:

3 8-ounce packages cream
cheese, softened

5 eggs

1 cup sugar

1 tablespoon flour

1½ teaspoons vanilla

Cream the cheese. Beat in eggs, one at a time. Add flour to sugar. Mix sugar and flour into cheese and egg mixture. Add vanilla. Beat thoroughly. Pour onto graham cracker crust. Bake at 325 degrees for 1 hour.

Topping:

3 cups sour cream

½ teaspoon sugar

1 teaspoon vanilla

Mix topping ingredients together. After 1 hour, remove cake from oven. Pour on topping. Bake at 325 degrees for 10 minutes. Turn off oven. Leave cake in oven with door closed for 45 minutes. Open door; leave cake in oven for 45 minutes. Remove cake from oven. Let cool before refrigerating.

NOTE: This cooling process keeps cake from cracking.

Judith Diehl

NO CRUST CHEESECAKE
(Simple and light)

Serves: 10

2 8-ounce packages cream
cheese, softened

⅔ cup sugar

½ teaspoon vanilla

3 eggs

Topping:

1 cup sour cream

½ teaspoon vanilla

4 teaspoons sugar

Cream the cream cheese and sugar. Add vanilla and eggs. Mix until lemon colored and fluffy. Pour into a well-buttered 9-inch pie plate. Bake at 375 degrees for 25 minutes.

Topping:

Mix sour cream, vanilla and sugar together. Cool cake for 20 minutes. Pour topping onto cheesecake. Bake at 375 degrees for 10 minutes. Cool cake for 6 hours in refrigerator before serving.

Jo Ann Pulcini

CHEESE CAKE

Serves: 8 to 10

Crust:
1½ cups graham cracker crumbs
  (2 double sections of a box)

½ cup butter or margarine,
  melted
4 tablespoons sugar

Filling:
3 8-ounce packages Philadelphia
  Cream Cheese, softened
5 eggs

1 cup sugar
1 tablespoon vanilla (less can be
  used if so preferred)

Topping:
2 cups sour cream

4 tablespoons sugar
1 teaspoon vanilla

Crust:
Mix graham cracker crumbs, butter or margarine and sugar. Place in spring form pan on bottom and sides. Pre-buttering sides of pan makes it easier for crumbs to adhere. Set aside.

Filling:
Beat cream cheese until smooth, add eggs one at a time, beating after each addition. Add sugar and vanilla. Pour gently into pan with crumb crust. Bake for 40 minutes at 375 degrees. Remove from oven, set oven thermostat to 450 degrees. Add topping, if desired.

Topping:
Mix together sour cream, sugar and vanilla. Pour topping on cake and bake only 5 minutes longer at 450 degrees. Chill overnight and serve with canned cherry pie filling or thawed frozen strawberries.

NOTE: If topping is not used, do not remove cheese cake from oven. Turn temperature to 450 degrees for about 5 minutes, just enough to slightly brown. Chill as above.

Fern Jagger

Don't throw away your empty frosting cans and some yogurt containers (such as Breyer's). They are wonderful for storing playdough, mixing paint, corralling small toys, holding crayons, or holding puzzle parts.

APPLE CAKE

Serves: 12 to 16

2 cups sugar
½ cup brown sugar
1 cup oil
3 eggs
1 teaspoon vanilla

3 teaspoons cinnamon
1 teaspoon salt
1 teaspoon baking soda
3 cups flour
4 apples, diced

Thoroughly blend sugars and oil. Mix in eggs and vanilla. Add the dry ingredients in the order given. Add the apples last. Pour into greased and floured 9 x 13 inch pan. Bake at 350 degrees for 1 hour.

Monica and Stuart Hall

APPLE NUT CAKE

Serves: 12 to 16

1¾ cups sugar
1 cup oil
3 eggs
1 teaspoon salt
1 teaspoon vanilla

2 cups flour, sifted
1 teaspoon baking soda
1 cup walnuts, chopped
5 apples, chopped

Mix the ingredients in the order given. Pour into greased and floured 9 x 13 inch pan. Bake at 350 degrees for 45 minutes.

Loretta Lucas

APPLE-RAISIN CAKE

Serves: 12 to 16

1 cup butter or margarine,
   softened
1½ cups sugar
4 eggs
2 cups sifted flour
2 teaspoons cinnamon

1 teaspoon baking soda
¼ teaspoon salt
4 cups peeled, sliced apples
1 cup raisins
1 cup chopped nuts

Cream butter and sugar. Add eggs. Mix until fluffy. Sift dry ingredients together. Add dry ingredients. Fold in apples, raisins and nuts. Pour into greased and floured 9 x 13 inch pan. Bake at 350 degrees for 1 hour.

Elizabeth Pasquantonio

CAKES

DARK APPLE CAKE

Serves: 12

¾ cup shortening, butter or
   margarine, softened
¾ cup sugar
¾ cup brown sugar
2 eggs
1 teaspoon vanilla

Topping:
¼ cup sugar
¼ cup brown sugar

2 cups flour
1¾ teaspoons baking soda
¼ teaspoon salt
½ teaspoon cinnamon
1 cup sour milk
2 cups peeled, diced apples

1 teaspoon cinnamon
½ cup chopped nuts

Cream shortening and sugars. Add eggs, one at a time. Add vanilla to egg mixture. Mix dry ingredients together. Alternately add dry mixture and sour milk to egg mixture. Mix until well-blended. Add apples. Stir gently.

Topping:
Mix topping ingredients together. Grease and flour tube pan. Pour cake mixture into a 10-inch tube pan. Sprinkle with topping mixture. Bake at 350 degrees for 1 hour.

Diana Smith

PRIZE WINNING APPLE CAKE
(Should win any contest it enters!)

Yields: 2 to 2½ dozen pieces

½ cup butter, softened
2 cups sugar
2 eggs
2 cups flour
1 teaspoon baking powder

1 teaspoon salt
3 to 4 apples, peeled and sliced
cinnamon
sugar

Cream butter and sugar until fluffy. Add eggs. Sift together flour, baking powder, and salt. Add to creamed mixture. Place batter in greased 9 x 13 inch pan. Press apple slices, in overlapping rows, over the top of the batter. Sprinkle with cinnamon and sugar. Bake at 325 degrees for 1 hour.

Dorothy E. Christiansen

BLUEBERRY TEA CAKE

Serves: 8

¼ cup butter, softened
¾ cup sugar
1 egg
½ cup milk

Crumbs:
½ cup sugar
¼ cup flour

2 cups flour
2 teaspoons baking powder
½ teaspoon salt
2 cups blueberries

½ teaspoon cinnamon
¼ cup butter

Cream butter and sugar until fluffy. Add egg and milk, and beat until smooth. Sift together flour, baking powder and salt. Add to creamed ingredients. Mix well. Fold in blueberries. Pour into a greased 7 x 11 inch pan.

Crumbs:
Combine sugar, flour and cinnamon. Cut into butter until crumbly. Sprinkle over batter. Bake at 375 degrees for 40 to 45 minutes.

Dorothy E. Christiansen

CARROT CAKE

Serves: 12 to 16

2 cups sugar
4 eggs
1⅓ cups oil
2 cups sifted flour
¾ teaspoon salt

Icing:
1 8-ounce package cream
   cheese, softened
½ cup margarine, softened

2 teaspoons baking powder
2 teaspoons baking soda
2 teaspoons cinnamon
4 cups grated carrots
¾ cup broken nuts

1 16-ounce package
   confectioners' sugar
1 teaspoon vanilla

Beat sugar and eggs until thick and pale in color. Stir in oil. Sift dry ingredients, then add to egg mixture. Fold in carrots and nuts. Grease and flour a 9 x 13 inch pan. Bake at 350 degrees for 35 to 40 minutes. Test center with a toothpick for doneness.
Icing:
Beat all ingredients until creamy (1 or 2 minutes). Spread on cake. Refrigerate cake after it is frosted. Remove shortly before serving.

Bev and Dick Schultz

DELICIOUS CAKE

Serves: 12 to 16

1 box yellow Jiffy cake mix
1 3½-ounce package instant
   vanilla pudding
2 cups cold milk
1 8-ounce package cream
   cheese, softened

1 20-ounce can crushed
   pineapple, drained
1 16-ounce container Cool Whip
chopped walnuts (optional)

Prepare cake mix according to package directions. Pour into greased and floured 9 x 13 inch baking pan. Bake at 350 degrees for 20 minutes. Mix pudding and milk. Beat until very thick. Add cream cheese and beat until very thick. Spread mixture over cooled cake. Top with pineapple. Spread Cool Whip on top. Sprinkle with chopped nuts. Refrigerate 2 to 3 hours before serving.

Sheila and Bob Pasquantonio

MOM'S PINEAPPLE CAKE
(For an old-fashioned treat)

Serves: 12 to 16

2 cups sugar
2 eggs
1 teaspoon vanilla
2 teaspoons baking soda
1 teaspoon salt

2 cups flour
1 20-ounce can crushed
   pineapple, undrained
½ cup chopped nuts

Cream sugar and eggs. Add vanilla. Gradually add dry ingredients. Fold in pineapple and nuts. Pour into a greased and floured 9 x 13 inch pan. Bake at 350 degrees for 35 minutes.

Millie McCathren

Short one egg? In a cake recipe calling for two eggs or more, substitute two tablespoons of mayonnaise for the missing egg. You'll never know the difference.

PINEAPPLE UPSIDE DOWN CAKE

Serves: 8

½ cup shortening
1 cup sugar
3 eggs, well beaten
2 cups sifted flour
3 teaspoons baking powder
½ teaspoon salt
⅔ cup milk
1 teaspoon vanilla

butter
1 cup brown sugar
8 slices pineapple, rinsed
8 teaspoons pineapple juice
4 teaspoons butter
8 maraschino cherries
walnut meats

Cream shortening and sugar. Add eggs. Sift together flour, baking powder and salt. Add to creamed mixture alternately with milk. Add vanilla and mix well. Grease a pudding pan or heavy skillet generously with butter and line with brown sugar. In the pan, place pineapple slices. In the center of each, place a teaspoon of pineapple juice and ½ teaspoon butter along with a cherry. If desired place walnut meats around pineapple slices. Pour cake batter over mixture in pan. Bake at 350 degrees for 45 minutes. When done, turn upside down, but do not remove from pan for a minute so as to allow butterscotch mixture to run down over cake instead of clinging to the pan.

Millie McCathren

When your child is in the in-between stage, too small for the tub but too big for the baby-tub, try this. Fill the tub with water. Place a plastic laundry basket with holes in the tub, and your child in the basket. Your child will be able to play in the tub and feel secure.

PINEAPPLE ICEBOX CAKE

Serves: 20 to 24

angel food cake
2 cups milk
1 cup sugar
2 egg yolks, beaten
1 3-ounce package lemon Jello

1 20-ounce can crushed
  pineapple
2 egg whites
1 cup heavy cream
shredded coconut

Cook milk, sugar and egg yolks to boiling. Pour into lemon Jello. Stir until Jello dissolves. Let it set in the refrigerator until thickened. Pour the pineapple and half the pineapple juice into the Jello mixture. Beat egg whites until stiff. Add heavy cream and whip. Stir into Jello and pineapple mixture. Cut angel food cake into slices. Use half of the slices to line a 9 x 13 inch pan. Spread half the liquid mixture on cake slices. Repeat. Cover with shredded coconut. Refrigerate overnight.

NOTE: This cake must be made a day ahead of time. The recipe can be cut in half.

Mary Ellen Weaver

PUMPKIN CAKE
(Nice alternative to pumpkin pie)

Serves: 12 to 16

1 package yellow cake mix
1 egg, beaten
½ cup margarine, melted
1 16-ounce can pumpkin
3 eggs, beaten

⅔ cup milk
½ cup brown sugar
2 teaspoons cinnamon
¼ cup margarine, softened
½ cup sugar

Reserve 1 cup cake mix. Mix remaining cake mix with 1 egg and melted margarine. Press into bottom of 9 x 13 inch pan. Mix pumpkin with eggs, milk, brown sugar and cinnamon. Pour on top of cake mixture. Mix reserved cake mix with margarine and sugar. Cut with pastry blender. Sprinkle on top of cake. Bake at 350 degrees for 45 to 50 minutes.

Loretta Lucas

PUMPKIN CRUNCH

Serves: 12 to 16

Pumpkin Mixture:
3 eggs, beaten
1 16-ounce can pumpkin
1 5.3-ounce can evaporated milk

Topping:
1 package Pillsbury Yellow
 Pudding Cake Mix

1 cup sugar
1 teaspoon nutmeg
1 teaspoon cinnamon
1 teaspoon cloves

1 cup margarine or butter, melted
1 cup nuts, chopped

Pumpkin Mixture:
Mix all ingredients together. Grease and flour a 9 x 13 inch pan. Pour batter into pan.

Topping:
Mix all topping ingredients together. Sprinkle topping on top of pumpkin mixture. Bake at 350 degrees for 50 to 60 minutes.

Sheila and Bob Pasquantonio

ZUCCHINI CAKE

Serves: 12

3 eggs
1 cup oil
2 teaspoons almond flavoring
2 cups grated zucchini
2 cups sugar
½ teaspoon cinnamon

½ teaspoon nutmeg
½ teaspoon salt
2 teaspoons baking soda
3½ cups flour
1 cup raisins
1 cup nuts, chopped

Mix eggs, oil and almond flavoring. Add zucchini and sugar. Mix dry ingredients together. Add dry ingredients to egg mixture. Add raisins and nuts. Place in greased and floured 10-inch tube pan. Bake at 350 degrees for 75 minutes.

Loretta Lucas

For a quick and easy topping for cakes try this: First, save and freeze the syrup from canned fruit. Take from the freezer, add 1 tablespoon butter, 1 tablespoon lemon juice to 2 cups of syrup. Heat until bubbly. Add 2 tablespoons flour to help thicken the topping. This is particularly good for gingerbreads or coffeecakes.

PINA COLADA CAKE

Cake:
1 3½-ounce package coconut
  cream instant pudding
1 package Pillsbury Plus white
  cake mix

½ cup Bacardi Rum (dark)
4 eggs
½ cup water
¼ cup oil
1 cup flaked coconut

Icing:
1 8½-ounce can crushed
  pineapple with juice
⅓ cup dark rum

1 3½-ounce package coconut
  cream instant pudding
1 8-ounce container Cool Whip

Cake:

Mix all ingredients except coconut in large bowl. Beat 4 minutes on medium speed. Grease and flour 2 9-inch round cake pans. Pour batter into pans. Bake at 350 degrees for 25 to 30 minutes. Remove from oven. Cool in pans for 15 minutes, then remove and cool on racks.

Icing:

Combine pineapple, rum and pudding until well blended. Fold in whipped topping.

Frost cake. Sprinkle with coconut and chill. Keep cake refrigerated after frosting.

Judy Tulley

BISHOP'S CAKE
(Pound cake with a touch of almond flavor)

Serves: 12

1 cup butter, softened
2 cups sugar
5 eggs

2 cups cake flour
1 teaspoon vanilla
1 teaspoon almond flavoring

Cream butter and sugar until smooth. Alternately, add eggs and flour. Beat after each addition. Add vanilla and flavoring. Mix thoroughly. Place in greased and floured 10-inch tube pan. Bake at 325 degrees for 1 hour and 15 minutes.

Betty Douglass Campbell

ME-MAW'S COUNTRY POUND CAKE

Serves: 12 to 16

1 cup butter, softened
½ cup shortening
3 cups sugar
1 cup milk
1 teaspoon vanilla

1 teaspoon lemon extract
5 eggs
3 cups flour
1 teaspoon baking powder

Glaze:
1 cup confectioners' sugar

orange juice

Cream butter and shortening. Gradually add the sugar. Add the vanilla and the lemon extract to the milk. Put half the milk mixture into the creamed mixture. Add eggs, one at a time, beating after each addition. Blend in the flour and baking powder until the batter is smooth. Add the remainder of the milk. Blend well. Pour into a greased and floured 10-inch tube pan. Bake at 350 degrees for 1 hour and 20 minutes.

Glaze:
Blend confectioners' sugar with enough orange juice to make a syrup. Pour over warm cake.

Maude "Me-maw" Holliday

GOLDEN POUND CAKE

Yields: 1 loaf

1 cup shortening
1⅓ cups sugar
5 eggs
1½ tablespoons lemon juice

½ teaspoon almond extract
2 cups cake flour
½ teaspoon salt

Slowly cream shortening and sugar. Add eggs one at a time. Beat well after each egg. Add lemon juice and almond; beat well. Add sifted dry ingredients. Line 5 x 10 inch loaf pan with waxed paper. Bake at 325 degrees for 70 minutes (300 degrees if using Pyrex).

NOTE: If using large eggs, it may take 10 to 20 minutes longer to bake.

Fern Jagger

CRUMB CAKE

Serves: 8

2½ cups flour
½ cup butter, softened
2 cups brown sugar
1 egg

¾ cup sour milk
1 teaspoon baking soda
1 teaspoon cinnamon

Mix together flour, butter and brown sugar. Reserve ¾ cup of mixture for topping. To the remainder add egg, sour milk, baking soda, and cinnamon. Beat until creamy. Pour into a greased 9-inch round pan. Sprinkle reserved crumbs on top. Bake at 350 degrees for 25 to 30 minutes.

Millie McCathren

SOUR CREAM CAKE
(An old time, well tried favorite)

Serves: 12

1 cup butter or margarine,
  softened
2 cups sugar
2 eggs
½ teaspoon vanilla

2 cups flour
½ teaspoon salt
1 teaspoon baking powder
1 cup sour cream

Cream butter and sugar. Add eggs and vanilla. Alternately add dry ingredients and sour cream. Grease and flour bundt pan. Bake at 350 degrees for 1 hour. Immediately remove from pan.

Judith Diehl

SOUR CREAM COFFEE CAKE

Serves: 9

2 eggs
¾ cup sour cream
2 cups yellow cake mix

1 7½-ounce dry frosting mix,
  pecan, almond or coconut
  flavor
2 tablespoons margarine

Combine eggs, sour cream and cake mix. Spread half in bottom of greased and floured 8 x 8 inch pan. Sprinkle 1 cup dry frosting over batter. Repeat layers until batter and frosting are gone. Dot with margarine. Bake at 350 degrees for 30 minutes.

Ruth Miller

SUGAR CREAM CAKE
(For those with a sweet tooth)

Serves: 12

1 package yellow cake mix
4 eggs
½ cup butter or margarine,
   melted

1 8-ounce package cream
   cheese, softened
1 pound confectioners' sugar
nutmeg

Beat together cake mix, 2 eggs and butter. Pour into a greased and floured
9 x 13 inch pan. Mix 2 eggs, cream cheese and confectioners' sugar.
Spread on top of cake mixture. Sprinkle with nutmeg. Bake at 350 degrees
for 35 to 40 minutes.

Millie McCathren

MORAVIAN SUGAR CAKE
(Light cake)

Serves: 36

2 packages active dry yeast
½ cup lukewarm water
½ cup lukewarm milk (scalded,
   then cooled)
¾ cup unseasoned lukewarm
   mashed potatoes
½ cup sugar

½ cup margarine, softened
2 eggs
1 ¼ teaspoons salt
4 ½ cups flour
butter
brown sugar
cinnamon

Dissolve yeast in warm water. Stir in milk, potatoes, sugar, margarine, eggs,
and salt. Add 2½ cups flour. Beat until smooth. Mix in remaining flour to
form soft dough. Turn onto lightly floured board. Knead until smooth and
elastic, about 5 minutes. Place in greased bowl. Cover. Let rise in warm
place until double, about 1½ hours. Punch down. Spread out evenly into 3
greased 9-inch round cake pans or 1 large greased cookie sheet. Allow to
rise for 30 to 45 minutes. Form holes or deep depressions into the dough
spaced at 1 inch intervals. Fill holes with liberal quantities of butter and
brown sugar. Dust with cinnamon. Bake at 375 degrees for 20 minutes or
until golden brown.

Mary Ellen Weaver

APPLESAUCE FRUIT CAKE

Yields: 2 loaves

1 pound mixed fruit
1 cup white raisins
brandy or rum (optional)
2 teaspoons baking soda
1 cup sour milk or buttermilk
2 cups unsweetened applesauce,
  warmed
¾ cup butter, softened

3 cups flour
1 tablespoon cocoa
1 cup walnuts
1 teaspoon cinnamon
1 teaspoon cloves
1 teaspoon allspice
1 teaspoon nutmeg

Soak fruit in brandy or rum (optional). Add baking soda to milk. Let stand for a few minutes. Warm applesauce; add butter. Sift flour and cocoa. Dredge fruit, raisins and nuts in dry mixture. Add spices to dry ingredients. Add sugar to applesauce. Alternately add milk and dry ingredients to applesauce mixture. Add fruit. Pour batter into 2 greased and floured 5 x 9 inch loaf pans. Bake at 300 degrees for 1½ hours. Test for doneness.

Gerri Bartelme

CHRISTMAS FRUIT CAKE
(For those who generally don't like fruit cakes)

Yields: 1 loaf

12 ounces dates, cut lengthwise
8 ounces green and yellow
  pineapple, cut
8 ounces whole red and green
  cherries
1 cup unsifted flour

1 teaspoon baking powder
¼ teaspoon salt
2 large eggs
½ cup sugar
1 pound walnuts and pecans,
  mixed

Combine the fruits and set aside. Stir baking powder and salt into flour. Sift over the fruit and stir gently. Beat eggs well, gradually adding sugar and beating again. Pour over fruit and flour mixture, mixing well. Add walnuts and pecans, mixing with hands until everything is coated. Grease 5 x 9 inch loaf pan, then line with brown paper, lightly greasing the paper. Pack firmly into loaf pan. Bake at 275 degrees for 1½ hours. Top should look dry, but not brown. After cooling 30 minutes, remove from pan and peel paper off.

NOTE: If the cake has been overbaked, wrap in a damp towel, then cover with plastic wrap to keep moist.

Bev and Dick Schultz

MINIATURE RUM FRUIT CAKES

Yields: 50

2 cups sugar
1 cup butter, softened
1 teaspoon ground cloves
2 cups applesauce
2 teaspoons cinnamon
1 teaspoon allspice
1 teaspoon nutmeg
2 teaspoons baking soda

2 eggs
3½ cups flour
½ cup nuts, chopped
2 cups raisins
1 cup dates, chopped
2 cups candied fruit
1 cup rum

Cream sugar and butter. Stir in remaining ingredients. Pour into greased and floured miniature cup cake tins. Bake at 350 degrees for 7 to 10 minutes.

Elizabeth Pasquantonio

WHITE FRUIT CAKE

Serves: 16

½ cup butter, softened
1 cup sugar
2 cups sifted cake flour
½ teaspoon salt
½ teaspoon baking powder
6 egg whites

½ cup slivered almonds
½ pound shredded coconut
1 cup candied cherries
½ cup candied pineapple
1 cup candied mix (citron, orange
      peel and lemon peel)

Cream butter and sugar. Sift flour 3 times with salt and baking powder. Beat egg whites until dry. Fold in flour gently. Fold in nuts and fruit. Pour into ungreased 10-inch tube pan. Bake at 350 degrees for 1½ hours. Invert pan to cool and remove cake when it is cooled.

NOTE: Can be made in 4 small pans to make 1 pound cakes to be used as gifts.

Doris S. DePierre

To soften brown sugar, dampen a piece of paper towel. Put it inside the lid of your brown sugar container, and close the lid.

MAPLE CREAM CHEESE ICING

¼ cup margarine, softened
2 3-ounce packages cream
  cheese, softened

4⅓ cups confectioners' sugar,
  sifted
1 teaspoon vanilla
1 teaspoon maple flavoring

In small mixing bowl, blend margarine and cream cheese. Gradually add confectioners' sugar · continually beating until smooth and creamy. Stir in vanilla and maple flavoring.

NOTE: Great on carrot cake.

Teresa Meyer

7-MINUTE ICING

1 cup sugar
¼ teaspoon salt
½ teaspoon cream of tartar

2 egg whites
3 tablespoons water
1 teaspoon vanilla

Blend all ingredients, except vanilla, in top of double boiler. Place over boiling water. Beat constantly with electric beater until icing stands in peaks (5 to 7 minutes). Remove from heat. Add vanilla. Beat until thick.

Maude Holliday

WHIPPED FLUFFY ICING

1 cup milk
2 tablespoons flour or cornstarch
½ cup shortening

½ cup margarine, softened
1 cup sugar
1 teaspoon vanilla

Stir flour into milk. Cook over medium heat until mixture is thick like a pudding. Cool. Cream shortening, margarine, and sugar until sugar dissolves. Add creamed mixture to pudding mixture. Add vanilla. Beat well.

NOTE: This can be tinted with food coloring or 2 to 3 squares of melted chocolate can be added.

Teresa Meyer

BIRTHDAY CAKE ICING

1 3½-ounce package instant
  French vanilla pudding
1 cup milk
1 cup unsalted butter, softened
½ teaspoon vanilla

1 ¼ cup sugar
½ cup Cool Whip
1 18-ounce jar strawberry or
  raspberry preserves
2 9-inch round cake layers

Mix pudding and milk until thick. Add butter, ½ cup at a time. Beat well. Add vanilla. Gradually add sugar. Mix well. Stir in Cool Whip. With a piece of thread, cut each 9-inch round cake layer in half. Spread bottom quarter with ½ of the preserves. Top with second quarter. Cover with ½ of the icing. Repeat procedure to complete the top ½ of the cake.

NOTE: To be used on any yellow or white cake. Makes enough frosting to cover tops and sides of 2 9-inch round layers.

Jean Kmiecik

CREAM CHEESE ICING

1 8-ounce package cream
  cheese, softened
¼ cup margarine, softened

2 cups confectioners' sugar
1 teaspoon vanilla

Blend margarine and cream cheese in a small mixing bowl. Add confectioners' sugar and vanilla. Beat until smooth.

Phyllis Fox

Peanut Butter Playdough: Everybody scrub your hands! Take ½ jar of peanut butter and add powdered milk and honey until the consistency of playdough. Place on paper plates or waxed paper and let your children go to work. Your child might mold the dough into balls, snakes, snowmen, or a variety of other shapes. Provide some toothpicks and you'll immediately see some birthday cakes. This is a great opportunity to introduce some number concepts. With this playdough the children can munch as they play. Have their cake and eat it too?

STRAWBERRY ICING
(A Valentine's Day treat)

3 to 4 cups confectioners' sugar
2 tablespoons butter, softened
2 tablespoons shortening
1 to 2 teaspoons lemon juice

1 10-ounce package frozen
strawberries in syrup, thawed
3 to 4 tablespoons syrup from
the strawberries

In a mixing bowl, stir together confectioners' sugar, butter, shortening and lemon juice. Drain as much syrup from strawberries as possible using a strainer. Reserve juice. Blend ingredients in mixer adding strawberry syrup 1 tablespoon at a time. Beat well to a good spreading consistency. Add more confectioners' sugar if icing is too thin. If too thick, add more syrup. To assemble cake, frost the bottom layer leaving the icing thick in a 1 inch rim around the edge of the cake. Spoon drained strawberries onto the bottom layer, within the rim of icing. Place second layer on the first. Frost top and sides of cake. Frosts a 9-inch round layer cake or a heart shaped layer cake.

Dorothy Baker

MAPLE WALNUT ICING

3 cups confectioners' sugar
2 tablespoons butter, softened
2 tablespoons shortening
1 teaspoon vanilla

dash of salt
3 to 4 tablespoons maple syrup
1 cup chopped walnuts

In a mixing bowl, stir together confectioners' sugar, butter, shortening, vanilla and salt. Blend ingredients in mixer, adding maple syrup 1 tablespoon at a time. Beat well to a good spreading consistency. If icing is too thin, gradually add more confectioners' sugar. If too thick, add more syrup. When assembling cake, frost the bottom layer and sprinkle with ½ cup nuts. Place the second layer on the first, frost and sprinkle with remaining nuts. This icing is recommended for use on a 9-inch round golden yellow layer cake.

Dorothy Baker

Pies

Gary G. Boker

CHAPTER XII

Snow White's ... Pies

SNOW WHITE:
Mirror, mirror on the wall,
Which is fairest of them all?
Meringue or chiffon,
Apple or chess?

Mincemeat, lemon
or a pecan success?

Peach, grape, pear,
or
Deep dish cherry?

Pineapple, rhubarb,
or
Rare gooseberry?

MIRROR:
Any one is a slice of heaven,
As long as there is enough for seven!

Cook's Note: Sleepy, Sneezy, Dopey, Doc, Happy, Grumpy, and Bashful
have done our taste-testing here and their only recommen-
dation was that the cook double every recipe!

ALASKA MINT PIE
(More than refreshing)

Serves: 8

1 5-ounce package shortbread cookies, crushed (about 1⅓ cups)
½ cup pecans, finely chopped
⅓ cup light brown sugar, firmly packed
6 tablespoons butter or margarine, melted
½ cup water

10 tablespoons sugar
2 tablespoons green crème de menthe
1 quart vanilla ice cream, softened
½ cup whipping cream
few drops green food coloring
3 egg whites
⅛ teaspoon cream of tartar

Blend shortbread crumbs, pecans, brown sugar, and butter or margarine in a medium-sized bowl. Press mixture firmly over bottom and sides of a 9-inch pie plate. Bake at 325 degrees for 10 minutes or until set. Cool completely on a wire rack.

Combine water with 4 tablespoons of the sugar in a small saucepan. Cover and bring to boiling. Uncover. Continue boiling without stirring, 7 minutes. Remove from heat and cool slightly. Stir in crème de menthe. Cool completely.

Spread half the ice cream in an even layer in cooled pie shell. Cover; freeze until firm.

Combine cream with food coloring in a small bowl; beat until stiff. Fold in 2 tablespoons of cooled crème de menthe syrup into the cream. Spread evenly over firm ice cream in pie shell. Freeze until firm. Top with remaining ice cream. Freeze until firm. Pie may be wrapped in foil or plastic wrap and kept frozen for a week before a buffet.

Beat egg whites with cream of tartar until foamy-white and double in volume in a medium-size bowl. Beat in remaining 6 tablespoons sugar, 1 tablespoon at a time, until meringue stands in firm peaks. Pile meringue onto filling, sealing firmly to crust edge and swirling into peaks. Freeze overnight.

Just before serving, brown meringue until lightly golden at 450 degrees for 4 minutes. Drizzle with remaining crème de menthe syrup. Serve at once.

Gerri Bartelme

BOB'S FAVORITE CHOCOLATE PIE

Serves: 8 to 10

1 9-inch pie shell, baked
2 egg whites
¼ teaspoon salt
¼ teaspoon cinnamon
½ teaspoon vinegar
½ cup sugar

6 ounces chocolate bits
2 egg yolks
¼ cup water
1 package Dream Whip
milk
¼ teaspoon cinnamon

Beat together egg whites, salt, cinnamon and vinegar until fluffy. Add sugar gradually. Line the baked pie crust (top and sides) with the meringue, making a second crust. Bake in 325 degree oven for 15 minutes. In double boiler, melt chocolate bits. Add egg yolks and water. Cool slightly. Spread 3 tablespoons of mixture on meringue crust. Reserve remainder. Whip package of Dream Whip, adding milk as directed, and cinnamon. Spead ½ of this mixture on top of the 3 tablespoons of chocolate mixture. Fold remaining chocolate mixture into Dream Whip. Add to pie. Chill a few hours.

Dottie Pierson

CHOCOLATE ALMOND CREAM PIE
(Fit for a King!)

Serves: 8

Crust:
1 ½ cups graham cracker crumbs
  (18 crackers)

3 tablespoons sugar
½ cup butter, melted

Filling:
1 4½-ounce Hershey almond bar
20 large marshmallows

⅓ cup milk
1 cup whipping cream
1 teaspoon vanilla

Crust:

Mix graham cracker crumbs and sugar. Add melted butter and mix thoroughly. Save ¼ cup for topping, if desired. Press mixture into 9-inch pie pan, firmly and evenly. Bake at 350 degrees for 10 minutes. Cool.

Filling:

Combine Hershey bar, marshmallows and milk. Melt and stir until smooth and creamy. Cool. Whip cream and add vanilla. Add to cooled chocolate mixture. Pour into baked crust and chill several hours. Garnish with whipped cream when served.

Bonnie Emerick

CREAM CHEESE PIE

Serves: 8 to 10

Crust:
20 graham crackers, crushed

½ cup sugar
¼ cup butter, melted

Filling:
4 3-ounce packages cream
   cheese, softened
¾ cup sugar

2 eggs
pinch of salt
½ teaspoon vanilla

Topping:
1 cup sour cream

2 tablespoons sugar
½ teaspoon vanilla

Crust:
Mix together crushed crackers, sugar and butter. Press into 9-inch pie plate and chill.

Filling:
Beat together cream cheese, sugar, eggs, salt and vanilla. Pour into chilled crust. Bake at 350 degrees for 20 minutes. Cool 15 minutes.

Topping:
Spread topping on cooled pie. Bake at 450 degrees for 5 minutes. Cool, then chill.

Gerri Bartelme

AMISH VANILLA PIE
(From the heart of Pennsylvania)

Serves: 16

Crust:

2 9-inch pie shells, unbaked

Filling:
1 cup sugar
1 cup light molasses or ½ cup
   molasses and ½ cup honey

4 tablespoons flour
1 egg, beaten well
2 cups water
1 teaspoon vanilla

Topping:
2 cups flour
1 cup brown sugar
1 teaspoon cream of tartar

1 teaspoon baking soda
¼ cup butter or margarine
¼ cup shortening

Combine filling ingredients in saucepan and bring to a full, rolling boil. Set aside to cool. For crumb topping, combine flour, brown sugar, cream of tartar, and baking soda. Cut in butter or margarine and shortening. Pour half of the filling into each unbaked pie shell. Sprinkle ½ of the crumbs onto each pie. Bake at 350 degrees for 40 to 45 minutes.

Mary Ellen Weaver

217

FAIRY PIE

Serves: 8 to 10

Filling:
½ cup sugar
½ cup butter or margarine,
   softened

4 egg yolks
4 tablespoons milk
½ cup plus 2 tablespoons flour
1 teaspoon baking powder

Meringue:
4 egg whites
1 cup sugar

1 teaspoon vanilla
½ cup chopped nuts

Topping:
1 8-ounce can crushed pineapple,
   drained

½ pint container whipping cream

Filling:
Cream sugar and butter or margarine. Beat egg yolks. Add ½ cup flour and milk alternately. Mix 2 tablespoons flour and baking powder. Add to mixture. Set aside.

Meringue:
Beat egg whites very stiff. Stir in sugar, vanilla and chopped nuts.

Procedure:
Divide filling between two 8-inch cake pans. Spread evenly. Divide meringue and spread over first mixture in each pan. Bake at 350 degrees for 20 to 25 minutes. Stir drained pineapple into small container of whipped whipping cream. Spread between cake layers and use as topping.

Gerri Bartelme

PEANUT BUTTER PIE
(Very rich, very good!)

Serves: 8

⅔ cup powdered sugar
4 ounces cream cheese
⅔ cup chunky peanut butter

1 8-ounce container Cool Whip
1 graham cracker crust

Blend sugar and cream cheese. Add peanut butter and Cool Whip. Whip with mixer until smooth. Pour into crust. Chill.

Nancy McCloskey

COCONUT PIE
(For those unexpected guests)

Serves: 8

¼ cup margarine, softened
¾ cup sugar
2 cups milk
½ cup Bisquick

½ teaspoon salt
1 cup coconut (angel flakes)
1 teaspoon vanilla
4 eggs

Put all ingredients in blender, and mix for 1 minute. Pour into 1 greased 9-inch pie pan. Bake at 350 degrees for 40 minutes.

Margaret Getz

PECAN PIE

Serves: 8

3 eggs
¾ cup sugar
1 cup honey
2 tablespoons butter, melted
2 teaspoons vanilla

1 teaspoon salt
2 cups pecan halves (option: can
   be chopped)
1 9-inch pie shell, unbaked

Beat eggs. Add sugar, honey, butter, vanilla, and salt. Mix well. Place pecans in pie shell. Pour mixture on top of pecans. Gently stir pecans. Bake at 350 degrees for 50 minutes. Serve with whipped cream.

Bill Kasavage

PUMPKIN PIE
(For a large family get-together)

Yields: 3 pies

3 9-inch pie shells, unbaked
3 cups fresh pumpkin
1½ cups sugar
1 teaspoon salt
1½ teaspoons ginger
2 teaspoons cinnamon

½ teaspoon nutmeg
½ teaspoon cloves
6 eggs
2½ cups milk
1 13-ounce can evaporated milk

Combine pumpkin, sugar, salt and spices. Add eggs, milk and canned milk. Pour into 3 9-inch unbaked pie shells. Bake in 400 degree oven for 50 minutes.

Doe Clark

SHOO-FLY PIE (Dry)
(A Pennsylvania Dutch coffee cake)

Serves: 16

Crust:
2 9-inch, single pie shells,
   unbaked

Crumbs:
4 cups flour
2 cups brown sugar

1 tablespoon cinnamon
   (optional)
1 cup butter or margarine,
   softened

Liquid:
1 cup boiling water

¾ cup molasses
1 teaspoon baking soda

Mix flour, brown sugar and cinnamon. Cut in butter or margarine until crumbly. Mix boiling water, molasses and baking soda. Alternate layers of crumbs and liquid in pie crust, ending with crumbs. Bake at 350 degrees for 45 minutes.

NOTE: This is a Pennsylvania Dutch idea for coffee cake - not a dinner dessert. Wonderful with coffee or milk. A treat for your family.

Judith Diehl

SOUTHERN PECAN PIE

Serves: 8

1 9-inch pie shell, unbaked
5 eggs
1 cup sugar
6 tablespoons butter or
   margarine, melted

1½ cups corn syrup
½ teaspoon salt
1½ teaspoons vanilla
1½ cups chopped pecans
16 pecan halves for garnish

Beat eggs. Add sugar and beat until well blended. Add butter, corn syrup, salt, vanilla, and chopped pecans and mix thoroughly. Pour into unbaked pie shell. Bake at 350 degrees for 1 hour and 15 minutes. When done, garnish with pecan halves.

Gladys Douglas

APPLE PIE
(Try it with a slab of cheddar cheese)

Serves: 8

Crust:

1 ⅓ cups sifted flour
½ teaspoon salt

½ cup shortening
3 tablespoons water

Filling:
9 apples, cored, peeled, sliced
thin (McIntosh are excellent!)
½ teaspoon salt

1 cup sugar
2 teaspoons cinnamon
3 teaspoons butter

Bottom Crust:
Combine flour and salt. Cut in shortening with pastry blender or 2 knives. Gradually stir in water. Mixture should be coarse. Work mixture into a firm ball with your hands. Press it into a flat circle. Ease dough into a 9-inch pie plate, allowing some loose edges for sealing top crust later.

Filling:
Arrange apples in pie crust. Sprinkle with salt, sugar and cinnamon. Dot with butter, 5 or 6 pieces.

Top Crust:
Make a second crust following same instructions as bottom crust. Roll out dough and cover apples. Seal to bottom crust and flute edges with fingers or a fork. With a fork, poke holes in the top crust 8 or 9 times. Bake at 350 degrees for 1¼ hours. Cool before cutting.

Monica and Stu Hall

FRENCH SILK CHOCOLATE PIE

Serves: 8

½ cup margarine, softened
¾ cup sugar
2 squares unsweetened
chocolate, melted and cooled

1 teaspoon vanilla
2 eggs
1 8-inch pastry shell
whipped cream

In mixer bowl, cream margarine. Gradually add sugar, creaming until light. Blend in chocolate and vanilla. Add the eggs, one at a time, beating 3 minutes after each addition. (Use the medium speed on an electric mixer.) Turn into pastry shell. Chill for several hours. Garnish with whipped cream and chocolate curls, if desired.

Teresa Meyer

ELEGANT APRICOT PIE

Serves: 8

Crust:
1 ¼ cups graham cracker crumbs
   (18 squares)

¼ cup sugar
6 tablespoons butter or
   margarine, melted

Filling:
1 cup dried apricots
1 cup water

⅔ cup sugar
1 cup Ricotta cheese
1 teaspoon vanilla

Topping:
½ cup whipping cream
1 tablespoon confectioners' sugar

½ teaspoon vanilla
snipped dried apricots, optional

Crust:
Stir together cracker crumbs and sugar. Stir in melted butter or margarine until moistened. Press crumbs into 8-inch pie plate and chill 1 hour.

Filling:
Combine the apricots and water and bring to boiling. Cook apricots covered, over low heat for 5 minutes or until tender. Add sugar to apricots. Simmer uncovered about 5 minutes or until slightly thickened, then cool. Place apricot mixture, Ricotta cheese, and vanilla into food processor or blender. Process mixture until smooth. Spread mixture in crust. Chill several hours.

Topping:
Just before serving, beat cream. Add confectioners' sugar and vanilla. Pipe or spoon a whipped cream border on top of the filling. If desired, garnish with snipped dried apricots.

Sherry Wilson

An apple has two "surprises" inside: If you cut through from the stem to the blossom end, you will find a heart in the middle. If you cut crosswise, you will find a star.

NO-ROLL CHERRY PIE

Serves: 8

Crust:
½ cup butter or margarine
1 teaspoon sugar
1 cup flour

Topping:
1 egg
½ cup sugar

1 21-ounce can cherry pie filling
(apricot or apple pie filling may
be used)

¼ cup flour
¼ cup milk

Crust:
Melt butter with sugar over low heat. Add flour until mix forms a soft ball. Press into pie plate. Pour pie filling into crust.

Topping:
Beat egg. Add sugar, flour, and milk. Mix well with mixer. Spoon over filling. Bake in 350 degree oven for 50 to 60 minutes until golden brown.

Debbie and Frank McKenna

CURRANT PIE

(Kitchen farm recipe, where currants have to be picked
before the birds get them)

Serves: 8

Crust:

Filling:
3 egg yolks
4 tablespoons water

Meringue:
3 egg whites
6 tablespoons sugar

1 9-inch pie shell, unbaked

2 tablespoons flour
1 cup sugar
1 ½ cups fresh currants

¼ teaspoon cream of tartar
½ teaspoon vanilla

Filling:
Beat egg yolks. Add water, flour, sugar and currants. Stir and pour into pie shell. Bake at 375 degrees for 40 minutes. Remove from oven and prepare meringue.

Meringue:
Beat egg whites until stiff. Gradually add sugar, cream of tartar and vanilla. Cover baked pie with meringue. Bake at 375 degrees for 10 minutes or until brown.

Nancy Latshaw

LEMON MERINGUE PIE
(Tart and refreshing)

Serves: 8

Crust: 1 9-inch pie shell, baked

Filling: 3 tablespoons cold water
1 cup sugar   6 tablespoons lemon juice
1¼ cups water   1 teaspoon grated lemon rind
1 tablespoon butter   3 egg yolks
¼ cup cornstarch   2 tablespoons milk

Meringue: 6 tablespoons sugar
3 egg whites   1 teaspoon vanilla
¼ teaspoon salt

Filling:
Combine sugar, 1¼ cups water and butter. Heat until sugar dissolves. Blend cornstarch with 3 tablespoons water. Gradually add to sugar, water, butter mixture. Cook slowly, stirring constantly until clear, about 8 minutes. Add lemon juice and rind. Cook 2 minutes. Slowly add egg yolks beaten with milk. Bring to boiling. Cool. Pour into baked pie shell.

Meringue:
Add salt to egg whites. Beat to a stiff foam. Add sugar - one tablespoon at a time. Stir in vanilla. Continue beating until mixture forms moist, lustrous peaks. Spread over cooled filling, sealing to edge of crust. Bake at 350 degrees for 12 to 15 minutes.

Fern Jagger

CREAMY PEACH PIE

Serves: 8

1 9-inch pie shell, unbaked   2 eggs, beaten
2 to 2½ cups fresh peaches,   ¼ teaspoon salt
  sliced   2 tablespoons butter
1 cup sugar   1 teaspoon cinnamon
1 tablespoon flour

Place peaches in pie crust. Mix sugar, flour, eggs and salt. Pour mixture over peaches. Dot with butter. Sprinkle with cinnamon. Bake at 450 degrees for 15 minutes, then turn oven down to 350 degrees for 30 minutes.

Sally Joiner

FRESH PEACH CHIFFON PIE
(The fresher the peaches, the better)

Serves: 8

Crust:
1 cup crushed cornflakes
  (graham crackers or vanilla
  wafers may be used)

Filling:
2¼ cups chopped, fresh peaches
¾ cup sugar, scant
1 tablespoon unflavored gelatin
¼ cup cold water

¼ cup sugar
⅓ cup butter or margarine,
  melted

½ cup hot water
1 tablespoon lemon juice
dash of salt
½ cup heavy cream, whipped

Crust:
Roll cornflakes until well crushed. Add sugar and melted butter or margarine. Press firmly in 9-inch pie plate. Chill.

Filling:
Peel and chop fresh peaches. Add sugar and allow to stand for ½ hour. Soften gelatin in cold water. Add hot water and cool. Add peaches, lemon juice, and salt. Chill until partially set. Fold whipped cream into peach mixture. Pour into chilled crust.

Ada Bates

PATTY'S PEACH PIE

Serves: 6 to 8

Crust:
¾ cup flour
½ teaspoon salt
3 tablespoons butter, softened
1 teaspoon baking powder

Topping:
1 8-ounce package cream
  cheese, softened

1 3½-ounce package instant
  vanilla pudding
1 egg
½ cup milk
2 cups peaches, drained (reserve
  juice)

½ cup sugar
3 tablespoons peach juice

Crust:
Mix all ingredients except the peaches. Beat together for two minutes. Press into a 9-inch pie pan. Drain peaches well. Lay peaches on top of crust.

Topping:
Mix topping ingredients together well. Pour over peaches. Sprinkle with sugar. Bake at 350 degrees for 35 minutes.

Pat Smetanka
225

FRESH STRAWBERRY CHEESE PIE
(The dwarfs' favorite)

Serves: 8

Crust: 1 8-inch pie shell, lightly baked

Filling:
1 8-ounce package cream
  cheese, softened
2 eggs

2 tablespoons lemon juice
½ cup sugar
1 quart fresh strawberries, clean
  and reserve 1 cup for glaze

Glaze:
1 cup small strawberries
¾ cup cold water

1 cup sugar
3 level tablespoons cornstarch
1 tablespoon lemon juice

Filling:
Beat cream cheese; add eggs, lemon juice and sugar. Beat until smooth. Pour into shell and bake at 350 degrees for 20 to 25 minutes. Cool on a cake rack. Filling does not need to be set in center. Arrange whole fresh strawberries on cooled filling.

Glaze:
Place small berries in saucepan. Add cold water and cook to a boil. Mix sugar and cornstarch, add to boiling water and simmer. Stir 5 minutes or until mixture is clear. Remove from heat and add lemon juice. Cover pie with hot glaze. Refrigerate. Garnish with whipped cream when serving.

Nancy McCloskey

STRAWBERRY CHIFFON PIE

Serves: 6 to 8

1 9-inch pie shell, baked
1 cup crushed strawberries
1 cup sugar
1 package unflavored gelatin
¼ cup cold water

¼ teaspoon salt
½ cup hot water
1 tablespoon lemon juice
2 egg whites, stiffly beaten
½ cup heavy cream, whipped

Add sugar to strawberries and let stand for ½ hour. Soften gelatin in cold water. Add gelatin mixture and salt to hot water. Stir until dissolved. Add gelatin to strawberry mixture with lemon juice. Refrigerate until it begins to set. Fold in beaten egg whites. Fold in whipped heavy cream. Pour into baked pie shell and refrigerate.

Barbara Cooledge

EIGHT-MINUTE LIGHT 'N FRUITY PIE

Serves: 8

Crust: 1 8 or 9-inch graham cracker pie
            shell

Filling: 2 cups ice cubes
1 3-ounce package Jello, any   1 8-ounce package Cool Whip
   flavor   *fruit (type optional)
⅔ cup boiling water

Completely dissolve Jello in boiling water. Stir about 3 minutes. Add ice cubes and stir constantly until gelatin is thickened, 2 to 3 minutes. Remove any unmelted ice. Using wire whip, blend in whipped topping and whip until smooth. Fold in fruit. Chill, if necessary, until mixture will mound. Spoon into pie crust. Chill 3 hours, until firm.

*Suggested fruits:
1 cup diced, peeled fresh peaches or apricots
1 cup fresh raspberries or blueberries
1 cup diced orange sections or fresh strawberries or bananas
1 8¾-ounce can apricots, sliced peaches, or fruit cocktail, drained
1 8¼-ounce can crushed pineapple, drained.

Eileen Joll

NANA'S PIE CRUST
(Roll thin for a better crust)

Yields: 2 8-inch double-crusts

2 cups flour   1 teaspoon salt
1 cup butter   ½ cup ice cold water

Cut butter into the flour with a knife until the mixture is the size of small peas. Add salt. Gradually mix in water with a fork. Handle as little as possible. Form into a ball. Wrap in waxed paper. Refrigerate for 1 hour before rolling.

Dorothy E. Christiansen

NEVER-FAIL PIE CRUST

Yields: 1 9-inch double crust

2¼ cups flour
2 tablespoons sugar
¼ teaspoon salt

1 cup margarine, cold
2 tablespoons plus 2 teaspoons
ice water

Sift flour, sugar and salt. Cut margarine into ⅔ of flour mixture until well blended. Add remaining flour. When light and flaky, add ice water. Handle as little as possible. Chill before rolling out.

Bev and Dick Schultz

PASTRY
(From Snow White's kitchen)

Yields: 6 8-inch single crusts or
3 8-inch double crusts

4 cups flour
½ teaspoon salt
1 teaspoon baking powder
1 tablespoon sugar

2 cups shortening
1 egg
½ cup cold water
1 teaspoon white vinegar

Sift together flour, salt, baking powder, and sugar. Cut shortening into flour mixture with fork or pastry blender until size of peas. Mix together egg, water and vinegar. Add to flour mixture, mixing with a fork. Roll out on well-floured surface.

Eleanor Towers

 The next time you are making pie crust, give a few scraps of dough to your children and allow them to pound, roll, and cut to their heart's content. Then you can get that pie into the oven!

Desserts

Gary G. Baker

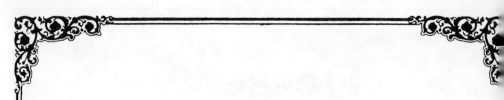

CHAPTER XIII

Hansel and Gretel's ... Desserts

This witch will get her just desserts
For not treating those babes as she should!

Give her blueberry buckle
And raspberry dream,
Peppermint pudding
And Bavarian cream,
Artificial beans vanilla
All washed down with sarsaparilla

Then dribble on another cup
Of hot fudge and **make her eat it up!**

A trembly tummy and a sweet tooth that hurts,
Will help her learn to be good!

Cook's Note: A dessert smorgasbord may be a tempting idea, but any
one of these will exercise the golden rule quite nicely.

BAVARIAN APPLE TORTE
(A "honey" of a dessert)

Serves: 8

4 to 5 Golden Delicious apples (4 cups)
1/3 cup sugar
6 tablespoons butter, softened
1/8 teaspoon salt
1/4 teaspoon vanilla
1 cup flour
1 8-ounce package cream cheese, softened

3 tablespoons honey
1 egg
1/2 teaspoon grated lemon rind
1/4 teaspoon vanilla
1/8 teaspoon salt
2 tablespoons sugar
cinnamon
almonds

Peel, core and slice apples to measure 4 cups. Turn into a shallow pan. Cover with foil and bake at 400 degrees for 15 minutes. In a mixing bowl, cream 1/3 cup sugar, butter, 1/8 teaspoon salt and 1/4 teaspoon vanilla. Blend in flour. Pat pastry mixture onto bottom and up the sides of a lightly greased 10-inch spring form pan. In a separate bowl, beat cream cheese with honey until creamy. Beat in egg, lemon rind, 1/4 teaspoon vanilla and 1/8 teaspoon salt until smooth. Pour cream cheese filling into pastry lined pan. Top with warm, partially cooked apple slices. Sprinkle with 2 tablespoons sugar mixed with cinnamon. Sprinkle almonds on top. Set pan on baking sheet. Bake at 400 degrees for 40 minutes, until apples are soft and crust is set. Cool before cutting.

Nancy Latshaw

ALICE'S CHERRY DESSERT

Serves: 10 to 12

1 3/4 cups shredded coconut
1/2 cup sugar
1/2 cup butter, melted
1 1/2 cups sifted flour
1 cup sugar

3 tablespoons cornstarch
1 1/2 cups juice from cherries
2 16-ounce cans sour cherries
a few drops red coloring
(optional)

Blend together coconut, 1/2 cup sugar, melted butter, and flour. In a large saucepan, mix 1 cup sugar, cornstarch, and cherry juice. Cook over medium heat, stirring constantly until thickened. Allow to cool. Stir in cherries and red coloring. Place 1/2 of dough in buttered 9 x 13 inch pan. Cover with cherry mixture. Add remaining dough. Bake at 400 degrees for 30 minutes.

Fern Jagger

CHERRY DELIGHT

Serves: 10

1 14-ounce can sweetened
  condensed milk
1 20-ounce can crushed
  pineapple, drained

1 8-ounce container Cool Whip or
  substitute topping
1 21-ounce can Thank You brand
  cherries
½ cup chopped walnuts

Mix together milk, pineapple, and Cool Whip. Add cherries and nuts. Mix thoroughly. Pour into a 9 x 9 inch square pan. Chill overnight.

Bill Kasavage

QUICK COBBLER
(A favorite recipe from grandmother)

Serves: 12 to 16

½ cup margarine
1 cup sugar
1 cup flour

3 teaspoons baking powder
1 cup milk
1 quart fruit, sweetened

Melt margarine in a 9 x 13 inch baking pan. Mix sugar, flour, baking powder, and milk until smooth. Pour over margarine. Pour fruit over batter. Do not stir. Bake at 375 degrees for 50 to 55 minutes or until golden brown. Serve with ice cream or whipped cream.

NOTE: Crust creeps to the top as it bakes. Great with any fruit - raspberries, blueberries and peaches are family favorites.

Maude "Me-maw" Holliday

For a quick way to whip cream, add a pinch of salt to the cream just before whipping. This will strengthen the fat cells, making them more elastic, and help the cream stiffen more quickly.

NUT ROLL
(A time filler for those long winter days!)

Yields: 6 nut rolls

Dough:
2½ packages dry yeast
1 cup warm milk
½ cup sugar
1 teaspoon salt

6 cups flour
1 cup margarine, softened
4 egg yolks
1 5.3-ounce can evaporated milk

Filling:
3 pounds finely chopped walnuts
3 cups sugar

4 egg whites, stiffly beaten
1 cup milk

Dough:
Dissolve yeast in warm milk. Add a pinch of sugar. Cover for 5 minutes. Mix sugar, salt and flour. Blend in margarine, egg yolks and evaporated milk. Blend in the yeast mixture. Knead for 5 minutes until shiny and smooth. Place in a buttered bowl. Let rise overnight in refrigerator.

Filling:
Mix together nuts and sugar. Fold in stiffened egg whites. Stir in milk until mixture is of spreading consistency.

To Assemble:
After allowing dough to rise overnight, form into 6 balls. Allow to rise for 2 to 3 hours. Roll each ball into a 9 x 12 inch rectangle. Spread ⅙ of the filling onto the dough and roll up. Seal the ends. Place seam down on a large cookie sheet. Place 2 rolls on each cookie sheet. Let rise for 1 hour. Bake at 350 degrees for 40 minutes, until brown. Brush with margarine.

Jo Ann Pulcini

When scalding milk, rinse the pan first with water. This keeps the milk from sticking to the pot. Milk is scalded when little bubbles appear around the edges.

PEACH ROLL
(Tricky but yummy!)

Serves: 9

1 ½ cups flour
3 teaspoons baking powder
½ teaspoon salt

2 tablespoons butter or
    shortening, softened
⅜ cup milk
peaches, peeled and sliced

Syrup:
1 cup light brown sugar

1 cup sugar
1 ½ cups warm water

Mix dry ingredients with butter. Add milk to form soft dough. Roll out to ¼ inch thickness. Lay peaches on top. Roll up jelly-roll fashion. Cut into 1 ½ inch slices. Mix syrup ingredients together. Pour into 9 x 9 inch pan. Place slices of peach roll in pan, cut side down. Add more peaches between slices, if desired. Sprinkle with cinnamon (optional). Bake at 450 degrees for 15 minutes, then turn oven down to 325 degrees for 15 minutes. Serve warm with whipped cream.

Doris S. DePierre

STRUDEL

Serves: 24

Dough:
1 cup margarine, softened
2 cups flour

Filling:

¼ cup water
1 tablespoon vinegar
3 egg yolks, beaten

1 21-ounce can favorite prepared
    fruit pie filling

Combine dough ingredients. Roll dough into 8 x 12 inch oblong shape. Place on greased and floured cookie sheet. Pour filling into center of dough. Fold dough over filling. Bake at 350 degrees for 30 minutes or until brown. Sprinkle with powdered sugar or drizzle icing on top if desired.

NOTE: Can be made into 2 smaller strudels. Can freeze.

Ruth Miller

GRAHAM CRACKER SQUARES
(The kids will love it, but you will want to hide it)

Serves: 8

18 graham crackers, finely crushed

1 6-ounce package chocolate chips

1 14-ounce can sweetened condensed milk

Mix all ingredients well. Batter will be stiff. Press into a buttered 8 x 8 inch pan. Bake at 325 degrees for 30 minutes. Cut immediately and remove from pan.

Mary Jane Roderick

BROWNIES

Serves: 12 to 16

4 squares unsweetened baking chocolate

1 cup shortening or butter

3 cups sugar

4 eggs

1 ½ cups sifted flour

1 ½ teaspoons salt, if shortening is used

2 teaspoons vanilla

1 to 2 cups chopped nuts

Melt chocolate and shortening together. Add sugar. Mix thoroughly. Add eggs one at a time, mixing well after last egg. Blend in flour, salt (if shortening is used), vanilla, and nuts. Mix together. Bake in a greased 9 x 13 inch pan at 350 degrees for 35 to 40 minutes.

NOTE: Recipe can be cut in half. For an 8 x 8 inch pan, bake 25 to 30 minutes.

Fern Jagger

Children enjoy polishing pennies with salt and lemon juice, and a small toothbrush. This will keep them busy while you're working.

BANANA SPLIT DESSERT
(This dish will make you flip!)

Serves: 16 to 20

2 cups crushed graham crackers
⅔ cup butter, melted
1 cup margarine, softened
2 eggs
2 cups confectioners' sugar
1 teaspoon vanilla

3 large bananas
1 16-ounce can crushed
   pineapple, reserve juice
1 16-ounce container Cool Whip
chopped nuts
maraschino cherries

Mix together graham cracker crumbs and melted butter. Press into the bottom of a 9 x 13 inch glass pan. In a medium bowl combine margarine, eggs, confectioners' sugar and vanilla. Beat until firm. Spread egg-sugar mixture over the crust. Thinly slice bananas, and dip in pineapple juice. Arrange slices over the egg-sugar layer. Top sliced bananas with drained crushed pineapple. Spread Cool Whip over pineapple. Sprinkle with chopped nuts and maraschino cherries. Chill for 8 hours.

Elaine Axelson

CHOCOLATE ICE BOX PUDDING
(Expensive, but well worth it . . . a family favorite)

Serves: 16

2 4-ounce bars German sweet
   chocolate
2 tablespoons hot water
6 egg yolks

6 rounded tablespoons sugar
1 teaspoon vanilla
6 egg whites, stiffly beaten
18 whole lady fingers

Melt chocolate in double boiler, add water and stir. Add 1 egg yolk and 1 tablespoon sugar at a time, stirring after each addition. After all egg yolks and sugar have been added, remove from heat and add vanilla. Cool slightly and add stiffly beaten egg whites. Split lady fingers. Place half of them, rounded side down, in shallow casserole dish or 9-inch square cake pan. Pour half of chocolate mixture over them. Place remaining lady fingers, rounded side up, on top of the chocolate mixture. Cover with remaining chocolate. Refrigerate before serving, preferably overnight. Serve with whipped cream. Sprinkle with nuts, if desired.

NOTE: A 9 x 13 inch pan will hold 24 lady fingers (2 large packages), but you must make 1½ times the recipe to cover them (3 bars chocolate, 9 eggs, etc.).

Judy Douglass

CRANBERRY PUDDING
(Especially great for a holiday treat)

Serves: 9

Pudding:
2 cups flour
1 cup sugar
4 teaspoons baking powder

1 cup milk
3 tablespoons butter, melted
2 cups raw cranberries

Sauce:
1 cup milk
⅔ cup sugar

1 tablespoon cornstarch
2 to 4 tablespoons butter or
  margarine

Pudding:
Mix together all ingredients. Pour into a greased 9 x 9 inch pan. Bake at 400 degrees for 30 minutes. Serve hot with sauce.

Sauce:
Scald milk. Mix sugar and cornstarch. Add to milk, stirring constantly. Add butter. Bring to boil. Simmer until slightly thickened. Continue to stir until thickened. Serve in pitcher, and pour hot sauce over pudding.

Barbara and Rick Heinze

LEMON PUDDING SQUARES

Serves: 10 to 12

1 cup flour
½ cup margarine, softened
½ cup chopped nuts
1 cup unsifted confectioners'
  sugar
1 8-ounce package cream
  cheese, softened

1 10-ounce container Cool Whip
2 3½-ounce packages instant
  lemon pudding
3 cups cold milk
1 10-ounce container Cool Whip
chopped nuts

Mix together flour, margarine and ½ cup nuts. Press into the bottom of a 9 x 13 inch pan. Bake at 350 degrees for 20 minutes. Cool completely. Blend together sugar, cream cheese, and Cool Whip. Spread over crust. Refrigerate for 15 minutes. Whip together pudding and milk. Set aside for several minutes. Spread over middle layer. Refrigerate an additional 15 minutes. Top with Cool Whip. Sprinkle with nuts. Refrigerate before serving.

Mary Benson

DESSERTS

EASY SOUFFLÉ GRAND MARNIER

Serves: 8

1 8-ounce package cream
  cheese, softened and cut in
  cubes
5 eggs
½ cup sugar

¾ cup whipping cream
¼ cup Grand Marnier liqueur
1 10-ounce package frozen
  raspberries, thawed

Beat cream cheese and eggs until smooth. Add sugar, whipping cream and Grand Marnier. Beat until thoroughly combined. Butter a 2 quart soufflé dish and sprinkle the bottom and sides with sugar. Pour batter into dish. Bake at 375 degrees for 50 minutes until golden brown. Serve immediately with raspberries spooned over the top.

Joan Clark

CHOCOLATE CREAM TORTE

Serves: 12 to 16

1 box Betty Crocker Sour Cream
  Chocolate Cake Mix
2 bars German Sweet Chocolate
¾ cup margarine, softened

½ cup toasted, slivered almonds
2 cups whipping cream
1 tablespoon sugar
1 teaspoon vanilla

Bake cake according to directions on package. Cool completely. Cut each layer into 2 layers to make 4 thin layers. Melt 1 ½ bars chocolate in a double boiler. Cool completely. Blend in margarine and almonds. Whip cream together with sugar and vanilla in electric mixer. Assemble torte as follows. Place 1 cake layer on a plate. Spread ½ of the chocolate mixture over cake. Place second layer on plate. Cover with ½ the whipped cream mixture. Repeat steps ending with whipped cream on the top layer. Do not frost sides of cake. Make chocolate curls with the remaining ½ bar of chocolate. Decorate top of cake with curls. Cover with waxed paper and refrigerate until ready to serve.

NOTE: May be frozen.

WALNUT TORTE

Serves: 8

1 cup sifted flour
½ teaspoon salt
2 teaspoons baking powder
½ cup shortening

Meringue:
4 egg whites
⅛ teaspoon cream of tartar

Frosting:
1 ½ cups heavy cream

⅓ cup milk
½ teaspoon vanilla
4 egg yolks
½ cup sugar

¾ cup sugar
1 cup walnuts, chopped

⅓ cup cocoa
½ cup sugar

In large mixing bowl sift together flour, salt and baking powder. Place shortening, milk, vanilla, egg yolks and ½ cup sugar in electric blender. Blend for 1 minute. Add dry ingredients and mix well. Pour into 2 9-inch round pans which have been lined with waxed paper and greased around the edges.

Meringue:
Beat egg whites and cream of tartar until stiff. Gradually add ¾ cup sugar and beat until glossy. Fold in chopped nuts. Spread over cake batter in pans. Bake at 300 degrees for 1 hour.

Frosting:
Combine heavy cream, cocoa and sugar. Chill for 1 hour. Whip. Frost bottom layer. Place layers together and frost.

Millie McCathren

Spices should be stored in a cool dry place away from heat. Ground spices lose most of their flavoring after a year.

QUICK CHOCOLATE MOUSSE
(A fancy dessert that's quick and easy)

Serves: 4

1 6-ounce package chocolate chips
3 tablespoons strong brewed
  coffee, hot

2 eggs
3 tablespoons rum (optional)
¾ cup milk, scalded

Put all ingredients in blender. Blend at high speed for 2 minutes. Pour into dessert cups. Chill.

Mary Jane Roderick

CHOCOLATE FONDUE AND FRESH FRUIT
(A perfect dessert and coffee event)

fruit, cut into bite-size chunks or
  slices (recommend fruit such
  as: fresh apples, bananas,
  grapes, peaches, pears,
  pineapple or angelfood cake)

1 12-ounce bag Hershey Real
  Chocolate Chips
1 cup sour cream
¼ cup Grand Marnier or Crème
  de Cacao

Arrange fruit attractively on a platter. Cover, and place in refrigerator. Melt chocolate chips in saucepan or microwave, taking care not to scorch. Add sour cream to chocolate. Whisk cream and chocolate quickly with a wire whisk. Add liqueur, and whisk until blended well. Place warm fondue in attractive bowl. Use fondue forks to dip cool fruit or cake into chocolate.

Lora T. Spence

JELLY CREAM CUSTARD
(A bit of fruit is a perfect complement to this light custard)

Serves: 10

2½ teaspoons unflavored gelatin
2 cups milk
2 egg yolks
2 tablespoons sugar

2 egg whites
2 tablespoons sugar
few drops of vanilla

In a saucepan, dissolve gelatin in milk over very low heat. Beat egg yolks with 2 tablespoons sugar. Put beaten egg yolks in milk-gelatin mixture. Heat just to a boil. Beat egg whites with remaining sugar until stiff. Remove milk-gelatin mixture from heat and stir in beaten egg whites. Add flavoring. Stir well. Pour into mold or serving dish.

NOTE: Serve with fruit, strawberries, peaches or blueberries.

Gladys Douglas

EASY PLUM PUDDING
(An old-fashioned holiday dessert)

Serves: 12

1 cup English walnuts, chopped
1 cup suet, grated
1 cup raisins
1 cup sugar
1 cup flour
1 cup bread crumbs
1 cup chopped apples

1 cup milk
1 teaspoon baking powder
1 teaspoon baking soda
    dissolved in ¼ cup water
1 teaspoon cinnamon
1 teaspoon salt
1 2 or 3-pound coffee can

Sauce:
1 cup brown sugar
½ cup butter
4 cups milk

pinch of salt
1 teaspoon vanilla
½ cup flour

Mix ingredients in the above order. Stir after each addition. Grease coffee can with shortening and fill ¾ full with the pudding mixture. Cover can with aluminum foil. Place can in a large pot. Fill pot with water to cover ⅔ the height of the can. Cover large pot. Bring water to a boil. Simmer for 3 hours, checking water level occasionally. Serve with favorite sauce.

Sauce:
In top of a double boiler, dissolve brown sugar in butter. Add all but a small portion of milk, salt and vanilla. In a separate bowl, beat flour with the remaining milk. Mix until smooth. Stir milk and flour mixture into the sugar mixture. Slowly bring to a boil. Continue stirring until thickened.

Marjorie H. Gray

KIDDIE PEANUT BUTTER:

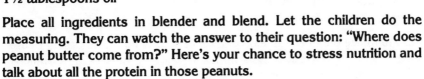

1 cup roasted peanuts
1½ tablespoons oil

½ teaspoon salt

Place all ingredients in blender and blend. Let the children do the measuring. They can watch the answer to their question: "Where does peanut butter come from?" Here's your chance to stress nutrition and talk about all the protein in those peanuts.

STEAMED CUP PUDDING
(From my grandmother's kitchen)

Serves: 12

1 cup flour
1 teaspoon baking soda
1 teaspoon salt
1 teaspoon cinnamon
1 teaspoon nutmeg
1 cup fine bread crumbs

1 cup sugar
1 cup cold water
1 cup suet, finely chopped
1 cup seedless raisins
1 cup walnuts, finely chopped

Nutmeg Sauce:
¼ teaspoon salt
2 cups water
½ cup butter

4 tablespoons flour
¾ cup sugar
1 teaspoon nutmeg

Sift together flour, baking soda, salt, cinnamon, and nutmeg. Add bread crumbs and sugar. Stir in cold water. Add suet, raisins and walnuts. Stir. Pour into a greased 10-inch tube pan. Place tube pan in a large pot. Fill large pot with water to cover ⅔ the height of the tube pan. Cover the large pot. Bring water to a boil. Simmer for 2 hours, checking water level. Serve hot with nutmeg sauce and whipped cream.

Nutmeg Sauce:
Combine salt, water and butter in a saucepan. Bring to a boil. In a separate bowl mix flour, sugar and nutmeg. Stir flour mixture into water mixture. Heat for 3 minutes. Serve hot.

Doris S. DePierre

FROZEN BANANA DESSERT

Serves: 1

1 banana
1 tablespoon peanut butter
cinnamon or nutmeg to taste

walnuts, peanuts or raisins to
    taste
pure maple syrup

Peel and freeze banana. Place on dish. Spread peanut butter on top of the banana. Sprinkle with cinnamon or nutmeg. Add walnuts, peanuts, raisins or similar garnish. Cover with pure maple syrup.

Larry Pearson

EASY BUTTERMILK ICE CREAM
(Light and refreshing ice cream without the taste of buttermilk)

Yields: 1½ quarts

1 quart buttermilk
1 cup sugar
1 8-ounce can crushed pineapple,
   drained

½ jar maraschino cherries,
   drained and quartered

Beat together buttermilk and sugar. Freeze until almost solid. Remove from freezer and break into lumps. Beat with electric mixer until creamy. Add pineapple and cherries. Mix well. Refreeze.

NOTE: For a beautiful pink color add cherries before second beating.

Doris DePierre

INDIVIDUAL BAKED ALASKA
(A tempting make-ahead dessert)

Serves: 4

4 large cookies, preferably sugar
   cookies
4 scoops ice cream

3 egg whites
¼ teaspoon cream of tartar
½ cup sugar

Place cookies on small cookie sheet. Top each cookie with a scoop of ice cream. Freeze. Separate eggs. In a mixing bowl, beat egg whites with cream of tartar until frothy. Gradually beat in sugar until stiff peaks form when beater is slowly raised from bowl. Spread over ice cream, covering completely. Return to freezer. Bake "Alaskas" until golden at 400 degrees for 3 to 5 minutes. Remove to plates. Return to freezer until served.

Mary Jane Roderick

LEMON ICE

3-pound container
2 cups sugar
warm water

½ cup Real Lemon juice
½ cup milk
dash of salt

In a 3 pound container, dissolve sugar in a small amount of warm water. Add lemon juice, milk and salt. Fill the container with water. Freeze, shaking occasionally until frozen.

Jo Ann Pulcini

243

RASPBERRY ICE CREAM

Yields: 1 quart

1 cup cream (light or heavy)
2 cups evaporated milk
¼ cup sugar

almond extract
1 10-ounce package frozen
   raspberries, thawed

Combine cream, evaporated milk, sugar, almond extract and juice from frozen raspberries. Stir until sugar is dissolved. Churn in manual or electric ice cream freezer. Add mashed frozen raspberries. Serve immediately or return to freezer.

Sherry Wilson

SUE'S ICE CREAM TREAT
(For ice cream lovers, young and old!)

Serves: 16

3 cups crushed Rice Krispies
½ cup chopped nuts
1 cup shredded coconut
¾ cup brown sugar

½ cup plus 2 tablespoons
   margarine, melted
½ gallon soft ice cream (butter
   pecan is best)

Mix the Rice Krispies, chopped nuts, coconut and brown sugar. Pour melted margarine over mixture and stir. Remove ⅓ cup for topping. Place mixture into a 9 x 13 inch pan. Top with ice cream. Sprinkle reserved mixture on top. Cover with aluminum foil and freeze. Remove from freezer 20 to 30 minutes before serving. Cut into serving pieces.

Nancy McCloskey

 An easy way to get "coordinated" color and flavor when baking a chocolate cake or cookies is to use cocoa instead of flour to dust greased cake pans and cookie sheets.

Cookies & Candies

Gary G. Baker

CHAPTER XIV

The Gingerbread Boy's ... Cookies and Candies

She rolled and mixed and patted,
Cut and baked his child-like form.
To her husband she said warmly,
"Our boy will soon be born!"

But the ginger boy was feisty
With molasses adding zest.
So these parents learned that children
When **real,** are at their best!

Cook's Note: The cookies and candies presented here will not roll or run away like the gingerbread boy. However, they **will** quickly disappear and that's why we have absolutely no information about how well they keep.

AGGRESSION COOKIES

(The best method for mixing these cookies is by hand, thus,
the name aggression cookies. A great outlet for frustration!)

Yields: 7 to 8 dozen

3 cups butter, softened
3 cups sugar
3 cups flour

1 tablespoon baking soda
6 cups oatmeal

Mix all ingredients by hand until well blended. Shape into small balls. Place on greased cookie sheets. Flatten cookies with the bottom of a glass which has been buttered and dipped in sugar for each cookie. Bake at 350 degrees for approximately 10 minutes. Let stand 1 to 2 minutes before removing from cookie sheet.

Judith Diehl

CHOCOLATE CHIP OATMEAL COOKIES

Yields: 4 to 5 dozen

1 cup shortening
¾ cup brown sugar
¾ cup sugar
2 eggs
1 teaspoon vanilla
1 teaspoon hot water
1½ cups flour

1 teaspoon salt
1 teaspoon baking soda
2 cups oatmeal
1 6-ounce package chocolate
  chips
¾ cup chopped nuts

Cream shortening and sugars. Add eggs, vanilla, and hot water. Sift together flour, salt and baking soda. Add flour mixture to shortening and sugar. Add oatmeal, chocolate chips, and nuts. Drop by rounded teaspoon onto ungreased baking sheet. Bake at 350 degrees for 8 to 10 minutes.

Elaine Axelson

Oil the cup with cooking oil and rinse with hot water before measuring honey or syrup.

GINGERSNAPS

Yields: 5 dozen

¾ cup shortening
1 cup sugar
¼ cup light molasses
1 egg
2 cups flour

¼ teaspoon salt
2 teaspoons baking soda
1 teaspoon cinnamon
1 teaspoon cloves
1 teaspoon ginger

Cream shortening and sugar until smooth. Add molasses and egg; beat well. Add sifted dry ingredients. Roll into small balls. Dip into sugar. Place about 2 inches apart on greased cookie sheet. Bake at 350 degrees for 12 minutes.

LaRue Weber

MARY'S SUGAR COOKIES

Yields: 3½ dozen

1 cup confectioners' sugar
1 cup butter or margarine,
  softened
1 egg

⅛ teaspoon salt
½ teaspoon baking soda
1 teaspoon cream of tartar
2 cups flour

Cream sugar and butter. Beat in egg. Add dry ingredients and stir. Chill. Roll into walnut-sized balls. Roll balls in granulated sugar. Flatten slightly with fork. Bake at 350 degrees for 10 to 12 minutes or until lightly browned on edges.

Mary Benson

OLD FASHIONED MOLASSES COOKIES
(A big, soft cookie!)

Yields: 8 to 10 dozen

1 cup butter, softened
1 cup margarine, softened
3 cups sugar
1 cup molasses
3 eggs
8 cups flour

1½ tablespoons baking soda
1½ tablespoons ginger
1 tablespoon ground cloves
1 tablespoon cinnamon
1 teaspoon salt

Cream butter, margarine, and sugar until smooth. Add molasses, and 1 egg at a time. Sift dry ingredients together. Mix dry ingredients with the creamed mixture. Make large balls, the size of 2 walnuts and roll in sugar. Bake at 350 degrees for 10 minutes.

Sally Joiner

POPPIN' FRESH COOKIES
(A good and nourishing treat)

Yields: 4 dozen

2¼ cups flour (reserve 1 cup)
2 cups brown sugar, packed
   firmly
1 teaspoon baking soda
1 teaspoon salt
2 teaspoons vanilla

2 eggs
1 cup margarine, softened
2 cups oatmeal
1 cup chocolate chips
1 cup raisins
½ cup chopped nuts

Mix 1¼ cups flour, brown sugar, baking soda, salt, vanilla, eggs, and margarine in a bowl. Beat 1 to 2 minutes at medium speed. Stir in remaining ingredients by hand. Drop by tablespoonful about 2 inches apart on greased cookie sheet. Bake at 350 degrees for 15 to 20 minutes, until lightly browned.

Judith Diehl

SOFT SUGAR COOKIES
(Get a jump on the holidays)

Yields: 3 dozen

2 tablespoons lemon juice
½ cup plus 2 tablespoons
   evaporated milk
1 cup sugar
½ cup margarine, softened
1 egg

1 teaspoon vanilla
3¼ cups flour
1 teaspoon baking soda
½ teaspoon salt
1 10-ounce can prepared apricot
   filling

Add lemon juice to canned milk; set aside. Cream sugar, margarine, egg, and vanilla until smooth. Sift flour, baking soda and salt. Alternately add the milk mixture and flour mixture to the creamed mixture. Chill for 4 hours. Roll out ¼ inch thick on a floured and sugared surface. Cut out 3 inch rounds. Place 1 teaspoon of prepared apricot filling in center. Fold in half and crimp with fork. Bake at 400 degrees for 10 minutes. (Check after 7 minutes.)

NOTE: These stay soft when placed in an airtight container and they freeze easily.

VARIATIONS: Cut 3 inch rounds, press thumb in center and fill with grape jelly, pecans, Hershey kisses or M&M's.

Eleanor Towers

249

SOUR CREAM COOKIES

Yields: 5 dozen

4 cups cake flour
1 teaspoon baking soda
1 teaspoon baking powder
1 teaspoon salt
1 cup shortening

1 cup brown sugar
1 cup sugar
3 eggs, beaten
1 cup sour cream or buttermilk

Sift cake flour, baking soda, baking powder and salt together. Cream shortening and sugars together. Add eggs to creamed mixture. Add dry ingredients and sour cream alternately to creamed mixture until smooth. Drop by teaspoonful onto greased cookie sheet. Bake at 350 degrees for 5 minutes.

NOTE: Cherries and/or nuts can be added to batter, or jelly can be spooned into indentation on top of unbaked cookies before baking.

Doris S. DePierre

THUMBPRINT COOKIES

Yields: 3 to 4 dozen

1 cup margarine, softened
½ cup brown sugar
2 egg yolks
1 teaspoon vanilla

2 cups flour
½ teaspoon salt
egg whites, slightly beaten
finely chopped nuts

Combine margarine, sugar, egg yolks and vanilla. Mix well. Add flour and salt. Roll dough into 1 inch balls. Dip in egg whites. Roll in nuts. Place on ungreased cookie sheet. Bake at 375 degrees for 5 minutes. Remove from oven and press thumb in center. Return to oven for 8 minutes.

Bev and Dick Schultz

While sorting the family's socks, your children can learn their colors.

JELLY COOKIES

Yields: 5 dozen

1 cup butter, softened
1 ½ cups sugar
5 eggs
4 cups flour

5 teaspoons baking powder
½ cup sour cream
strawberry jam

Cream together butter and sugar. Add eggs, flour and baking powder. Mix together well to form soft dough. Add sour cream and more flour, if needed. Knead until soft and smooth. Roll out to ⅛-inch thickness. Use round cookie cutter or glass to cut circles. On half of the circles, using a thimble, cut out a smaller hole in the center. Bake at 350 degrees for 10 to 12 minutes.

Heat strawberry jam till hot, but do not melt or boil. Spread on bottom of cookies, put top on cookies.

These cookies freeze well.

Jean Kmiecik

ORANGE DROP COOKIES

Yields: 5 dozen

2 cups sugar
1 cup butter, softened
2 eggs
1 cup milk

1 teaspoon baking soda
2 teaspoons baking powder
4 cups flour
juice and grated rind of 1 orange

Frosting:
1 pound confectioners' sugar

2 tablespoons butter
juice and grated rind of 1 orange

Cream sugar and butter. Add eggs and milk; beat well. Sift dry ingredients together. Add, with juice and rind, to the creamed mixture. Drop by spoonful on greased cookie sheet. Bake at 350 degrees for 10 to 12 minutes. Cool. Blend frosting ingredients. Spread on baked cookies.

Teresa Meyer

To keep your cookies fresh, place crushed tissue paper on the bottom of the cookie jar.

THE WORLD'S BEST COOKIES

Yields: 10 dozen small cookies

1 cup butter, softened
1 cup sugar
1 cup brown sugar, firmly packed
1 teaspoon vanilla
1 egg
1 cup oil
1 cup rolled oats

1 cup crushed cornflakes
½ cup shredded coconut
½ cup chopped walnuts or
   pecans
3½ cups sifted all-purpose flour
1 teaspoon baking soda
1 teaspoon salt

Preheat oven to 325 degrees. Cream together butter, sugars and vanilla until light and fluffy. Add egg, mixing well, then oil, mixing well. Add oats, cornflakes, coconut, and nuts, stirring well. Add flour, baking soda and salt. Mix well and form into balls the size of small walnuts. Place on an ungreased cookie sheet. Flatten with a fork dipped in water. Bake for 12 minutes. Allow to cool on cookie sheet before removing.

Nancy Johns

SANDWICH COOKIES
(Color the filling to match the occasion)

Yields: 3 dozen

Cookie:
1 cup butter, softened
¼ cup thick cream

Filling:
¼ cup butter, softened
¾ cup confectioners' sugar

2 cups sifted flour
sugar

1 egg yolk
1 teaspoon vanilla

Cookie:
Mix butter, cream and flour and chill. Roll out ⅛ inch thick on floured board. Cut into small circles. Coat with granulated sugar. Prick 3 times with a fork. Bake at 350 degrees on an ungreased pan for 7 to 9 minutes.

Filling:
Cream butter and sugar. Add egg yolk and vanilla. If desired, add a touch of food coloring to filling. After cookies cool, fill in sandwich style.

Marilyn Hayes

BUCKEYE COOKIES

Yields: 5 dozen

2 cups margarine, softened
2 pounds peanut butter
2 pounds confectioners' sugar

½ pound graham cracker crumbs
1 12-ounce package semi-sweet chocolate chips

Mix together margarine, peanut butter, sugar and graham cracker crumbs by hand. Form into balls. Refrigerate for 8 hours or overnight. Melt chocolate chips in top of double boiler. Put a toothpick in the peanut butter balls and dip in chocolate until ¾ covered. Place on waxed paper to cool.

Florence Tabor

CHEESECAKE COOKIES

Yields: 16 2-inch square cookies

Crust:
1 cup whole wheat flour
⅓ cup butter or margarine, softened

Filling:
1 8-ounce package cream cheese, softened
¼ cup honey
1 egg

Garnish (optional):
fruit slices - oranges, apples, bananas, strawberries

⅓ cup brown sugar
½ cup chopped walnuts or toasted sesame seeds or roasted sunflower seeds

2 tablespoons milk
1 tablespoon lemon juice
grated peel of 1 lemon
½ teaspoon vanilla
½ teaspoon nutmeg (optional)

chopped nut meats - almonds, walnuts, brazil nuts

Crust:
Blend flour, butter and brown sugar together with pastry cutter until crumbly. Mix in nuts or seeds. Reserve ½ cup for topping. Press remainder into 8 x 8 inch pan. Bake at 350 degrees for 12 to 15 minutes.

Filling:
Blend together cream cheese and honey. Blend in egg, milk, lemon juice, lemon peel, vanilla and nutmeg, and beat well. Spread over baked crust. Sprinkle reserved topping over cream cheese mixture. Garnish with fruit slices and/or nut meats. Bake at 350 degrees for 25 minutes. Cool and cut into 2 inch squares.

NOTE: If using strawberries for garnish, place on cheesecake after baking.

Janine and Mike Murphy

CHOCOLATE DROP COOKIES WITH ICING AND COCONUT

Yields: 4 dozen

Cookies:
2 squares unsweetened baking
   chocolate
½ cup butter, softened
1 cup light brown sugar
1 cup sour cream
1 egg, beaten

2 cups plus 4 tablespoons cake
   flour
1 teaspoon baking soda
½ teaspoon salt
1 teaspoon vanilla
1 cup chopped nuts

Icing:
1 cup sugar
4 tablespoons cold water
1 egg white

1 teaspoon cold water
1 teaspoon sugar
½ teaspoon vanilla
coconut

Cookies:
Melt chocolate. Cream butter and sugar until smooth. Add chocolate, sour cream, and egg. Sift together cake flour, baking soda and salt. Fold into mixture. Fold in vanilla and nuts. Drop by teaspoon onto greased cookie sheet. Bake at 350 degrees for 15 minutes. Frost with icing and top with coconut.

Icing:
Mix sugar with 4 tablespoons cold water in pan. Bring to a boil. Cook until it spins a thin thread. Beat egg with 1 teaspoon cold water, until very stiff. Beat in sugar. Slowly add syrup to egg white while beating. Beat until cool. Add vanilla. Continue beating until spreadable.

Doris S. DePierre

MINIATURE CHEESECAKES

Yields: 34

2 8-ounce packages cream
   cheese, softened
2 eggs
½ cup sugar

1 teaspoon vanilla
1 box Sunshine vanilla wafers
1 21-ounce can "Thank You"
   cherry pie filling

Mix cream cheese, eggs, sugar and vanilla until smooth. Place wafer, flat side down in foil cup. Fill ¾ full with mixture. Place cups on cookie sheet. Bake at 350 degrees for 15 minutes. Top with cherry pie filling when cool.

Doe Clark

CLOTHES PIN COOKIES
(Off the line into the oven!)

Yields: 5 dozen

Cookies:
3 cups flour
2 tablespoons sugar
dash of salt

2 egg yolks
1 ¼ cups cold water
1 ½ cups shortening

Filling:
5 tablespoons flour
1 cup milk
½ cup butter, softened

½ cup shortening
2 cups confectioners' sugar
6 tablespoons marshmallow
    cream

Cookies:
Mix flour, sugar, salt, egg yolks and water. Spread on floured surface by hand or with rolling pin. Spread with ½ cup shortening and fold in half. Refrigerate ½ hour. Repeat shortening application 2 more times. Roll thin. Cut in ½ inch strips and wrap around clothes pins. Bake at 375 degrees for 20 minutes or until brown. Remove clothes pins.

Filling:
Cook flour and milk. Cool. Add butter, shortening and confectioners' sugar. Fold in marshmallow cream. Fill cookies.

Doe Clark

MERINGUE-NUT COOKIES

Yields: 3½ dozen

½ cup shortening
1 cup sugar
2 eggs
1 ½ cups flour
½ teaspoon salt
1 teaspoon baking powder

½ teaspoon vanilla
1 cup chopped pecans
2 egg whites
1 cup brown sugar
1 teaspoon vanilla

Mix together shortening, sugar, eggs, flour, salt, baking powder and vanilla. Spread on greased cookie sheet. Sprinkle with chopped nuts. Set aside. Beat egg whites until stiff. Fold in brown sugar and vanilla to form meringue. Spread meringue over nuts. Bake at 350 degrees for 15 to 25 minutes. Do not overbake. Cut in bars while still warm.

Carolyn Heaton

COOKIES

PEACHES

Yields: 6 to 7 dozen

Cookie:
12 eggs
12 teaspoons baking powder
3 cups oil

3 cups sugar
2 tablespoons vanilla
6 cups or more flour (enough to
    make a soft dough)

Filling:
6 egg yolks
12 tablespoons sugar
8 tablespoons flour

4 cups milk
juice from ½ of a lemon
cocoa

Coating:
Red Vermouth and red food
    coloring mixed together

sugar
paper cupcake holders

Cookie:
Mix ingredients in order given. Mix until dough is soft. Shape into balls. Bake at 350 degrees for 10 to 15 minutes.

Filling:
Mix egg yolks and sugar in top of a double boiler. Add flour and milk. Stir till smooth. Add lemon juice. Cook for 1 hour or until thick. Divide filling in half. In one half, add a little cocoa to make the filling chocolate.

Assembly:
Scoop the bottom out of each cookie, leaving a hollow shell. Fill holes of ½ the cookies with vanilla filling and the other ½ of the cookies with chocolate filling. Form a round ball by placing vanilla and chocolate halves together. Dip into Vermouth and food coloring mixture. Roll into sugar. Place in cupcake paper.

If desired, scrape a bit of lime peel to look like a stem.

Jean Kmiecik

PIZZELLES

Yields: 5 dozen

12 eggs
2 cups sugar
2 cups oil

4 cups flour
1 teaspoon vanilla or anise

Mix all ingredients in order given. Heat pizzelle maker. Pour 1 tablespoonful for each pizzelle onto the pizzelle grill.

Jean Kmiecik

STRAWBERRY CHRISTMAS COOKIES

Yields: 4 to 5 dozen

1 8-ounce package pitted, diced
  dates
½ cup flaked coconut
½ cup sugar
¼ cup butter or margarine
1 egg, slightly beaten

dash of salt
1½ cups Rice Krispies
½ cup chopped walnuts
1 teaspoon vanilla
1 jar red sugar
green cake frosting

In frying pan, combine dates, coconut, sugar, butter, egg and salt. Cook over medium/low heat until mixture thickens. Remove from heat. Stir in cereal, nuts and vanilla. Cool. Use 1 tablespoon of mixture for each cookie. Roll in ball and form into strawberry shape. Roll in red sugar. Trim top of cookie with green frosting to make leaf.

Sheila and Bob Pasquantonio

FROSTED CASHEW COOKIES
(A delicious, rich cookie which cashew lovers will be crazy about)

Yields: 4½ dozen

Cookies:
2 cups sifted flour
¾ teaspoon baking powder
¾ teaspoon baking soda
¼ teaspoon salt
½ cup butter, softened

Golden Butter Icing:
½ cup butter
3 tablespoons light cream

1 cup brown sugar
1 egg
½ teaspoon vanilla
⅓ cup sour cream
1⅓ cups salted, whole cashew
  nuts, chopped

¼ teaspoon vanilla
2 cups sifted confectioners' sugar
salted, whole cashew nuts

Cookies:
Sift flour, baking powder, baking soda and salt together. Cream butter and sugar until fluffy. Add egg and vanilla. Alternately add dry ingredients and sour cream. Fold in nuts. Drop by spoonful on cookie sheets. Bake at 400 degrees for 10 minutes. Cool and frost with Golden Butter Icing, topping each cookie with a cashew.

Icing:
Lightly brown butter and remove from burner. Add cream, vanilla and sugar. Beat until smooth and thick enough to spread.

NOTE: Do not overbake. This cookie adds a touch of variety to the usual Christmas assortment.

Judy Douglass

DATE DAINTIES
(Very light with a delicate flavor)

Yields: 3 dozen

1 cup chopped dates
3 eggs, well beaten
1 cup sugar
1 cup flour
pinch of salt

1 teaspoon baking soda
   dissolved in 3 tablespoons hot
   water
1 teaspoon vanilla
confectioners' sugar

Mix all ingredients except confectioners' sugar in order given. Spread thinly in a greased 10 x 15 inch pan. Bake at 300 degrees for 15 to 20 minutes. Cool. Cut in squares. Roll in confectioners' sugar.

Doris De Pierre

PECAN PIE COOKIES

Yields: 4 dozen

Dough:
1 cup butter or margarine,
   softened
½ cup sugar

Filling:
½ cup confectioners' sugar
¼ cup butter or margarine

½ cup dark corn syrup
2 eggs, separated
2½ cups unsifted flour

3 tablespoons dark corn syrup
½ cup chopped pecans

Dough:
Mix butter and sugar in large mixing bowl on low speed. Add corn syrup and egg yolks. Beat until thoroughly blended. Stir in flour gradually. Chill several hours.

Filling:
Combine sugar, butter and corn syrup in saucepan. Stir to blend. Cook over medium heat, stirring occasionally until mixture reaches a full boil. Remove from heat. Stir in pecans. Chill.

Assemble Cookies:
Beat egg whites slightly. Roll about 1 tablespoon of dough into a ball. Brush lightly with egg white. Place balls on greased cookie sheet about 2 inches apart. Bake at 375 degrees for 5 minutes. Remove from oven. Roll ½ teaspoon of chilled filling into a ball and press firmly into center of partially baked cookie. Bake 5 minutes longer or until lightly browned. Cool on cookie sheet for 5 minutes. Remove to rack and cool completely.

Sue and Bill Law

TEXAS ALMOND COOKIES
(A healthful handful of cookies and a mouthful of crunch)

Yields: 4 to 5 dozen

1 cup sugar
1 cup confectioners' sugar
1 cup margarine or butter,
  softened
1 cup light oil
1 tablespoon almond extract
2 eggs
3½ cups unbleached flour

1 cup whole wheat flour
1 teaspoon baking soda
1 teaspoon salt
1 teaspoon cream of tartar
2 cups chopped almonds
1 package butter brickle chips or
  3 crushed Heath bars

Blend sugars, margarine, oil, almond extract and eggs. Mix well. Add flour and dry ingredients. Add almonds and butter brickle. Blend well. Roll by tablespoons into balls. Place on cookie sheet and press with fork making X's. Bake at 350 degrees for 12 to 18 minutes. Cool before removing from cookie sheets.

Lora T. Spence

VANILLA KIPPLES
(A lot of vanilla is the key)

Yields: 4½ dozen

1 cup butter, softened
3 cups flour
½ cup confectioners' sugar
½ pound walnuts, chopped

½ cup vanilla mixed with 2
  tablespoons water
confectioners' sugar

Cream butter. Work in flour and sugar until crumbly. Blend nuts into mixture. Add vanilla-water mixture a little at a time until dough can be formed into little crescents or balls. Bake on ungreased cookie sheets at 425 degrees for about 15 minutes. Roll baked cookies in confectioners' sugar.

Terri Piatek

PECAN DAINTIES

Yields: 5 to 6 dozen

1 cup butter, softened
½ cup sugar
2 cups sifted flour
1 teaspoon vanilla

1 tablespoon water
2 cups ground pecans
pecan halves

Cream butter and sugar until light. Add flour, vanilla, water and ground pecans and mix well. Chill until firm; about 1 hour. Shape dough into ¾-inch balls. Either top unbaked cookies with pecan halves or roll warm baked cookies in sugar. Bake at 325 degrees for 20 minutes.

Dorothy Baker

JAN HAGELS

Yields: 4 dozen

1 cup sugar
1 cup butter, softened
1 egg yolk
2 cups flour

½ teaspoon cinnamon
1 egg white
½ cup chopped nuts

Cream sugar and butter until smooth. Add egg yolk and beat thoroughly. Gradually add flour and cinnamon. Mix well. Spread and press dough into 2 9 x 13 inch cookie sheets, about ¼ inch thick, (dough will be very thin). Brush tops with egg white. Sprinkle with nuts. Bake at 300 degrees for 20 to 30 minutes. Cut into squares while still hot. Remove from pans immediately.

Dorothy E. Christiansen

ALMOND BARS

Yields: 3 to 4 dozen

1 cup butter, softened
1 cup sugar
3 egg yolks
4 cups sifted flour

3 teaspoons almond extract
2 tablespoons milk
egg whites
½ cup slivered almonds

Cream butter and sugar. Add egg yolks. Mix in flour, almond extract and milk. Form into 2 long bars; 3 inches by ¼ inch by length of cookie sheet. Place on greased cookie sheet. Brush the top of each bar with egg white. Sprinkle with almonds. Bake at 350 degrees for 30 minutes. Take from oven and cut into bars ¾ inch width.

Dorothy E. Christiansen

SPRITZ COOKIES

Yields: 5 dozen

1 cup butter, softened
⅔ cup sugar
3 egg yolks

1 teaspoon almond extract
2½ cups flour

Cream butter and sugar until smooth. Add egg yolks one at a time. Add almond extract, then gradually add flour. Dough should be very stiff. Chill for 1 hour. Squeeze dough through cookie press onto greased cookie sheet. Bake at 400 degrees for 8 minutes.

Dorothy Baker

SCOTCH SHORTBREAD

Yields: 20 to 30 pieces

1 cup butter, softened
½ cup sugar

2½ cups flour
¼ teaspoon salt

Cream butter. Add ¼ cup sugar; cream, then add remaining sugar. Sift together flour and salt. Gradually add to creamed butter and sugar until mixture is dry enough so as not to adhere to hands when handled. Knead. Place on cookie sheet and pat into one round cake about ⅜ inch thick. Bake in a 325 degree oven until light brown. Cut on the diagonal while still warm.

Dorothy E. Christiansen

Instead of the kids going into the refrigerator all day long, fill a picnic-size jug with their favorite drink and place on the kitchen counter. It is best to use jugs with spouts. Put a supply of paper cups next to the jug and the kids can help themselves.

Place a slice of bread with your soft cookies. It will help prevent them from becoming hard.

BISCOTTI
(A true Italian cookie)

Yields: 6 dozen

6 cups flour	1 cup shortening
3 tablespoons baking powder	4 eggs
1¼ cups sugar	1 cup milk
1 teaspoon salt	1 tablespoon vanilla

Mix flour, baking powder, sugar and salt. Cut shortening into dry ingredients until crumbly. Add eggs, milk, and vanilla and mix lightly. Roll out dough the length of cookie sheet (not too wide). Bake at 350 degrees until lightly browned. Cut on an angle 1 inch thick. Return to pan, cut side down. Place in oven until lightly browned.

Elizabeth Pasquantonio

OAT CAKES
(Old Scotch recipe)

Yields: 5 dozen

3 cups flour	1 cup brown sugar
3 cups rolled oats	½ teaspoon salt
1 cup butter, softened	¼ cup maple syrup
1 cup shortening	

Mix all ingredients except maple syrup in a bowl. Add maple syrup and mix well. Roll between waxed paper to ½ inch thickness. Cut into squares. Bake on ungreased cookie sheet at 350 degrees for about 15 minutes.

Judith Diehl

BAKELESS COOKIES
(A rainy-afternoon project)

Yields: 24 to 30 pieces

1 cup margarine or butter	½ cup peanut butter (chunky or
2 cups sugar	regular)
½ cup milk	1 teaspoon vanilla
	3 cups oatmeal

Heat margarine, sugar and milk and boil for 1 minute. Add peanut butter, vanilla, and oatmeal. Spread in 9 x 9 inch pan, or drop by teaspoonful onto waxed paper. Cut in squares when cool. Refrigerate.

VARIATION: Add 5 tablespoons of cocoa.

Ada Bates

HOLIDAY WREATHS

⅓ cup butter
1 package of 40 marshmallows
1 teaspoon green food coloring

6 cups Kelloggs corn flakes
red hots

Melt together the butter and marshmallows. Add the green food coloring and stir. Add the corn flakes and coat well. Help your children shape this mixture into "holiday wreaths" and decorate with red hots.

Joan Fullwood

ROCKY ROADS

Yields: 2 to 3 dozen

graham crackers
1 cup chocolate chips
1 cup pecan pieces

1 cup miniature marshmallows
½ cup margarine
2 tablespoons brown sugar

In a 9 x 13 inch pan layer graham crackers, chocolate chips, pecan pieces, and marshmallows. Melt margarine and stir in brown sugar. Pour over layered mixture. Bake at 350 degrees for 10 minutes.

Joan Fullwood

Instant Picnic Kit: Roll a paring knife, can opener and plastic silverware in paper towels and place in a cardboard tube from paper towels. Pinch the tube ends shut. When out for a drive at the beach or park, you'll be ready for an instant picnic. Just buy the drinks, fruit and cheeses.

No white sugar in the house? Use brown sugar in the same proportions. It will give the cookie or cake a light molasses flavor.

COCONUT PEANUT BUTTER BARS

Yields: 32 bars

1 cup sifted flour
1 teaspoon baking powder
¼ teaspoon salt
⅓ cup butter or margarine,
   softened
1 cup sugar

½ cup peanut butter (creamy or
   chunky)
2 eggs
1 teaspoon vanilla
1 cup flaked coconut
confectioners' sugar (optional)

Grease 8 x 8 or 7 x 10 inch pan. Preheat oven to 350 degrees. Sift flour, baking powder and salt together. Cream shortening, sugar and peanut butter together. Stir in eggs and vanilla and mix well. Add dry ingredients. Add coconut. Mix and spread in pan. Bake 25 to 30 minutes or until top springs back when lightly touched. Cut into 1 x 2 inch bars. If desired, roll in confectioners' sugar while still warm.

Ada Bates

FRYING PAN COOKIES

Yields: 4 dozen

½ cup butter
1 cup brown sugar
1 cup chopped dates
1 teaspoon vanilla

1 egg, beaten
3 cups Rice Krispies
coconut

Mix butter, sugar, dates and vanilla in frying pan over medium heat until smooth. Take pan off stove. Stir in egg. Cook over very low heat for 10 minutes and stir. Add Rice Krispies. Place coconut in bottom of 7 x 11 inch pan. Spread cookie mixtue on top. Top with coconut. Cut in squares.

Millie McCathren

PEANUT BUTTER CHOCOLATE BARS
(Great for an afternoon snack)

Yields: 20 bars

1 cup butter or margarine, melted
2⅓ cups honey
1¾ cups graham cracker crumbs

1 cup peanut butter
2 cups milk chocolate chips or 8-
   ounce chocolate bar

Mix together all ingredients except chocolate chips. Spread in a greased 9 x 13 inch pan. Melt chocolate in a double boiler. Spread chocolate over mixture in pan. Refrigerate for 1 hour. Cut into squares.

Linda Polito

GRANOLA MIX

Yields: About 15 cups

7 cups rolled oats	1 teaspoon cinnamon
2 cups shredded coconut	4 cups honey
1 cup wheat germ	1 tablespoon vanilla
1 cup sesame seeds	1 cup sesame oil
1 cup chopped walnuts	1 cup raisins

Mix dry ingredients, except raisins. Mix honey, vanilla and oil. Pour over dry ingredients. Mix well. Spread in oiled shallow pans. Bake at 350 degrees for 20 to 25 minutes or until evenly browned. Stir every 10 minutes. Add raisins after toasting.

NOTE: To insure even toasting, do not spread more than ½ inch deep in pans.

Linda Polito

CREAMY FUDGE

Yields: 36

3 cups (3 6-ounce packages) semi-sweet chocolate morsels	dash of salt
1 14-ounce can sweetened condensed milk	1½ teaspoons vanilla
	½ cup chopped nuts

Melt chocolate in the upper part of a double boiler, stirring occasionally. Remove from heat. Stir in sweetened condensed milk, salt, vanilla, and nuts. Spread mixture evenly into waxed paper-lined 8 x 8 inch baking pan. Chill 2 hours or until firm. Turn fudge onto cutting board. Peel off paper and cut into squares. Tightly cover any leftovers.

Bill Kasavage

The spring variety of clothes pins make fine construction tools for children three years and older. Just show them how to attach one to the other and wait to see the constructions that come from a batch.

CHOCOLATE MACAROON CANDY

Yields: 5 to 6 dozen

1 pound broken milk chocolate
  (purchase at the candy counter
  of a department store or use
  Hershey bars)
4 squares Baker's unsweetened
  chocolate
4 cups corn flakes
1 cup or more coconut
1 pound pecans, chopped
pinch of salt
1 teaspoon vanilla

Melt the milk chocolate and the Baker's chocolate in the upper part of a double boiler. The water should be hot but not boiling. While this is melting, mix the corn flakes, coconut, pecans and salt. Add vanilla to the chocolate mixture. Pour melted chocolate over the corn flakes mixture and mix quickly. Drop from spoon on cookie sheets covered with wax paper and put in refrigerator until hard. Store in cookie tin in refrigerator. Eat and enjoy.

Diana Smith

ENGLISH TOFFEE

Yields: 8 dozen

1 cup butter or margarine (not
  polyunsaturated)
1 cup sugar
3 tablespoons cold water
1 teaspoon vanilla
3 plain Hershey bars, broken
$\frac{1}{3}$ cup finely chopped walnuts or
  pecans

Bring butter, sugar, and water to a boil while stirring constantly. Reduce heat, but maintain at a slow boil until the hard crack stage (300 degrees). Remove from heat. Add vanilla and pour into a buttered 8 x 10 inch pan. Immediately top with Hershey bar pieces and gently spread with a knife as they melt. Top with nuts. Cool. Break into irregularly shaped pieces.

Bev and Dick Schultz

FRENCH TOFFEE BARS

Yields: 8 dozen

1 cup butter, softened
1 cup brown sugar
1 teaspoon vanilla
2 large chocolate bars (Hershey's
  or Nestle's)
1 cup chopped walnuts

Thoroughly cream together butter, sugar, and vanilla. Press mixture into a 9 x 13 inch pan. Bake in a 350 degree oven for 25 minutes. Remove from oven and place candy bars on top. Spread evenly when melted. Sprinkle liberally with walnuts. Let cool.

Pat Blair

PEPPERMINT CANDY

1-pound box light brown sugar
1 cup water
¾ cup Karo blue label syrup

pinch of salt
1 teaspoon peppermint
confectioners' sugar

Combine all ingredients in saucepan. Heat to 275 degrees using a candy thermometer. Stretch in confectioners' sugar. Cut into pieces.

LaRue Weber

POPCORN BALLS
(This is a Christmas tradition in the Smith house)

⅓ cup water
⅓ cup white Karo syrup
1 teaspoon salt
1 cup sugar

½ cup butter
1 teaspoon vanilla
popcorn

Stir all ingredients except vanilla and popcorn in a large deep saucepan. Boil to 250 degrees. Make 3 batches of popcorn. When candy syrup reaches 250 degrees, add vanilla and several drops of red or green food coloring. Pour over popcorn. Working quickly, form into balls.

CAUTION: Syrup is very hot. It may help to remove all rings and coat hands with butter. Store popcorn balls in baggies.

Diana Smith

PAT'S CARAMEL POPCORN

1 cup unpopped, popcorn
2 cups brown sugar
½ cup margarine

½ cup white Karo syrup
1 teaspoon salt
1 teaspoon baking soda

Pop corn. In a large pan combine sugar, margarine, Karo syrup and salt. Heat to boiling. Boil 5 minutes. Remove from heat and add baking soda. Stir well and pour over popped corn. Spread on baking sheet. Bake at 200 degrees for 1 hour, stirring every 15 minutes. Remove and cool on waxed paper.

Dottie Pierson

5 MINUTE FUDGE

Yields: 6 dozen

2 5.3-ounce cans evaporated milk
3 cups sugar
3 cups Marshmallow Cream (2 7½-ounce jars)

1 cup chopped walnuts
3 6-ounce bags chocolate chips
2 teaspoons vanilla

Put milk and sugar in large saucepan and heat to boiling, stirring constantly. Boil 5 minutes, continuing to stir. Remove from heat and add all other ingredients. Stir until they are dissolved (about 1 minute). Pour into 9 x 13 inch pan. Refrigerate.

Sheila and Bob Pasquantonio

NO BAKE COOKIES

½ cup Karo syrup
½ cup peanut butter

3 cups Rice Krispies

When it seems that the rain will never stop, take ten minutes to whip up these cookies with your little ones. Combine the syrup and peanut butter. Stir in the Rice Krispies. Shape into balls. Eat and enjoy. Happy smiles will brighten your whole day.

SEVEN LAYER CANDY

Yields: 3 dozen squares

½ cup butter
1½ cups graham cracker crumbs
1 cup chopped pecans
1 cup chocolate chips

1 cup butterscotch chips
1 cup coconut
1 14-ounce can sweetened condensed milk

Melt butter in 9 x 9 inch glass baking dish. Mix in graham cracker crumbs to form bottom layer. Add pecans as next layer. On top of pecans, put layer of chocolate chips, then add a layer of butterscotch chips. Sprinkle coconut on top of chips. Pour milk over these layers. Bake at 325 degrees for 30 minutes. Cool and cut into squares.

Teresa Meyer

 For sour milk, add 1 tablespoon vinegar or lemon juice to 1 cup of fresh milk. Let stand for five minutes before using.

Index

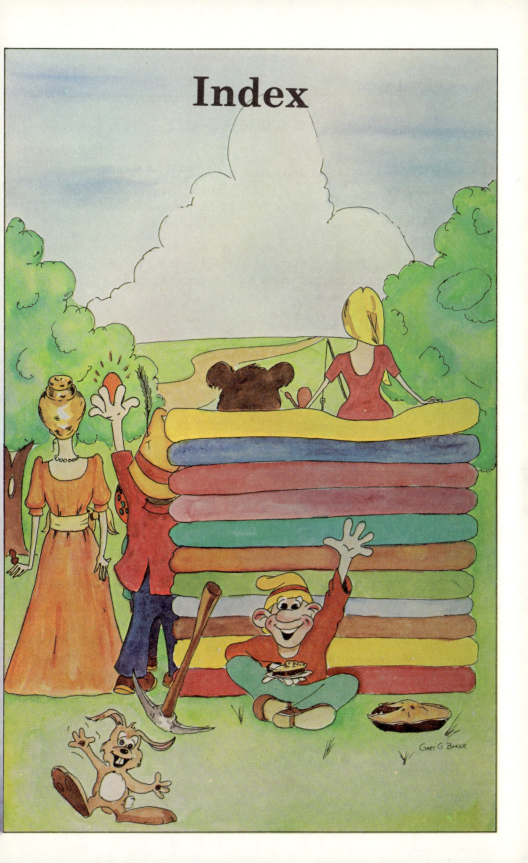

Gary G Baker

INDEX

INDEX

INDEX

INDEX

INDEX

INDEX

CONTRIBUTORS

Judy and William Alexy
Amel's Restaurant
Anne Austen
Elaine and Alan Axelson
Dorothy C. Baker
Elaine Baker
Geraldine Bartelme
Ada Bates
Mary Benson
Patricia Blair
Rose Bloom
Betty Douglass Campbell
Castle Tavern Restaurant
Cedar House Restaurant
Dorothy E. Christiansen
Doe Clark
Joan Clark
Nancy Conover
Barbara Cooledge
Elaine Cretekos
Marsha DeCaria
Doris DePierre
Doris S. DePierre
Judith Diehl
Frances Dortenza
Gladys Douglas
Judith Douglass
Jennifer Drummy
Bonnie Emerick
Susan Ferrell-Berman
Daniel Findley
Barbara Fisher
Phyllis Fox
Dottie France
Joan Fullwood
Ann Garner
Jean Getz
Margaret Getz
Margaret Gillick
Barbara Goldsmith
Penny Goldstein
Margaret Goodwin

Carolyn Graham
Marjorie H. Gray
Monica and Stuart Hall
Marilyn Hayes
Carolyn Heaton
Barbara and Richard Heinze
Delores Helm
Judy Helman
Suellen Hicks
Janet Holliday
Maude Holliday
Gail Holsinger
Joan and Gilbert Iacono
Fern Jagger
Twyla Jagger
Nancy Johns
Jeannette Johnson
Sally Joiner
Eileen Joll
Martha Juliano
William Kasavage
Vera King
Jean and Mike Kmiecik
Anne Knoell
Margaret and John Koltick
Patricia Krivonak
Patricia Kuehn
Nancy Latshaw
Sue and William Law
Anong Litwin
Loretta Lucas
Millicent McCathren
Nancy McCloskey
Deborah and Frank McKenna
Eleanor Marshall
Marty Matthews
William Metzger
Teresa G. Meyer
Ruth Miller
Nancy Morgan
Janine and Michael Murphy

Shirley Norman
Carolyn Novelly
Judy Oakley
Caroline O'Brien
Zuzanna K. O'Brien
Peggy Osborne
Elizabeth Pasquantonio
Sheila and Robert Pasquantonio
Grace H. Pearson
Lawrence Pearson
Sandy Pearson
Vivian Pennington
Dottie Pierson
Theresa Piatek
Cheryl and Donald Polito
Linda Polito
Jo Ann Pulcini
Holly Raulston
Brenda Reavis
Mary Jane Roderick
Shirley Rose
Rosemary Ross
Mary C. Ruffennach
Fran Schoemaker
Beverly and Richard Schultz
Sandra Simpson
Fran Smetanka
Patricia Smetanka
Diana and Dave Smith
Bobbi Snyder
Susan Spagnuolo
Lora and Eugene Spence
Florence Tabor
Eleanor and Joseph Towers
Judy Tulley
Katie VanHoozer
Mary Ellen Weaver
LaRue Weber
Janet White
Deborah and Ronald Wilcher
Sherry Wilson

THE WESLEY INSTITUTE

The Wesley Institute is a private, non-profit corporation located in suburban Pittsburgh, but serving children and youth from Pittsburgh and the four surrounding counties of Allegheny, Beaver, Washington, and Westmoreland in Southwestern Pennsylvania. The programs of The Institute have been developed to help young people with special needs, special needs which respond favorably to the caring attention, love, guidance, and instruction of sensitive professionals. Each day The Institute's programs serve 190 children and youth ages 6-21 who are unable to succeed in the regular path of life because of "hidden handicaps" which are not readily visible to the untrained eye. The Wesley Institute's professional staff of 80 helps fulfill the lives of these young people whose potential was nearly destroyed by emotional, social, or behavioral problems.

The Institute began with The Village Academy in 1965 which was followed the next year with Highland School. In the late 70's Highland Youth Services and Penn Residence were added, with the Oakdale Center becoming part of The Institute in 1980. As we look to the end of the 80's, we are actively pursuing further growth and development of The Wesley Institute.

Each year many of our young people are able to move on to the next step in their lives. After having mastered their problems, they are then able to pursue their goals, because we have given them the care and confidence to do so.

Additional information about our programs and services is available by writing The Wesley Institute, Inc., 243 Johnston Road, Pittsburgh, PA 15241.

ILLUSTRATOR

Gary Baker, creator of the illustrations in There Once Was a Cook ..., is in his second year at the Reformed Presbyterian Theological Seminary in Pittsburgh, Pennsylvania. He holds a Bachelor of Arts degree in Communications and Business from the University of Pittsburgh. Although he has had no formalized training in art, he has actively pursued drawing as a hobby. The artistic creations seen throughout There Once Was A Cook ... are Gary's first published works. Gary is the husband of Wesley Institute employee Dorothy Baker, who is the Speech-Language Pathologist at Highland School.

VIGNETTIST

The charming vignettes accompanying the fairy tale illustrations in There Once Was A Cook ..., are creations of the lively mind of Lora Spence. Lora serves as the Clinical Reading Specialist and Learning Styles Specialist for the Bethel Park School System, Bethel Park, Pennsylvania. In addition, she writes the school district's federal program grants, and has written an alternative high school curriculum for students with learning difficulties. Lora has published two books of her own, and is working on a third book. Lora is the wife of Dr. Eugene Spence, Development Officer for the Wesley Institute and former Superintendent of the Bethel Park School System.

NOTES:

THERE ONCE WAS A COOK ...

The Wesley Institute
P.O. Box 113445
Pittsburgh, Pennsylvania 15241

Please send me _____ copies of **THERE ONCE WAS A COOK...** at $12.95 per copy plus $1.75 for postage and handling. (PA residents add $.78 sales tax)

Enclosed is my check or money order for $ _____ Make check payable to: The Wesley Institute.

Name _____

Address _____

City _____ State _____ Zip _____

All proceeds from the sale of this book will benefit children and youth serviced by The Wesley Institute, Pittsburgh, Pennsylvania.

- -

THERE ONCE WAS A COOK ...

The Wesley Institute
P.O. Box 113445
Pittsburgh, Pennsylvania 15241

Please send me _____ copies of **THERE ONCE WAS A COOK...** at $12.95 per copy plus $1.75 for postage and handling. (PA residents add $.78 sales tax)

Enclosed is my check or money order for $ _____ Make check payable to: The Wesley Institute.

Name _____

Address _____

City _____ State _____ Zip _____

All proceeds from the sale of this book will benefit children and youth serviced by The Wesley Institute, Pittsburgh, Pennsylvania.

- -

THERE ONCE WAS A COOK ...

The Wesley Institute
P.O. Box 113445
Pittsburgh, Pennsylvania 15241

Please send me _____ copies of **THERE ONCE WAS A COOK...** at $12.95 per copy plus $1.75 for postage and handling. (PA residents add $.78 sales tax)

Enclosed is my check or money order for $ _____ Make check payable to: The Wesley Institute.

Name _____

Address _____

City _____ State _____ Zip _____

All proceeds from the sale of this book will benefit children and youth serviced by The Wesley Institute, Pittsburgh, Pennsylvania.